Kaleidoscopic of A Entrepreneur

JOHN PETER MASSE

Copyright © 2014 John Peter Masse

All rights reserved.

ISBN: 1495229130
ISBN-13: 978-1495229138

DEDICATION

I would like to dedicate this book to my children Connie, Kelly, Julie, Penny, Patti, and Jason.

CONTENTS

DEDICATION III
CONTENTS V
ACKNOWLEDGMENTS VII
INTRODUCTION 1
THE INSTITUTIONAL MUSIC CAREER: 7
POST MARRIAGE SEPARATION: 21
KING ARTHUR'S COURT: 28
TARALEIGH INVESTMENTS COMPANY: 32
POST TARALEIGH INVESTMENTS: 44
MOVIE HUT/CINEMA KID OF CANADA: 63
COMPUTE-A-SIGN CANADA LTD: 68
NU-MEDIA SYSTEMS INC: 76
OCOM CORPORATION: 113
FLORIDA STATE CONSERVATORY OF MUSIC: 127
THE MORTGAGE BUSINESS: 142
FINAL THOUGHTS AND SUMMARY CONCLUSIONS: 197

ACKNOWLEDGMENTS

This writing exercise, while intended for the young people in our family is for you Fran. No one could love and respect you as I. A large "thank you" for your encouragement and help with this book.

CHAPTER ONE

INTRODUCTION

After a near million cocktail conversations with Fran concerning my working career she has steadfastly encouraged me to write a book, claiming the stories I related to her were fascinating and could be a teachable lesson to my grand children and others.

So, this is an attempt to put into a script the history of a working career spanning some 55 years. From the early farming years to the daunting experience of finding my first job, through the middle productive years, and through to retirement.

The story will reveal the near million $ deals to the failures and success's of an entrepreneur. Entrepreneur was my calling card for most of my working life. Be it direct sales commissions, salaries and bonus, to sharing company profits, income was almost always production driven. And there were times when paychecks were not available or were very tiny.

Having only a high school education I cannot be considered "educated". One of life's wishes would have been more pro-active parents toward my education. Many of my early schoolteachers would always repeat the same mantra "he should apply himself, he has the ability". While this may have been my own failure I believe, Pete and Gene did engage me in other forms of training and education, as I hope you soon will discover and agree.

And of course on my side of the equation there was an easy deterrent of the always ever presence of playing sax in a rock band. Oh, the sheer joy and fun a teenager experiences playing rock music in a dance hall or in a jam-packed bar, winking, smiling at all the pretty, hot looking girls.

I believe whatever moderate success I accomplished was primarily based on self-belief, self reliant, positive attitude and a knowing if you put your mind to it, you will succeed. That coupled with the teachings of solid work ethics and an inherited sales ability.

And so the journey I have put off for several months, if not years, will now begin.

The early, early years:

The beginning really starts growing up on a farm on the 14th concession in Huron County, address: RR 2, Zurich Ontario.

The geographical location, a mile or so from the shores of Lake Huron, was a true blessing, as the fertile land would grow almost anything one planted. The original 100 acre farm and later a second farm were both purchased by my father and mother from my paternal grandfather. The latter being the original homestead of my father.

Regular chores and duties were a natural progression of a boy growing up on any farm. In the early years chores were both barn and field related. For some reason, at an early age I possessed an advanced sense of operating anything that was a motor driven vehicle. Dad used to say to anyone listening "if it makes noise, burns oil and makes smoke, don't worry John can handle it". Sometime around the age of twelve I would regularly be given tractor driven jobs working a field in preparation of sowing the intended crop or mowing a field of hay in preparation of harvesting for the animals during the winter months. As I developed more experience the degree of responsibility grew to operating a combine harvester that local farmers would hire Dad to harvest for them, called "custom work". I protected the position of confidence Dad gave me because to my way of thinking sitting on your ass operating a tractor was much preferred to hard, back breaking, physical field labor. In addition to school this schedule continued until I was seventeen years old at which time Dad realized he could not pass the farm onto me since I had absolutely no interest in farming. The consequences of this now known fact coupled with what now had become serious arthritic knees, drove him to a sales career in the automotive field beginning with the local Pontiac/Buick, Cadillac dealer. He possessed no prior sales experience but was a natural at it and soon it became his sole employment, quickly becoming and earning the GM "master salesman" award. It was General Motor's recognition of their top million dollar sales club. I believe he annually earned this prestigious recognition right up to his near retirement.

Earlier I mentioned "solid work ethics". I would be totally remiss if I did not say how my mother and father magnificently instilled, by example, their work skills and habits. I easily recall how they worked 15 –16 hour days including Saturday and Sunday so there were definitely no days off. It was common local gossip that no one could out work Pete and it is not lost on my memory of watching Dad urinate while walking (well certainly not against a north wind) so as to not loose any working time. If I attained any moderate success as an entrepreneur, by comparison, Dad had a master's degree. When one considers how they began arriving on the original farm (1941 I believe) with no plumbing, no electrical power, no equipment and little money, it is mind boggling to realize their meteoric accomplishments. I think for the reader to get a sense of this I should list a few of the major acquisitions and accomplishments.

They purchased 2 farms and paid for them, purchased 4 tractors, 2 trucks, a threshing machine, a combine harvester, piped in 2miles of spring water to feed the animals, built a concrete silo, expanded the barn and added electric milking machines eliminating hand milking cows. Not to mention completely renovating the house including installing electricity, plumbing and running water. All accomplished in a span of 18 years. He was my hero and remains so to this day.

The early years:

Dad was now entirely in the car business and coupled with the success he enjoyed he discontinued farming, leasing both farms to local farmers, while continuing to live at the farm home. It wasn't until 1959 that they sold the farms and moved to Grand Bend.

My first job away from the farm was a "summer one" working for the township operating a tractor cutting grass along the side of the township roads. It was real easy, just 8:00 to 5:00, giving ample time to being a Grand Bend teenager. Although I was asked to continue with the township (operating a snow plow was said to be fun) I knew my future was not with the township.

I still did not know what I wanted to do but clearly non-employment was not an option. Vic Denomy, "Ducky" Denomy and I began interviewing together for what was our first non summer school job employment (other than working on the family farm). Our limited skill level gave us few options. Not surprising offers did not come our way so I decided better results would come by looking for work on my own. Off I went to London. With the help of our dear Aunt Win I found factory work at Canadian Westinghouse. I couldn't believe how boring and uninspiring these 12 hour shifts were and I knew this would be temporary allowing just enough time to build a little reserve money. Not long after beginning with Westinghouse I was solicited by a union agent to join the new union he was forming. Coming off a farm and not knowing diddle-do-daw about unions, I soon learned the consequences of joining a non-union plant. I went from 12-hour shifts to no shifts. I was laid off.

Incidentally, during my entire time in London living as a single person I roomed and board with a Mrs. Murray at 1429 Brydges Street. Four years I believe, with this wonderful Irish den mother who always had my best interest at heart.

The early Years Part 2:

I still had no idea what I wanted to do – but I knew factory work was not going to cut it. Office work seemed to have some appeal, so I began scouting want ads in the paper – without any results.

What happened next was, by my guess, my first experience with "Divine Intervention" because without the "union" issue I most likely would have continued with Westinghouse factory work for a much longer period than would have been productive to my self-development

While working at Westinghouse, right next door, was a large handsome new factory, Wolverine Tube, recently built and just after I drew my final check from Westinghouse they went into production building seamless copper tubing. Since nothing was happening on the job front I mustered enough nerve to put on my only suit, shirt and tie and presented myself, past security, to the front personnel office - now known as Human Resources – stating I was applying for an accounting position. The logic of applying for a position in accounting was due to the fact my high school teachers were always commending me and telling me " I had an aptitude for figures" – not to be confused with the always mind presence of girl figures.

Well, they said that was okay as they were looking for accounting personnel and gave me an application form to complete and would I be willing to take an aptitude test. I was to return the next day, take the test and turn in the completed application.

Needless to say nothing about my application remotely suggested anything resembling any accounting skills, particularly when a college degree was or almost required. But, as luck would have it "I blew the top off" the aptitude test. HR were impressed with my test scores but could not accept me to an accounting position due to my lack of education but expressed an interest in hiring me. "Could I start soon"? "Sure, what's the position"? Thinking they were going to put me somewhere in the plant. "Office Messenger" was the reply. It was a beginning position that would eventually lead me to advanced office positions. Starting salary $37.50 per week. Of course that part was the bummer but, five or so days after knocking on their door I was employed.

My initial responsibility was sorting the mail and distributing it and inner office communications, to the different departments – twice a day. Given a choice of office messenger or some other office position I would have elected something other than the messenger position. Actually, it was a hidden blessing. Meeting, talking and observing all facets of the office, afforded me extraordinary learning opportunities and a wonderful perspective of office procedures, foreign to most teenage farm boys. I learned what the production and trafficking department did, the functions of sales, engineering, shipping and what was occurring in the executive offices. Great orientation. And by the way, this is when my young eyes were first opened to extramarital activities. With the exception of one secretary all were "doing" most everyone. Nothing like that on the 14th concession I'll tell you!

Soon my responsibilities grew to picking up executives who arrived in the corporate jet from their Kentucky Head Quarters flying into the London Airport to attend company meetings. I would pick up the executives in the company station wagon and deliver them to the office and plant, always listening and learning from their company chatter. I also volunteered to handle the switchboard after 4:30 to 7:00 and that did not go unnoticed. The downside to all this of course was the $37.50/ week. Paying $10 for room and board left little for fun and entertainment. Thankfully, I guess for the past years of farm work a generous father and mother gave me a 2 year old green and white Pontiac and unlike most of my friends, no car payments. Secondly, the dance band (the Melody Masters would you believe) Vic Denomy and I formed three years earlier, gained a solid reputation of being one of the best in the local area so most weeks we had Friday and Saturday night gigs. Happily, the $37.50 was augmented by an additional "music money" of $20 -$30. More if we could convince the dance venue to kick in some gas and expense money. So with the combined income it was much more manageable. Also, when you adjust the $60 weekly to today's income it rounds out to something in excess of $500. Gas was like .50 a gallon, a case of beer was like $5 and lunch was no more than .75cents. So, it wasn't bad.

Soon I received promotions eventually leading to the coveted accounting department only to learn that working with figures for 8 hours, every day, became very boring. My salary had increased to some $60 weekly and it became clear after a "come to Jesus meeting" with the company Comptroller, no less, that I would soon have to decide to advance my education level by enrolling in night classes at a local college and the classes were 2 – 3 times per week. And to achieve this accounting degree would take 7 years. Ugh! The accounting dream was fast loosing its luster.

It was shortly after that I decided to leave and look for something else. Just a short side bar story, the night before my final day and in advance of the customary "good bye" company lunch, I was taken ill with a high fever and abdominal pains. Mrs. Murray called Dr. Bruckshwager and he admitted me to St. Joseph Hospital for an immediate appendectomy.

While recovering from my appendectomy I began checking the newspapers for employment notices. No factory. No accounting. An advertisement caught my eye, only because it was about music. Something else. Sales!

CHAPTER TWO

THE INSTITUTIONAL MUSIC CAREER:

I am not totally certain, but I believe this time frame was early spring 1960.

In responding to a newspaper advertisement I spoke with a Rand Green. Basic information was provided and I agreed to meet him at a restaurant. At this time an office was not available.

The company, 'The Audio School of Music', out of Toronto, taught guitar and accordion lessons in the student's home, and attended by a teacher on a monthly basis. Obviously the market was for interested students who were not located near teaching facilities (country bumpkins) such as would be found in larger cities and towns. Teacher training was aided by usual music book material, and pre-recorded lessons available by the old thirty three and a third records that you listened to on a portable record player. The customer would purchase in addition to the books, a series of records, record player, a music stand and the selected instrument. Cost $299. Financing was available by way of a provided consumer finance company. Fortunately no one was ever declined a contract or financing! Commission: $100 per sold package.

Rand Green was a 40 year old, low-key, quiet and a laid back non high-pressure person. Nothing ever seemed to bother him. He explained he was the new local manager for the company and he was putting together a sales staff to sell and market this service and product. Rand explained a basic simple plan. He and I would visit country public schools, distribute blank lead forms to the students and the attending teacher. Students interested would return a completed signed form the following day for immediate follow up. (No way would this be possible in this day and age) My job training included watching Rand do actual sales presentations.

My interest level in music greatly affected my thought process and I agreed I would start after first watching some presentations. Rand was in total agreement saying this would be part of my training anyway.

Part of the presentation was administrating a 'music aptitude test' to the perspective student by way of the student(s) listening to a test given through a record played on the portable record player. There would be no intra action by the salesman other to mark the resulting answers on a provided "test report" form.

I watched about 4 or 5 presentations and Rand closed 2 of them. Well, the math was pretty simple. One week= $200. Done deal! I started immediately.

I began setting up my appointments and doing actual presentations. I couldn't believe the results. No one was saying "no". I racked off about 8 or 10 sales before someone said "no thank you". It was mind boggling to me. $800 in a little less than a month! By the way, there was no one else to share the leads with, as it turned out Rand & I were the only staff (hah).

Well, after something like 3 months "the worlds your oyster" mentality soon began to get fuzzy. We were running out of schools not previously visited. Hence, fewer sales lead to work with.

It was then that Rand arranged a meeting with the "Ontario Conservatory of Music". This was a real school with teachers, receptionists, actual music studios with active students and more than 50 studios throughout southwestern Ontario. The company, at the time, had been in business for 20 years. In this meeting I met the co-founder of the company, Keith Turner. The most dynamic person I had never met.

Their program was simple. An enrolled student paid a $10 enrollment registration fee and $1.95 per attended lesson taken at the studio, plus required music material. The program provided the enrolled student with a beginner instrument for 6 months. "Hey what a deal!" If I could sell the Audio Music deal I sure as hell could sell this program.

Commission per enrollment: $10.

I agreed to a weeks training in Kitchener, Ontario where I agreed to start immediately.

Side bar story: It seemed peculiar to me that Rand was not part of the training. He was after all the person who arranged the meeting. I learned much later, that Rand had previously worked with OCOM and the parting was poor. Secondly, the only reason he was granted a meeting and rehired was because of me. (Keith Turner told me this directly some 5-6 years later)

Thirdly, I was made aware, much later in my OCOM career, that Turner took it upon himself personally to direct my development. During the initial first year of my employment, he met with me once per week, no matter where (area wise) I was working. Without question, next to my father and mother, I respected no one like I did this man. I cannot tell you the depths of business knowledge, salesmanship, leadership training, the value of respect, and general personal development he taught me. He always spoke of little euphemisms like," Always protect your integrity. In life, it will almost always precede you. If you damage it, it will always follow you". Or, "when you have completed most of your calls and you decide to call it a day. Make just one more call before you leave for home".

To this day, the first and foremost quantifier of any relationship that I look for is RESPECT. I just don't think it is lastingly possible without. He was one of a kind and anyone who knew him held him to this level of respect. I was very privileged to experience this tutorship – few people did and particularly the level extended to me. I called him Mr. Turner and meant it. But for him, certainly in the beginning years, I would have left the business. Providing for a family by way of direct sales commission is not easy, nor always productive.

The company referred to my sales position as Registrar. As previously stated I spent a week in training at the company's Kitchener office/studio. I completed the training successfully but my trainer said he was under instructions to continue the training for an additional week allowing him to monitor my enrollments. I finished the 2nd week with 7 enrolled students. Everyone seemed pleased.

I was to report to the London East studio and meet Rand Green the following Monday where I learned that the enrollment staff consisted of Rand and me. Not close to the level of business activity so evident at the Kitchener office. I don't recall my exact enrollment numbers but I do know that I was making much more money than the old office job. Enough that sometime in July, Ducky Denomy, who was now working for a finance company in London, called to tell me he had repossessed a 1958 Chevy Impala convertible. Black on black with red interior and powerful 348 cu inch engine – with dual exhaust yet. Well, one look at the back beauty and I knew it was mine.

Because it was repossessed by the finance company the purchase price was well below market value and I sold the 56 Pontiac to my uncle, Vic Masse, buying the Impala convertible leaving sufficient cash to replace the only required repairs, the entire exhaust system and best of all. Zero car payments.

Not long after I started in London and with no other sales people, Rand informed me that he was leaving, giving me a set of keys for the office/studio and told me to meet Jack Campbell and Keith Turner at 3:00 on the following Tuesday. There I was, me and only me, with about 2 months of experience to manage myself for the remainder of the summer and well into September. I managed to enroll about 7 to 10 students weekly, meeting Campbell and Turner every Tuesday for our weekly meetings. Mr. Turner told me early on if I could demonstrate managing myself he would offer me a promotion. I still don't know if it was a carrot to keep me on. I guess it worked.

Sometime during the early fall he did promote me to Sr. Registrar, which would increase my income by an additional $1 for each new student enrolled by any Registrars under my direction. I was to report to the Oakville studio the following Monday to manage a "floating" sales team of 3 or 4 Registrars. (floating, meaning they were not permanently located in Oakville but traveled as directed and needed)

I was probably the youngest team leader the floating team ever had and not un-expectantly, they did test me from time to time. I decided to lead by example and as much as I remember it worked out ok.

I had been in Oakville 3 or 4 weeks when one-day "black beauty's" transmission failed. The garage mechanic said the transmission had to be replaced. I do not remember the cost but know that it was expensive. What choice did I have other than to go ahead with the quoted price and on the condition that the dealership provide me with a loaner as part of the cost so I could continue to work. Reluctantly, the manager finally agreed. For some reason right after that, while still using the loaner car, I was shifted back to the London area to lead a newly formed Registrar staff and our initial area was Tillsonburg, just 35 miles from London. Not one week later as I was driving through one of the town's intersections, a driver did not stop as required and tee-boned me. Not real serious damage but sufficient to render the loaner non-drivable. I thought the Oakville dealer service manager was going to have a stroke lamenting that he would surely loose his job.

Anyway, as permanent London staff we remained in London for quite a long time. Upper management had hired a manager (Dennis Farthing was his name) and the person that I reported to.

That December I became engaged to a super-hot good-looking girl who I had been dating exclusively for some time. Not so in the early stage but certainly in the later term. Her name was Jane McNaughton. No marriage date was set but it seemed we were firm in our intentions. (I didn't know then but sooner would become sooner than originally thought)

I continued to blow a horn on weekends and by that time Vic and I had disbanded the good old Melody Masters and joined a new rock & roll group organized by Wayne Muck who later would find fame and notoriety as "Buddy Carlton and the StratoTones". The music now was no longer the dance band variety but hot rock & roll. We played mostly high school dances and liquor bars having to provide false proof that the bass player was of legal age.

In the mean time everything is percolating along fine with the student enrollment scene and upper management replaces Dennis Farthing with a real hotshot manager by the name of Thorne Vallas (more on him later) when Jane informs me that serious and immediate attention must be given to moving the yet to be settled marriage date. Yes! And more yes! In the back of your mind you always know this could happen but for some reason it will always be someone else – but definitely not you.

Leaving the band was not an issue for me as I had decided that I would not be part of the other band member's decisions to become professional musicians. Using the jargon of the day "to go on the road". I thought I had a better career and life than the storied one of constant bars, booze, girls and living out of a suitcase. That decision was reached long before Jane's memo.

So, moving foreword on April 22, 1961 Jane and I are married in my old parish church in St. Joseph, Ontario, honeymooned in Niagara Falls and moved into a one bedroom apartment, 511 Highbury Avenue (a address where I would years later set up an extensive office, showroom and warehouse right next door.)

I am doing ok with OCOM, experiencing some struggles with the more demanding money requirements but managing. One of life's realities was the decision to sell the gas guzzling black beauty and buy a more economical Volkswagon.

On September 23, 1961, Miss Connie comes along. She is healthy, very good looking, as far as newborn babies go and has red hair. Mother is just fine and remains beaming.

Sometime during the summer a guy form Seaforth, Ontario joins OCOM as a Registrar. His name is Lou Barry and we would remain friends and confidents for many years.

It is about this time an operational decision comes down the pike affecting studio ownership. Area Franchising. This allowed selected individuals to purchase existing, operating studio areas from the corporation under franchise agreements. The idea of the plan was to allow the corporation a method of better managing the ever-expanding business and territory. As part of this new methodology, I was approached to join the Simcoe franchise as a junior shareholder and as such become part of middle management and remain in the enrollment division. This division was always the most difficult to successfully maintain and yet vital to the success of the business.

Just prior to the February 1963 Simcoe move, Kelly pops into the world on December 2 1962. Blond, & blue eyes she comes packaged possessing an attitude of don't push me until I am ready. She is very healthy and now ... we are four.

Apart of the equity position in the franchise, the physical move and adhering to the operational plan were the least favorite to me. It was okay but the senior franchisee wanted to move me from exclusively enrollments to include selling instruments in the instrument sales division. I spoke against it but he was insistent, reasoning that the sales work load in addition to general management was too much and of course he won, as he was the boss. I never enjoyed selling instruments and frankly was never any good at it. This resulted in a most difficult financial period for my family. During the one and half years in Simcoe, Julie Genevieve is born, the only one of six born outside of London. The date. February 17, 1964. She is cute as a button and later on will always demonstrate her intense sense of independency and warrior mentality.

In the spring of 1964 I negotiated a move back to the London area. But before getting into that era I would like to reflect on one of the most likeable, helpful, making work fun, mangers I ever worked with. Eventually we went our separate ways, remaining in the business and friends for a long period of time. Thorne Vallas.

Thorne was in his mid to late 40s when we met, single, about 6.2, slim with an athletic build, very good looking with an engaging smile and personality. He had been previously married, I don't recall how many times. Women would flock to him and literally fight over him. He was the consummate salesperson. Lou Barry and I loved him. I introduced him to Dad and he purchased at least 2 cars from him. Dad would tell me Thorne would make him laugh whenever he would ask how I was doing and Thorne's answer, "he's a genius".

Less than a year after he came on board he partnered up with one of the senior teachers, leaving London to start a new franchise in Chatham Ontario. Lou, myself and several other OCOM registrars helped in the initial new student enrollment. He eventually left the company and the Chatham franchise (due primarily to the attitude of the partner teacher) joining a few ex OCOM persons and started a competitive company in Ottawa and later Winnipeg. He often asked me to join him in Ottawa saying he always respected me and would see to my greater success. I declined for a number of reasons; including my growing family and knowing that decision would hurt my relationship with Keith Turner. I often wondered if that decision was the wisest because Thorne became very successful retiring with a boatload of money. Would you believe when retiring he did so in Florida! I heard from him a few times, inviting me to visit him.

I was doing my thing primarily in the London area, taking on more responsibility and promoted to an area supervisor. June 23, 1965 Penny is born. Talk about a beauty, blond, blue eyes to this day. She would later become Julie's sidekick and the two of them would find mischief that humanity has yet to discover. We moved from the new town home on Sorrel Rd, that we rented when first in London to a single family home at 415 Merlin St. Penny's first home. (No new babies until Patti) Our family endured several health problems while living at the Sorrel Rd residence and the cause of our moving. The problem was determined to be poor construction and drainage causing water to seep into the lower level basement living area. The constant moisture caused illness to most of the family. After repeated requests to the builder/owner to repair the leakage with no satisfying results, I took him to civil court and chose to represent myself. No prior legal experience but I thought I could handle it, reasoning that I had a strong case. I assembled the evidence and Bob Broderick who lived with us for a short period, agreed to testify. Anyway the judge ruled on a 50/50 split. Meaning he did not award funds for medical expenses and suffering but the owner would be required to cancel the lease with no penalties or costs – which he previously refused to do.

Other than the supervisor promotion there were no particular changes in my work. We did move again this time to 7 Sumner Rd as we were served legal notice the homeowner was selling the Merlin property to clear land for a commercial development. The property sat on a corner lot with the main street.

I was involved in a peculiar car accident during a quick trip to the Ingersoll warehouse to pickup some needed supplies. I had borrowed Paul Bartha's new Ford station wagon, as my car was in for service and temporarily unavailable. On my way to the warehouse, driving on a county road, two deer suddenly jump out of the ditch that ran parallel to the road, right in front of the car. I had no time to brake or swerve, due to oncoming traffic and avert the collision. Bam, two dead deer and damage to Paul's new car that had less than 300 miles on it. Un drivable! I stopped some distance from the impact and walked back to the 2 carcasses. While discussing the accident with two men, who were drivers of the on coming traffic, we were all perplexed at how it happened. I noticed a rabbit only a few feet from one of the dead deer. Upon further observation I notice another and then yet another. I pointed this out to the two observers - one was a UWO professor and the other an industrial sales rep – when one of these intelligent men posed a mind-blowing question "do deer eat rabbit?" I couldn't believe the question and that is when it hit me. They were unborn dead fawns.

The police arrived followed by the game warden, who was non too happy with me. He explained he knew the deer, a couple of long standing and they were en route crossing the road to find their way to the woods, a distance of a football field away, where obviously the doe was preparing to birth her unborn fawn. He was distraught to near tears and told me and my two anointed friends, that one fawn birth is normal, two uncommon and three nearly unheard of. I somehow got a ride back to London and while at home that night the local TV news reported the killing of 5 deer just outside Dorchester. The London Free Press had it in their morning, paper with the headline "local music supervisor kills five deer".

1968 saw a number of major changes.

July 28 a premature Patti is born and spends the first few weeks of her life in the hospital. She is not in danger. The Doctors are following routine procedure. She was very small but grew normally thereafter. Premature birth did not alter her ability to do flips and unbelievable gymnastic maneuvers. She was always very athletic and possessed a unique sense of street smarts.

I had been in the London area for some time and had no desire of moving to another area. I transferred the Simcoe – Brantford franchise equity to the London franchise where Merv Thompson, Paul Bartha and I had formulated the original franchise. Vacant now of Thompson's and Bartha's shares. The why's your will soon learn.

A major event involved Jane & I purchasing our first home in May of that same year. 16 Westbury Grove located at the end of a cul-de-sac, a 4 level, 4 bedroom, 3 bath, 2 car garage with a living area of something around 3500 sq ft. Definitely upper middle class. Price? Get ready! $28,500. Amazing how the price of real estate has escalated. It was only 2 years old having been originally purchased by a Ford engineer who was returning to Dearborn MI. A quick sale was apparently necessary due to inner Ford issues but a huge financial break for the Masse family.

The other 1968 headline for me was the breakup of the original "StratoTones", after some 8 years on the road. It was such a throwback to my younger years watching them perform at the local Brass Rail and Campbells. The group was a solid R&R group with a strong following. Anyway, with the breakup, Vic Denomy finds himself at his London home – unemployed. We worked out a deal where my old friend joined OCOM organizing a new drum program. I was so proud of seeing my old trusted buddy in concert with me. Over the ensuing years he became recognized as a superior teacher elevating the drum program to one of the more popular programs we taught. He was awarded "teacher of the year" among his peers. If memory serves me correct it was 1974.

There were an abundance of changes in the educational music business surrounding OCOM. Newfound competitors and expansion fueled by giant egos. It resulted in me leapfrogging to the elevation of "the main honcho " in South Western Ontario.

I called it "the big shakeup". Here it is in abbreviated form and the "why's" referred to earlier.

Beginning in late 1969 the senior office executives decided on a major expansion outside of the Ontario market place. This was brought on by the ex OCOM mavericks who had started a successful competitive business's in Ottawa and Winnipeg. The Corporate expansion decision was to expand to Alberta under a new name "Dominion Conservatory of Music". Consequently, key middle management personnel and others who simple wanted a change, including Paul Bartha whose marriage was now disintegrating, left for new beginnings in Edmonton.

In the middle part of 1969 my other co-partner, Merv Thompson, who was a senior in the Simcoe/Brantford franchise, got in the preverbal wringer when he was caught messing with the wife (she chose to remain in the London area perhaps for that reason) of a major ex OCOM person (I originally hired during the early days in Simcoe) who now was a major player in the Ottawa operation. Well, of course all hell broke loose with Thompson's dysfunctional marriage and his OCOM position. I will shorten the process of the decision-making and just say he left his wife, family and franchise shares (a total hell to sort through) and became involved, in a senior position with Dominion Conservatory of Music in the province of Alberta. It is a fair notation while mentioning the marriage breakdowns of Bartha and Thompson; dark clouds were and had been forming in my own marriage too. More later.

I now was in a superior negotiating position for the control of the London franchise as the corporate office had taken back Thompson's share position in the London franchise in exchanged for an equity position in Alberta. They well understood that remaining in a shared position with me was not in their best interest. Added to that situation they wanted me to take over the general management of Simcoe/Brantford for a monthly fee.

As all this shit was hitting the fan, a friend, Neil Matheson started asking a lot of questions and showing interest in the music business.

Neil, Helen, Paul & Judy Lansing, Lyle & Jean Shields and Jane & I were all close friends partying and entertaining one another. We formed a 'Gourmet Club' where we alternately would host a monthly gourmet dinner party at each other's home. Neil elected himself as the elitist of the group always on top of the current music theme, meaning the music recording industry. He knew everything about the Beatles. He was the grand connoisseur of music, wine and food. Helen worked in a bank and he was in the municipal-insurance business traveling all over Ontario. They did not have children, as was the case with Paul and Judy. Paul & Lyle worked together in the garment industry, both in office positions. Judy worked in a real estate office close to the Westmount area where Jane & I lived. Jean and Jane were stay-at home moms. Anyway Neil asked to meet with me for a late night dinner where he, as expected, proceeded to tell me he was tired of the constant travel and had developed a high interest in my music business and wanted to join me in the business. He later in life told me that part of his reasoning was "if you could do it, I could do it". Over additional meetings we agreed to a business plan and in July he officially resigned the insurance business and joined the London franchise as an equal partner. St. Thomas and Simcoe were not part of the deal. His position would be the enrollment/marketing manager, relieving me of these management duties. He agreed to the standard OCOM pay plans for such a position. That is, commission on his enrollments and an override on all registrations generated by his enrollment staff. He was not opposed to direct commissions, as this was the basis for his income in the insurance business. On my side of the equation I was overwhelmed with work and could certainly use the assistance. I had great respect for his salesmanship and winning personality and here was the clincher for my willingness to share the London deal. We had agreed in principal of a business deal but I still had not fully decided. Of course I had to provide full disclosure to the corporate office so they would be well aware of the deal. In fact they were required to approve the deal. They had already asked me to be the Simcoe general manger so they said "John, you already have the responsibility of Simcoe/Bantford why don't you buy the franchise, joining Margaret Thompson". She was the bookkeeper and office manger and already had a minority share position. So in the big picture I was giving up half of London and gaining most of the Simcoe Area Franchise.

With the addition of Simcoe added to existing St. Thomas and London we were teaching about 800 students weekly generating over $10,000 in monthly lesson revenue plus instrument sales and music publication revenue.

There is an old saying "be careful what you ask for – you might get it".

In July 1969 Neil joined the company and by the middle of the following year he left the London Franchise, unable to perform his responsibilities by accepted company standards.

Resulting in a horrific financial position for both Neil and Helen. They had refinanced their home to generate the needed funds to purchase half of the franchise. They eventually left London moving to Stratford and started a music records/ reproduction equipment retail shop and did very well with it. He remains in the same business today.

I mostly blame myself for this failure. He should never been allowed to become engaged in ownership without first spending time learning that side of the business. The notion, that he was a good salesman with a beaming personality is distinguishly flawed as qualifying credentials to entering ownership. Spending time in this elected position as an employee would have given him insight as to what was necessary and given me, and others, the opportunity to assess his effectiveness. We would have all learned of his lack of staff leadership. It also serves as a reminder that going into business with friends is dangerous. Working with friends is one thing. Business is quite another.

So, here I was faced with yet another dilemma of reconstructing and reassembling partnership and right of survivorship agreements. It's less than a year for a second such execution. Finding the fair and equitable arrangement is never fully acceptable to all. Somehow you do what you have to in resolving the unpleasant, distasteful occurrences in life.

The business was doing well and as we proceeded through 1970 and 1971, we were now collectively teaching just north of 1000 students weekly – 7 major studios and 11 satellite studios. Combining full and part time personnel represented more than 100 on weekly staff payroll. To add to the workload it is important to distinguish the difference in attitude and the countenance between music teachers, sales personal and administrative staff. Teachers always seemed to want to take shortcuts and do less than required. While sales people were always up, and in contrast to teachers, trouble always seemed to find them. Management seemed to be always solving one of their problems. Solve one and two more would appear and they never had enough money, no matter their income. I always seemed to have a negative slant towards administrative people, as they never were considered productive personnel in terms of generating income. For that reason, flawed as it sounds, I found it difficult to justify their personal income.

The workload and stress in keeping the balls in the air eventually took their toll. In the summer of that year I became sick with an unknown illness. I had an unusual headache, to this day I rarely ever get one, and the type of head pain was different as it was located in the back of my head. I finally took time off work trying to recover at home swallowing gobs of aspirin resulting in no change to the pain, vomiting a green fluid and I began running a fever. Jane became concerned and called Dr. Joe in Detroit. He told her to get me to his office as soon as possible. She in turn contacted Neil who immediately drove me to Joe's clinic. I remember my sister Joanne, who worked at his clinic, taking my personal information for the required medical file. As I was unable to give her the requested information, I noticed her hand beginning to shake. I then sensed something was quite wrong. Joe did a few tests and immediately checked me into Deaconess Hospital, next door to his clinic. The medical staff did more tests, and concluded I had spinal meningitis. Not good. Usually fatal if left unattended. The level of the virus in it's current stage was not fatal but definitely had to be treated. I remained in the hospital for 3 or 4 days and was released to recover at home. As usual with Joe, no doctor bill and no hospital bill. He was always there for our family no matter the circumstances or conditions. I recovered at home over the next week and returned to work with only minor reminders of my condition. However, to this day, if I am over stressed or run down I get that same feeling in the back of my head.

The personal "biggie" that year was the birth of Jason, December 28, 1970. Five girls and finally a boy! His arrival was like the arrival of the Messiah. He may not have been planned but he was sure welcomed. My male friends and I celebrated for days! Jane and baby were both in excellent condition. He has always been a treasure, loved by all and survived growing up amongst 5 older sisters. A near miracle!

In early 1972 we moved the office from 528 Dundas Street, across from Beal Tech High School to 479 Highbury. (remember, next door to 511 Highbury) The move was a definite upgrade from the 2nd floor, 800 square foot office to 2000 square feet. It was carpeted throughout giving us an accounting/reception area, 3 private offices, an instrument showroom, a new organ and advanced teaching area and our own instrument/supplies warehouse. Up to now we had to rely on warehouse facilities in Ingersoll, resulting in saving tons of driving and time. Shortly after the move I hired Lorne McNaughton, my father in law, to manage the warehouse and responsible for the instrument loaner inventories, saleable instrument inventories and all instrument deliveries. I had always been fond of Lorne, as most who knew him shared that same fondness. He had been unemployed for some time and he was eternally grateful for the break. I suppose Lorne would have been in his mid 50s at the time and in great physical shape. He did come with some baggage as he battled alcoholism acquired while serving his country during WW2. He was ever loyal and committed to his responsibilities. I did have some stressful times when he would be discovered severely impaired driving the company truck. He would feel terrible the next day, knowing he betrayed the trust given and would promise, over the last promise, to never, never again. I must have fired him a dozen times only to rehire him. How could I not? And besides he did a great job. The warehouse facilities necessitated the purchase of a company van, which we had painted with the company colors and inscribed with the company logo. He was so proud of "his truck" and maintained it better than anyone.

We are trucking along through 72 and 73 with no major company issues, always and it seemed forever, making franchise payments, scrambling to make payroll along with paying rents, utilities, phones and expenses that all go with running a business. During this time it seemingly became a Friday night after hours ritual for my buddies to all meet at my office and of course imbibe like this would be the last Friday night we would ever meet and we would almost always leave roaring drunk and continue the nonsense at one of the downtown bars. During one of these famous episodes we had all left agreeing to meet, I believe at the Iroquois Bar. Dale McAllister was left to drive with me. On our way down to the bar, we get pulled over by the local police. The probability of me in jail is next to a given, along with a loss of driving privileges. The attending lone officer is asking the usual questions along with were had we been? Explaining that we just left the office after a late day meeting. He asked me where I worked and were the office was located. I told him and he responds that his son takes advanced music lessons at this same location. God Almighty! So, of course this is my divine opening and I engage him with the expected yada yada. He explains they are very happy with their teacher and the musical progress their son is achieving and that his teacher has recently stated that he is to be moved up to the next advanced music level requiring an advanced instrument. God Almighty again! I can't believe this. The "opening" is seized upon and I tell the officer the instrument in question is quite expensive and I admit that following the letter of the law, one in my condition might result in not financially beneficial to my family and that given our mutual situations we might be able to help each others families. He looked at me for what seemed eternity, not saying anything and me being in total abstinence of speech. He finally said "I guess we could work something out". I gave him my business card and wrote on the back something akin to " retail instrument discount to 'company costs' from whatever selected advanced instrument chosen." Signed and dated it. He thanked me and I thanked him. We met several times through the following years, always cordial and friendly to each other and never ever mentioned our initial introduction.

Dale is beside himself, shaking his head in disbelief and we are both roaring in laughter.

The year, however, ends with life not so funny, gay and successful.

Jane's and my marriage relationship had been deteriorating for some time, gradually becoming unbearable for both and definitely not a healthy environment for our children.

I no longer recall the specific reasons or causes, but like sundown forms from the light of day to gradual less light to the faded colors of the evening, to perpetual darkness of the sunless night. It was not a sudden but a gradual occurrence. It seemed we had isolated each other to separate islands, miles and miles apart, hesitant to communicate, our egos not allowing civility or common sense. We had grown apart from the mutual paths we once happily shared. To my erroneous fault, my daily focus was the ever-consuming business that dominated my mind and thoughts. Wrong? Of course! To this day I marvel at married couples having successful working careers and combine that with a joyful, resourceful marital relationship. Not today, but at the time I remember wondering if I had been a bus driver would it have made a difference to life and marriage?

Just before Christmas Jane and I mutually agreed to a separation. Coping with the hardships that the cycles of life play on each other, we are faced with extreme difficult executions that drain our resolve and emotions. Sometimes we just don't know how we will get through. You just dig down to find the will.

On January 2nd or 3rd 1973 I faced the most gut-wrenching act I have ever been faced with then or since. With 4 of my oldest 6 children sitting on a couch facing me, with Jane in attendance, I told them I was leaving the family and our home so that their mother and I could work out some difficulties we were having. I would be leaving that night – right now, and I promised I would spend every weekend with them. I believed that Connie and Kelly where in expectation of this decision, though none ever indicated their suspicions. Watching the pain and disappointment register on their faces as I delivered the dreadful announcement was dreadfully horrific. If I live to a 122, I will never ever forget the awful, sickening feeling. I am certain neither they nor Jane will either.

CHAPTER THREE

POST MARRIAGE SEPARATION:

To find new living quarters I joined Vic Denomy, who too was separated, (must have been something in OCOM drinking water) and living in a furnished one bedroom, one bath, living room, no kitchen apartment. The apartment was part of a single family home owned by a former follower of the Strato Tones, whose name was "Maggie". A divorced, 30ish with hot pants, who continued trying to bag either one of us, without luck I might add. The temporary arrangement allowed us time to find something more permanent and more accommodating. The one bedroom apartment lasted only 6 weeks. Thank God! To complete the sleeping accommodations we weekly alternated the one bed and living room couch. Sometime in February we moved into a two-bedroom apartment on Adelaide Street putting a end to the alternate sleeping and no kitchen arrangement.

I really missed the kids and knew I was needed with their development. Throughout 1973 and 1974, Jane & I discussed reconciliation, all to no avail. I was haunted by guilt and kept thinking that maybe we could make it work, but Jane always deferred. She may have realized my attempts were for the wrong reasons.

Around this time I hired Ken Cassis, brother to Philip who unknowingly at the time would later become my partner in the electronic sign business. Ken lived in St. Thomas and as such he began his OCOM career in enrollment sales and later I promoted him to area manger for the St. Thomas area franchise. He had no previous sales experience but was an astute student who learned the business quickly and efficiently and we became good friends even to this day.

His sales success did not go unnoticed and two years into his institutional music career was recruited by the life insurance industry. I hated to see him leave but knew he would also shine in that industry. He became a star very early, selected to the "Million Dollar Round Table" and remains to this day in the insurance industry.

Some time late in this same year (1974) I met someone I grew to like a lot. As it happened she lived in the very next apartment complex to Vic and I. Dixie was a blond, slight of build, in her late 20s, divorced with two children, had a good heart and worked in an office. It wasn't a monogamous relationship on my part but I did inconsistently see her for the next 3 years. She was much more serious about us than I and wanted the marriage thing. At the time it was the farthest thing from my mind and the off and on relationship finally ended just after the Tramps Video arcade in Grand Bend – 1977.

As 1973 ended and wove into 1974 I found myself living the unfamiliar singles life. The music business continued to develop and do well with no startling negative or smashing effects. To generate more positive promotions and public awareness we had started to be more involved in the public eye doing street and community events making the public more aware of OCOM. One of our annual events was to rent display booth space in one of the commercial buildings at the "Western Fair". The fair was the major one in all of Western Ontario, very well attended and lasted for 10 days. One afternoon I was manning the booth when a blast from the past appeared – Jean Overholt. I casually dated her when I was 15 & 16 years old while living on the family farm. Her brother was a guitarist/singer in the original Melody Masters. Jean was in her mid 20s at the time, several years older than I. My Mother was having a fit not able to connect the dots of a 20 something year old having an interest in a mid teenager. She had cause to be upset as I of course was still in school and Jean worked in Windsor coming home weekends to see me. At one point Jean promised me a 57 Chevy convertible if I would agree to marriage. Somehow Mother learned of this, I suppose only by methods mothers know of. When she confronted me with this information I managed to calm her hysterics and assured her this was definitely not any of my plans. But it did prompt her to ask "what do you do to these girls?" Not an easy question to answer truthfully. Thankfully, like most early teen flings it passed. But back to the beginning of the Western Fair story. While I had not seen or spoke to Jean for what seemed eternity I immediately recognized her as she walked past the booth and motioned for her to come over, hoping to learn what she was doing and exchange a friendly visit. She gave me an ugly sneer, lazily flipping her hand toward me and continued to walk away. Long after ending our little fling, I had seen her at dances we (Melody Masters) played and I was a friend of her brother and never spoke ill of her. I could not understand her spiteful rudeness. I guess that measures teenage affairs.

Having lived in London for 15+ years I developed a number of male friends. One person in particular was a single guy by the name of Don Beynon. Don was in his late 20s and a sales rep for the Honda Small Engine Division. One day he called and said he had read an article about the Mardi Gras in New Orleans. I too had read several books on the rich history of N.O. and was fascinated with its 350-year history. It is one of the oldest cities in the U.S. For me, while the Mardi Gras sounded interesting, the city itself was more alluring. We decided to go.

We had a direct flight out of Detroit. Because of the OPEC gasoline embargo we were, for reasons still not clear, routed to Atlanta ostensibly for refueling? Anyway it was a 4 hour lay over and what a grand reason to get hammered. The moment we arrived in the French Quarters, even in my drunken stupor, I could not shake the sense and feeling that at some previous time been or visited N.O – knowing I had not. I won't get into a lot of the details but I was truly bothered by this Dejai-Vous sense that occupied much of my non-drinking time. One morning I took upon myself to explore the French Quarter. Walking alone, kind of meandering the streets, I somehow had a sense of direction to an undetermined place. After maybe an hour of walking I found myself standing in front of a historic landmark. Reading the historic marker informed me it that it once was an Ursuline Convent donated in the 17th century by King Louis 1V. I found the exterior of the building vaguely familiar and was able to visualize the interior. It was a bone rattling experience and one that still causes goose bumps. During the entire time in New Orleans, I never did shake that sense. Yet, in subsequent trips to the Quarters I never again experience the same powerful feeling, only a fraction of the original.

Mardi Gras is a gala happening that any first timer cannot imagine. People from every corner of the globe, intermingling with everyone in the streets, the bars, the restaurants, even the old basilica. The forever on-going parties. The parades sponsored by the various Krewes. (clubs) The unforgettable music at Pat O'Briens, Preservation Hall and dinner at the oldest U.S. restaurant "Antoines" and of course Jackson Square and Cafe de Monde. Just some of the places I remember for this story. I have revisited New Orleans, specifically the "Quarters" five times and urge anyone who have not treated themselves, to visit this remarkable city.

Not long after returning home, I believe the date was March 6 or 7th, the family home was gutted by not one, but two fires. I was in the process of getting another car. Since Dad was in the car business getting another leased car was simple procedure. Good, because of my extensive travel. I plowed on excessive miles. I had arranged for another Pontiac Grand Prix and the agreed plan was to meet Dad in Grand Bend late Saturday afternoon to complete the required paper work. I knew it would be a short trip and thought Mom and Dad would enjoy seeing Jane again. Wrong! The paper work was over in a flash and the meeting went on more as a visit and we ended staying for an early dinner. Just as we were preparing to leave for London the phone rang with mother nervously handing me the phone. It was a hysterical Connie screaming the kitchen was on fire! I physically sank to my knees in disbelief and ordered her to get the other children out of the house. The neighbors quickly took them into their homes and called the fire department. Driving well over the speed limit, we arrived some 45 minutes later at which time the fire had been extinguished. The damage was minor, more from water than that of the grease fire and limited to the kitchen. After discussion we decided it was best for some of the family to spend the night with Jane's sister, Joan. I took most of the children to my apartment. About 6:00 AM, the next morning, the phone woke me up. The home was fully ablaze with smoke and fire erupting from the roof and windows. The decision to leave was primarily due to the smell of smoke and again, not due to fire damage.

The 2nd fire re-ignited from a spark that found it's way into the attic above the stove. While a search of the attic by the fire department proved to be clear, undetected smoldering re-ignited during the later hours and gutted the entire home. We were all devastated but thankful for the blessings of the decision to leave. Parental guilt washed over me from head to foot.

We had first-rate home insurance through my uncle Ken Etue with 100% coverage for contents and building. Jane and the children were moved to a Howard Johnson's and eventually to a rented town home. She and children eventually moved to a purchased single family home on Chester Street in south London. They lived there until Jane sold the home 15+ years later.

It amazes me how children constantly demonstrate, their inner strength and courage, in overcoming huge challenges, set backs and failures. Exception to the above in my estimation, are the emotional tolls and scars of family divorces. The fire had another consequence. It permanently ended Jane and John's marriage.

1974 ended without further developments, but for one.

Corporate, head office management called a meeting notifying me that they wanted substantial payment towards the franchise by way of the home loss insurance settlement. Franchise payments were not in arrears. The conversation sent me reeling. I could not believe their insensitivity and I was further inflamed when they served written notice! I declined in clear terms and they never proceeded with it. But, to me the damage had been done. I would not ever forget that on the surface, some 14 years of service, was lost to the attraction of cash. This particular act would later become one of the corner stones of my decision to leave the company. And I did, the following year.

Early in 1975 I received a call from another OCOM franchisee, inviting me to join him in a weeks vacation in Florida. His name was Frank Zolnai. He had started with the company about a year after me and also in the enrollment division. He was based out of the Guelph/Kitchener area and coincidently about the same time as me became a franchisee. We were the youngest of all franchisee's and considered the "up and coming young bucks".

Frank had previously visited the upscale golf/tennis destination community in Apopka FL a suburb of Orlando, called Erroll Estates. It was during this vacation period that the seed of an idea began to form in connection with a project we titled "King Arthur's Court". The concept as the name implies, is a throw back to Mid Evil Times with the theme depicting a castle reflecting the era of 1100 – 1200. A moat would surround the castle and arena where spectators would watch live jousting. The visiting spectators would pick a "winning" jouster of the available six, selected from accompanying programs and warm up proceedings. The jousters would dress in the regalia uniform of the period, including chain mail and helmeted head gear. The horses would be dressed in the protective riding equipment all of us have witnessed watching movies of the era. The winning spectator would receive a photo taken with the winning jouster and horse. Receive gifts purchased with credits provided by the company and crowned "King Arthur and Queen Guinevere". The attraction venue also included customary vendors, gift shops, restaurants and pubs of the middle age era. All staff would be in costume.

The idea/concept was fueled around the consideration Orlando was the center of the newly developed Disney World. Added to this were the abundant rumors of additional coming attractions. The business plan would take into consideration access to the many tourists visiting Disney along with additional attractions seeking to also capitalize on the high tourist volume.

As the concept progressed we began connecting the dots to higher levels. We found contacts that put us in touch with commercial real estate parties and we quickly obtained a purchase option on 14 acres of raw land 4 miles from Disney and adjacent to Interstate 4. We were not ready to make this type of decision but the offer was so good we could not turn it down. I am not totally certain but believe the purchase price was $650,000, with a $5000 good will deposit with an option term of 6 months. We signed the option. Without exception, everyone who knew of our plans said we stole the land.

In May we were back in Orlando moving the project further. We hired architects to provide renderings and initial building designs, engineers providing flood and parking studies, traffic and sewer studies determining impact to the surrounding community. Accountants projected completion costs of $3.5 to $4.5 million – after land purchase. They business plan also supported a 5 to 7 year debt payoff. All of the above was necessary to obtain project financing. Before returning to Canada, we obtained the services of a law firm, at no costs, based on their firm representing the project, subject of course to financing. Their job was to find lending institutions before taking it to the backup plan of private investors who would insist on a company share position. We soon learned the "flaw" in the project. It was a period of high loan interest rates and banks became more conservative and selective towards commercial loans. The basis of any bank discussions were centered to not more than 50% loan to cost basis. Deadly. Not good for Frankie and Johnnie.

Undeterred, we determined to release the law firm and abandon the banks and seek private investors. We received positive responses from investors in Toronto, New York and New Jersey. More on these proceedings later.

I still had not recovered from the requested "money grab" of the home insurance settlement by head office. It bothered me to the point of affecting my belief, not in the industry, but in the company itself. I started thinking I was buying a job and that I would be forever paying off a franchise that without me would garner a much lower market value. Negative yes – but that was the reality of my mind. Additionally, I was tiring of the business having done nothing else in my business career. Resigning and negotiating a buyback from head office preoccupied my mind. I approached Frank with the idea of selling our franchisees and concentrating on finalizing the start up of King Arthur. He agreed. With the decision made, it allowed us to be in a "hands on" position and not having a direct presence in Florida did not appear to be an option. For me, leaving London became inviting. I knew our marriage was over and I was in a personal relationship that I saw as crowding me into a corner. To be honest I liked the arrangement but did not want marriage. Leaving the scene seemed like a good alternative.

Our initial ownership plan was simple and I am sure over time realty would have dictated modifications. Build the project, operate it and after providing positive cash flow sell it for a net profit. To my thinking having private investors rather than a lending institution opened more avenues in addition to the open market for Frank & I to finalize the project allowing us to return to our home country. I was not an American citizen and becoming one was not in my immediate plans. Leaving my family for long periods disturbed me but if we could complete the plan in the original time frame I would be able to return to some place closer to the family.

Head office had me over a barrel as they correctly figured that leaving the company was not an obstacle to our Florida plans. They always thought of Frank and me as mavericks and so the negotiations were really one sided. In the end I agreed to two and half years family support payments, plus free health insurance. Not much more than $45,000, which does not speak well of my negotiating powers. I just wanted out and move on.

As I read my day timer organizer, preparing and jogging my memory for this narrative, my final hour with OCOM was 2:00 pm June 27, 1975. I had started this journey on May 2, 1960. Fifteen years +2 months.

CHAPTER FOUR

KING ARTHUR'S COURT:

After the "Goodbye Boat Cruises" and "Farewell Birthday Parties" Frank and I, in separate cars, drove to Orlando Florida. It was our belief that this would be our last time in Ontario for a couple of years – save for Christmas Holidays and the like.

Throughout July and August we continued pitching and presenting King Arthur's to private investors and the never ending required studies to satisfy the government and municipal developmental requirements in obtaining permits and state licenses. All with a price tag.

Frank's family flew down for the better part of a month returning to the family home in Waterloo, sometime in mid August. I recall Dixie flew down for a long weekend visit only to get pissed off because she found a note left on my car windshield by a girl I had seen off and on, requesting that I please call her. The note was void of a phone number and that was not lost on Dixie, suggesting of course I had the number. I don't blame her for being mad but undoing that incident took a measured degree of selling.

All potential investors appeared very interested -but no one said "yes".

In the course of this project Frank and I each purchased identical 2bedroom, 2bath golf villa (Erroll Estates) with the understanding that when not in use by us the owners, management would rent the villa to parties who continually visited "Erroll" for golf vacations. The golf course itself, at the time was highly rated as a prestige course and bragged that it recently was the site for a PGA tournament. The villas were all finely furnished and located next to the clubhouse and the three distinctly different golf courses. The villas were rented on a weekly and monthly basis with the rental funds split on a 70/30 basis in favor of the owners. Ample rental history was provided evidencing that even a 6month annual rental covered the mortgage and association dues. The real attraction for Frank and me was providing us the necessary lodging and living accommodations while pursuing King Arthur's.

We were becoming increasingly concerned with the financing issue. During the course of investor meetings, 3 or 4 groups indicated they were interested in investing, leading us to believe a forthcoming commitment. But, sadly by mid September we still did not have a firm commitment to the funding issue. The situation became grave, particularly with the amount of time and financial resources spent.

During this 3month period, we became increasingly aware of an unusual series of a social attraction – for lack of a better term – performed before our very eyes. Of all things, Buddy Carleton was performing with his small group in Erroll's clubhouse lounge and restaurant. And yes, he too was renting one of the golf villas. For me it was like old home week. Not having much else to do, most evenings were spent watching and listening to Buddy and yes finding lots of trouble. While in the bar we could not believe the perceived phenomenon of watching the attending customers line up to play a tabletop video game. Every night customers lined up to play this damn game. As a matter of fact one night I watched two men get into a fight because one of them broke or crashed the line. I became so intrigued with this that I began keeping track of the number of plays in a given night. The following is a sample of explored math:

- Two players per game x .25cents x 6 to 10 plays per hour x 6-7 hours per night
- x at least 6 nights per week (not counting afternoons) = estimated $150/weekly.

We later learned the gross was generally in excess of $200 weekly.

We visited other bars, and lounges -any that had these tabletop videos. All locations we visited were engaged in similar action as observed at Erroll Estates. Unbelievable!

It is important to explain a little of the bar owners mind set as it applies to occupying a floor space in any given bar/lounge. Law permits an owner, to only have a certain number of tables to the total number of square feet in the said room. Given this legal formula if the owner gives up floor space for a game or a pool table this reduces the number of permitted serving tables, as floor space is now used for the selected game(s). Fewer tables, fewer customers= fewer dollars. So, it becomes a question of what will provide the best financial return per the ratio sited above.

The uniqueness of the tabletop video game is that it did not discount the table count as the video game also doubled as a serving table. Therefore the tabletop video game provided a double source of income for the same square footage. A win, win!

At this time I did not play golf (unlike today) and one day while Frank was playing I set out to explore who owned the "pong" game (as they were referred to) in the clubhouse and if possible who manufactured them. I will save the reader the boredom of how I got to the treasured end but just say I found the game distributor in Orlando, talked to him and arranged for a next day appointment.

The result of this meeting follows.

The video table cost $1300 and the split with the location was 50/50. The distributor, who also operated the game in question at Erroll, confirmed most location sites with this tabletop video game grossed an average of $250-$300 weekly.

The math wasn't hard to calculate.

- $800 (reduced from projected $1000) divide by 50% = $400
- Unit acquisition cost = $1300
- Cost reduction to 00 = 3.5 months
- Annual Gross profit= $3500 (after cost reduction and before site collection costs, labor and maintenance)

Neither Frank nor I could recall any type of this game type in Ontario. So, I called some friends in London and asked them to check some bars and lounges in the London area. They reported back that none they visited had any of this so-called game and indicated they had visited the major hotels/bars.

The Orlando distributor was happy to sell us a truckload of this game called "attack" and by purchasing a truckload (13 units) agreed to a discounted price of $1150 per unit. We arrived at this figure because the import duty tax paid to the Canadian government increased the combined price to $1300 as illustrated in the above example.

In late September with the funding still unresolved, we decided to return to Ontario, place the 13 games on location, operate them and wait out the financing delay.

In early October the games arrived and we stored them in Franks garage at his Waterloo home. I stayed with Frank and Sylvia for the following 6-8 weeks and then moved into a nice 2 bedroom, 2 bath, upscale apartment in Waterloo called the Waterloo Towers. Monthly rent $250. Can you believe it!

We easily located the original 13 units in less than a week.

Frank was an above average buyer – as a matter of fact he was superior. We quickly learned each other's attributes. I was not the proficient negotiator that Frank was but my people skills were vastly superior and better at selling the idea to hotel and bar owners. Result, Frank was inside and I was outside.

We hadn't given any idea to an operational name. Locating the units in the vendor's sites required simple paper work identifying the agreement between the two parties and specifying the revenue split. We knew we could not refer our operation to Frank and Johnny's machines and finally stumbled into naming the operation "Taraleigh" after Franks daughter Tara Leigh.

We rented a truck and installed the units with the installations taking longer than signing up the venue sites. We anxiously waited for the first week to pass so we could do the collections. When the collection day finally arrived the owners commented, "It gets played all the time". We opened the locked cash boxes inside the units and could not believe our eyes. Over the top full - $300-$400

That night we celebrated going to the Charcoal Steak House in Kitchener. (a popular bar and restaurant serving the best steaks) It was this very restaurant that OCOM would hold their Corporate Christmas parties for the companies franchisees and executives. While there whom should we run into but Jack Campbell, the president of OCOM. The same gentleman who tried to convince me to tap into the insurance settlement and pay off or at least pay down the franchise mortgage. He was definitely into the sauce and pleaded with me to come back. I couldn't be rude because the company was still paying Jane and providing medical insurance. But------ paybacks are hell. Besides, we could readily see the potential we currently had, not to mention the still in play King Arthur's and by comparison to the music business, I was really enjoying this totally different type of work and seemingly fitting into this new environment.

CHAPTER FIVE

TARALEIGH INVESTMENTS COMPANY:

By the beginning of 1976 we had 25-30 tabletop video games in operation all doing better than original expectations. Through our continued successful revenue history we gained the respect and confidence of the venue location managers/owners and began to branch into other vending products like pool tables, music jukeboxes, shuffleboards and pinball machines. In the beginning we knew little or nothing of these products or the coin operating business, however everything just seemed to fit and worked. We were able to purchase additional products from current cash flow meaning no bank or credit lines, which would be a large future advantage.

The accelerated growth of the company caused us to think less and less of King Arthur's.

Suddenly, in early March we were notified by our Orlando contact that a verified investment proposal was expected from a small group of US Arab investors. I no longer recall the reason but it never materialized. Additionally through our in-attention and possibly the intentional oversight by the Orlando contact, we allowed the land purchase option to expire, which was immediately purchased for a couple of thousand dollars over our option price of $650,000. The new owners later resold it for well over a million dollars. How reckless and careless and, the farewell to King Arthur's Court. Keeping the land option in play would have allowed us to possibly recapture some of the seed money and maybe allowed us a handsome profit. In closing the subject, permit me this last memento. A near perfect copy to our original plans and drawings emerged and was operational, two years later, but now under a new name, "Medieval Times", near Disney World and in the Kissimmee area. Ugh and enough!

*See newspaper article listed in Photo Gallery.

The lack of office space was becoming a daily handicap and we began searching for affordable office space. We lucked out and found an available, two- story building with basement, in a prime downtown Waterloo location - the vacant old Post Office building. This really handsome historic building was void of any tenants. We negotiated for a portion of the upstairs floor requesting some required minor renovations (some minor work had been done but was limited in scope, possibly adding to the lack of appeal) and we moved into this new office in January. The address was 35 King Street, Waterloo Ontario.

I attended a Super Bowl party at one of my old drinking buddies in London, Dave McGuffin, also a friend of Don Beynon. (Mardi Gras partner) Dave worked for a company that supplied electronic video equipment to institutions like/high schools, hospitals etc. He had arranged to borrow a 4foot projection Sony Television to watch the game. I was blown away in watching the difference in the game compared to a normal 21inch TV. As I watched the game, I was captivated by the marketing potential this ingenious invention represented to the new industry I was now engaged in. In all the bars and hotels I visited during the past 4-5 months I could not recall ever seeing anything resembling this.

I had Dave give me all the available Sony Commercial Product contact numbers. Back at the office I set to work contacting Sony's Commercial Distribution. It was like walking in the dark of dead-ended street. Nothing, or, at least no one prepared to share. They either did not know what I was referring to, and/or could not refer me to anyone corporation. However, I did manage to pickup little pieces of seemingly unimportant information. Undeterred, I began to put the pieces together and followed up the little bits of seemingly minor information. Near the end of giving up, I spoke with the newly formed video division of the Advent Corporation in Massachusetts. Bingo! They had only recently finalized a working proto type of a 7ft projection television called "Video Beam" and were near ready to begin distribution to their "Commercial Product" US Distributors.

They where astounded that someone in Canada had learned of this new product. I carefully declined answering their questions seeking more to protect my luck over their perceived level of our intellect and spying ability.

I was able to secure an appointment and the shortened story is they would wholesale to us in truckload form, and subject to us gaining written CAA approval, (a Canadian equivalent to United States UL approval) a consumer protection government agency. The landed cost was $3100 per unit or almost $40,000 per shipment.

To protect the Advent agreement we required a sizeable warehouse, and to obtain CAA approval we also had to hire an certified electronic technician who could prep the Video Beams for sale, talk the lingo of the CAA board, see to it that all sold Video Beams met CAA approval and provide evidence to Advent that we were not just a couple of hustling salesmen. Mort important, establish a bank line of credit allowing wire transfers for the product before it left Advent.

The business plan stated each Video Beam to sell for $6100 per copy. More marketing details to follow.

The bank determined the presentation acceptable and we secured the necessary line, the technical staff and the warehouse. To obtain the necessary office space we pursued leasing the entire main floor of the Post Office building and negotiated specific renovations, allowing warehouse, offices and receptionist areas with a simulated liquor lounge, including a full viewing area to demonstrate the video beam. We encouraged the owner's to upgrade the 2nd floor offices while construction crews were present thereby increasing the overall appeal of the building. Negotiations were successful and we moved into the new quarters sometime in May. Wow! It was only perfect.

Around this same time I required extensive dental work and began a series of scheduled appointments with a local dentist, a Dr. Weiler, who Frank referred me to. During one of the procedures Dr. Weiler asked how the new business was going. He had read a newspaper article on the tabletop video games in the local paper and knew Frank. One thing led to another and I stumbled on a plan to package a series of video games currently located at various sites. I was able to provide a "revenue history" of weekly collections providing a formula effecting a viable investment. I took the Doctor to several locations where the games were in operation and introduced him to the manager/owners and allowed him his choice of locations. I do not recall the specifics of the locations and games but remember the agreed upon price was something in the neighborhood of $15,000 and the collection data supported the price. At the time the sale was huge for us because it infused a clear profit, as the games were completely paid for through 3 months of operations and just as important it freed us away from collections and weekly site visits permitting more time for other expansions.

This set a new level of profit and set into motion a focus on duplicating the same type of franchising for other video game locations. In the end we repackaged that same scenario 5 or 6 times.

Sometime during this period Dixie and I decided to end our

relationship, I no longer remember the reason. We did get back together later in the year, around Christmas time I believe but permanently separated in the summer of 1977.

We received our first VB shipment sometime in early summer and went to work demonstrating the new product by inviting hotel/bar owners to the newly renovated office lounge, stocked with a full bar. The reception was outstanding and I think we moved the entire shipment within the first couple of months. In meeting with the club owners we learned more about their business as it related to club entertainment. We began coupling the sale/lease of VB with videotapes. By developing and stocking a library of tapes featuring past epic boxing fights, comedy hours, current and past rock & roll concerts hotel/lounge owners were able to promote special entertainment nights to attract patrons on other wise slow nights. Best of all this new entertainment was most affordable when compared to other sources of entertainment. Videotapes were rented on a weekly and biweekly basis.

This marketing package had a dynamic impact on sales and by years end we were well into our 3rd or 4th shipment.

In the course of working with the hotel/bar owners we discovered something else about them. Most, not all, were sexual fiends and deeply interested in pornographic movies. So, not an entity that did not listen to its customer base, we began purchasing porno tapes. The likes of Devil in Miss Jones, Deep Throat and host of others I no longer remember. The porno tapes were by far the most often requested videos.

Following the banks request we were obliged to provide a profit and lost statement on our first 6 months of operation. The bank was very pleased and we were ecstatic with a net profit approaching $90,000. A wonderfully successful first 6 months of operation.

Just a couple of sidebar stories to round out 1976:

In July Joe Burke and I took our two Jason's for a Montana vacation, where Joe owned a fish farm. It ranks as one of my all time very favorite vacation trips so thoroughly enjoying my son and this incredible magnificent state, raw with majestic views and true to its billing "big sky".

In that same summer we hired a local artist to paint a wall Muriel on the stairs leading to the downstairs lounge. One day after work we were all enjoying a drink and the subject rolled around to art. The artist, I forget her name, suggested that since the office had such cultural appeal we should hang art on the walls throughout the office. Frank, the ever opportunist, suggested we contact local artists inviting them to hang their art on a consignment basis and that the company might be able to sell some of their inventory for a 10% commission fee. At the very least the artist would gain public exposure without incurring any costs. Bingo, we were deluged with calls from artists wanting to be involved. One, I remember was a Toronto artist who insisted she be included (by this time little wall space remained available) and would call almost daily. We finally relented and it fell on me to call her and arrange to hang a limited number of her art pieces. She was maybe in her late 20s or early 30s and full of it – if you know what I mean. I do not know why she was all over me like white on rice and slowly became a distraction. I think, she somehow interpreted me as the "art director" and wanted the inside track to move her art. I don't recall how this ended other than she just kind of went away.

Upon my return from our Montana vacation I hired a sales rep to cover the Hamilton area, to help market the VB and possibly new venues where we could operate coin operated video games, pool tables etc. His name: Neil McKay. Why I hired him remains a mystery. He had limited experience in the hotel industry but did have a background in radio broadcasting resulting in strong affiliations with hotel owners. He possessed little or no sales experience. His true background: HORSES.

Before long he convinced us horse racing could be profitable and be a whole lot of fun. Further, due to his vast knowledge of buying/selling and managing horses would give us the inside edge in developing a successful "stable".

Listen to this. By December we formed Taraleigh Stables, purchased 5 or 6 standard bred horses, all of which required stable care, feed, veterinarian assistance and purchased a year old GMC pickup (from Dad) plus a horse trailer to haul the horses from stables to race tracks. Those f------ horses! They won a fair share of races but ate and ate and always needed the care of a vet. They never, ever validated their keep and maintenance. How I came to rue the day of Taraleigh Stables.

This is a good time as any to prepare you for eventual unraveling of TARALEIGH.

It's a lesson that deserves attention and learning. At this point, without exception, everything we tried, including placing an advertisement in the local paper to buy gold coins, just worked beyond any maximum expectations. HORSES the exception. We came to think of ourselves as "invincible". We could do no wrong. Our mindset was no fear. Try anything. Prudence and any sense of caution did not exit in our little world. This attitude and modus operandi, led to careless and dreadful business decisions that eventually took its toll resulting in the forced closing of the business. It started with the damn horses.

As 1977 entered, the business continued to thrive with the VB market enjoying marvelous and powerful media coverage. We were featured on all 3 national TV networks where yours truly would be interviewed, answer questions and make a brief presentation with an actual VB on display. We began exploring and opening new markets in the hospital and educational industry where the institutions would use the large screen to enhance teaching and training sessions. We did untold Hospitality Trade shows like the International Hostex show.

I am not sure of the month but sometime in early spring we were advised of an opportunity to purchase two GMC motor homes. The leasing company we utilized to leased VB's had repossessed both and were looking to resell both through the local GMC motor home dealer. They were in prime condition, only one or two years old and substantially discounted. We personally purchased both – one each. The GM Dealer had a contract with movie productions/producers and having our elite motor homes on location (Toronto) for use by the actors became part of the purchase agreement. This caveat to the deal was very attractive to us, as the rental income would provide the lion's share of purchase payments to the bank. For the most part it was a viable deal and not until the demise of Taraleigh did the motor homes fall to the same fate of almost anything connected to the company. An interesting side story: The Boy Scouts of Canada contacted Frank and I requested renting the two motor homes as they were providing, to a select boy scout group, a 10 day vacation trip to the Canadian East coast. We agreed to terms and they signed the necessary papers and paid their security deposit and rental fees. Along their travels, the driver of my unit forgot about the two roof mounted air condition units and the operating instructions I personally provided. The operating manual specified the required road clearance and this highly enlightened driver either did not read or forgot the bridge sign advisory of 10 feet did not meet the 11 feet of clearance required. "Bam" there went the two A/Cs. They were ripped clear off the roof and scattered onto the side of the road. Along with roof damage, the ever well-behaved scouts somehow removed the head and damaged the shower and dining table. All total an extensive and costly repair and definitely in excess of the collected security deposit and I no longer recall if I was successful in collecting the net difference.

In the pursuit of purchasing video and arcade games Frank became cognizant of "power buying" (volume buying) resulting in preferred cost pricing, allowing us to sell at "distribution prices" to companies that operated coin operated routes, like we did when we first began the business. Doing so meant we had to purchase product from the Chicago Manufacturing base, again, in volume and that dictated the need for additional warehouse space, service techs and a work force to assist in moving and picking up the volume purchased product. Enter a former friend of Franks, who became attracted to Taraleigh through our participation in horse racing. His name was Pat Hannigan.

Having lived my formal years in the Grand Bend area and my family name well known locally, I got the bright idea to pursue opening an arcade to operate during the summer months in "the Bend". Mother suggested the old closed movie theatre. It proved to be only ideal for a Video Arcade. Nothing, anywhere like it in the area. It would feature, in addition to the customary arcade products, a VB playing amplified rock music featuring musicians and groups of the day. We knew we had a winner.

We had in current inventory about half of the 60 required products to equip the arcade resulting in the necessity to purchase the remaining inventory. We drove to Chicago and Detroit and finalized the purchases with the understanding our staff would arrange pickup and remit payment, by way of cashiers checks the following week. Additionally, while in Chicago we negotiated the exclusive Canadian Distribution rights for all of Bally's pinball product line. Meaning any pinball operator/dealer, interested in Bally Pin Ball Product, would have to purchase the game(s) from Taraleigh. A huge win for us! And, Bally was considered the giant in the industry.

Pat Hannigan was to drive the company truck to Detroit to facilitate the physical pickup of the Grand Bend arcade equipment and was issued a series of "bank cashiers checks" in favor of the selected companies and submit payment ($25,000 in total) at time of pickup. Only problem, Pat did not make the trip. He parked the truck off site, went to the local TD Bank and had them cash the checks to liquid US currency on the premise that the American Companies would not accept Cashiers Checks drawn on a Canadian Bank and Frank and John were out of town (which we were) thereby unable to complete the pre arranged payments. The bank confirmed with the office that we were in fact away and cashed the checks, $25,000, advancing the liquid cash to Pat. He left town that very day with of course all of the money. Two weeks later the RCMP found Pat in Alberta, visiting an ex girlfriend, where he had bought her a diamond ring. He was apprehended, arrested and returned to Ontario where he was subsequently sentenced to a 3month jail term in addition to time served. In total about 6 months. We recovered most of the original money and while that seemed to abate the consequences of the theft we failed to fully realize the enormous damage that combined with future events, would eventually ring the bells of doom for Taraleigh.

In the course of importing multiple shipments of arcade products from the USA, government documentation was required affecting the description and cost of the imported goods. The paper work was necessary to establish the import tax paid to the federal government. The completed documentation we prepared was intentionally not fully accurate resulting in the true purchase cost fraudulently stated, thereby lowering the amount of import tax due to the Canadian Government. You could equate this to a person misrepresenting his/her personal income tax returns to lessen the amount owing in personal income tax. During the course of the theft investigation we were compelled to disclose the false documentation in order to finalize the Hannigan guilty verdict handed down by the court. In turn, this resulted in a guilty plea of tax fraud on behalf of Taraleigh. The ever- innocent bank, yes the one and same that cashed the cashiers check for Hannigan, temporarily froze our bank accounts and declined further credit lines. We attempted litigation against them for the freeze on our accounts but abandon it due mostly to the negative distractions to regular daily business operations and the associated legal costs. The "freeze" while temporarily, effectively closed business operations for a short period.

To compound things, in line with our "exclusive Bally Distributorship" a shipment of 500 Hang Glider pinball machines arrived (payment had been completed prior to the theft) with much of the shipment having been pre-sold when we discovered that the big boys in Chicago had not disclosed to us the Hang Gliders were the last of "electric mechanical" pin balls and new releases would be new "electronic" technology virtually making all previous "pins" antiquated. We were now unable to sell the remaining inventory without discounting at or below our landed cost.

While on the subject of what the big boys can do to "mom & pop" distributors like Taraleigh, the local newspaper ran a front page report, just around labor day, that ELECTROME, the large Kitchener Ontario manufacture of Canadian made home televisions, would be licensed to assemble a new revolutionary **Advent** home projection television. The new home system would be a large 6 ft TV, unlike anything in Canada and would retail for $3400. Advent notified us that our 7ft commercial VB would remain available to us for the commercial market. We had 7 units sold, but were undelivered due to "pre delivery procedures". When the Electrohome news broke all 7 orders were of course cancelled. We now had 12 unsold VBs in our warehouse.

Back to May 1977.

We were committed by a commercial lease for the old movie theatre and believed the Tramps concept would be very profitable. But now, due to the removed credit line, we had to find private money (while we secured a replacement credit line) to finance the remaining half of the required inventory. We were to open for the May 24 weekend, the weekend designated as the beginning of the summer trade and when "The Bend" opens for the season. That schedule gave us about 10 days to finalize the financing and pickup the product waiting for us in Detroit and Chicago.

We had long been selling video and other related coin operated equipment to a hotel in Seaforth Ontario. The hotel, owned by Les Seiler, owned other local businesses, including the Seaforth Creamery. I don't recall how, but Frank began speaking to Sieler and an investment deal evolved where he would finance the remaining half of the required inventory, thereby allowing us to open Tramps on time. The back part of the Seiler deal was complicated but essentially a separate company was formed, effecting only Tramps, and would allow Seiler 50% of the net profit and he would retain ownership of the arcade equipment purchased with his investment – but only *that* equipment. Not any of the equipment supplied by Taraleigh. Tramps proved to be successful and we had a good profitable season. To insure that the help hired to operate the business, while we were tending to everyday business back at the office, would not steal us blind - hard, cold cash can be real tempting, I hired Connie & Kelly, my two daughters, high school students at the time, to manage the operation from Monday to Thursday, when company management and service tech's where attending to "regular office business" and not available for the Tramps site. They would continue working behind the counter during the busy weekend when management (usually me) and technicians from head office where present. They worked a grueling 7day week without complaint and always met their obligations.

The girls did a superior job, never missing the required opening, making the bank deposits, the **books balanced** and, the equipment never grew feet. I will always be grate full for both Connie and Kelly's assistance and I know helping to operate a real business was helpful experience toward their future employment endeavors. On a separate note they could fill a small book of "stories" relating to that summer. I will leave it to them to enlighten anyone curious enough to engage their rendition of this part of their history. I guarantee most will be over the top entertained.

During the summer and well after closing Tramps we continued to pursue a bank credit line. The local banks were well aware of our weakened position in the projection television market. The Electrohome news was massive and we learned later in 1978 that our chances of bank line was slim and none. The local banks also knew the circumstances following the theft of the $25,000 and the culpability of the TD Bank in assisting Hannigan converting the bank cashiers checks to cash. The news we later received in 1978 were the banks were playing the "good old boys game" protecting their fellow competition knowing that a credit line would certainly be helpful prevailing a legal position against the TD Bank. They also viewed our financial position as "poor and unstable".

Forced with this negative position we entered into untold number of conversations with Seiler. We must have agreed to a half dozen agreements only to have Seiler change his mind at the last hour, requesting this change or that change. These requested changes would be renegotiated into the next agreement and again Seiler would again change his mind requesting again more changes.

To stay alive we began "packaging" arcade equipment and videotapes with VB customers to at least convert our VB inventory to cash and we also discounted the original selling price to mirror Electrohome's pricing.

Realizing our diminished presence in the projection television market and our growing presence in the distribution of arcade equipment our offices in the old converted post office, no longer adequately served our new business model. We sub-leased the Post Office offices and leased much larger facilities in an industrial mall complex. This new facility afforded us the larger warehouse and service area needed with only minor renovations to the front part giving us two offices and a showroom area.

We were struggling but manage to meet payroll and remain in business and successfully finding new customers to distribute arcade equipment. We closed 1977 hope-full and expectant of riding this storm to a fruit full and mildly successful 1978.

In October I met a very good-looking 26 year old divorced woman at an October Fest event. Her name was Rita Parrott.

In that very month our family celebrated a wonderful event, our parent's 40th wedding anniversary. It would mark one of the final grand family events before our father would soon begin his devastating and crippling health issues.

The relationship with Rita progressed rapidly – in hindsight too quickly – although we really fell for each other, I am not sure if the heavy negative business events influenced my caring. In any event we saw a lot of each other through the remaining months of 1977 and around February Rita resigned her nursing job with a Tillsonburg hospital and moved to reside with me. To be sure, not very good timing. You will appreciate even more as this story continues. In the course of our dating I had discussed my previous New Orleans Mardi Gras visit and agreed to take her there, conditions on the home front permitting.

As previously mentioned, a number of agreements with Seilor failed to materialize and both Frank and I grew to distrust his true intentions. In late 1977, as a means of generating alternative income in the event Taraleigh failed to survive, we formed a separate entity, Conestoga Amusements. We separately purchased and personally paid, a small inventory of arcade equipment and placed them in local hotels/bars to operate on the normally accepted split of revenue. In early 1978 I obtained a 5year second mortgage on Jane's London residence through my father. The written agreement stated "interest only" payments on the note and any possible principal payments were optional. In any event the entire principal was to be paid within the 60month term. There was another purpose for this mortgage as advised by my lawyer, and that was to secure any potential equity in the family home in the event Taraleigh went south – which of course it eventually did. The proceeds from the mortgage loan brought me current with Conestoga Amusements.

In January we finally had an agreement with Seilor that would secure a $160,000 credit line with the bank and would erase the companies bank debt. The proceeds would also insure that we would be able to purchase, in volume, products from Stern Electronics in Chicago and other wholesale providers. The final agreement stated that (a) Seilor would hold 50% of the company stock, (b) be listed as the CEO, and (c) sole signing authority.

Needless to say this was a major concession on our part, but Frank & I conceded we had no other viable alternative options. Following multiple meetings with Seilor's lawyers/ accountants the deal was on. Comfortable that we averted a financial storm and we could now go on to once again grow the company, I purchased flight tickets to New Orleans in time for the Mardi Gras.

The final new shareholders agreement was to be signed the day after my return from New Orleans. However during my "away time" Seilor once again, asked to revue the books. Frank did not hesitate in releasing the books as they were properly audited. On the Monday following, Seilor called saying there was something wrong with the books. He called later that day saying his accountants/lawyers misread the books and all was Ok, and we would sign the new approved shareholders agreement and required paper work later that week. I receive a Tuesday night phone call in New Orleans (we were leaving for home the next day) that Seilor appeared Tuesday at 5:00 PM with a bailiff and a TD Bank official who stamped a "TD" sticker on every piece of equipment, furniture and personal affects. Taraleigh was no more. Dead and we were out of business. I would soon be broke without any viable income.

To further complicate life Seilor, referencing Conestoga Amusements, issued a conflict of interest and possible company theft of Taraleigh funds and/or equipment with the local police. In simple terms Corporate Fraud. Totally inaccurate and false as documentation would later prove. In the ensuing months we concentrated on clearing the fraud charge and we eventually prevailed. Further, we felt we had sufficient evidence to sue Seilor for the false charges and his intentional misleading manipulation. It was our position that the continued agreement alterations were intentional and designed to capitulate the company, acquiring it for costs well below market value. The legal back and forth went on into the ensuing years and I honestly am no longer certain how it concluded although I highly suspect we discontinued the legal course due to insufficient funds.

Selective memory? I do know I remained on the hook for $25,000 personal guarantee to the TD Bank, personal guarantee to Tawco Leasing towards any delinquent VB lease payments and the yet to be resolved bank note for the GMC motor home. Clearly, I no longer had personal income to meet the above guarantees and any personal financial obligations. 1978 would become and remain the lowest point in my business career.

It truly is a tragic ending to what was a sunshine success story of entrepreneurial business. Some of the mishaps yes, were not our doing and one might say "the wrong place at the wrong time". But we were negligent in many areas of good stewardship and falsely assumed we had no enemies and committed some stupid moves supported by a mind-set of "we can do no wrong". Hopefully, much of this narrative can be a valid lesson to young people who maybe reading this.

CHAPTER SIX

POST TARALEIGH INVESTMENTS:

Before continuing with 1978, I would like to comment on the continuous letters and expressions of support and love from my separated family – all of them. I have letters from Connie who helped keep the family lights on (an unbelievable one written in 1977) and copious notes from Julie expressing her "I am always with you" mantra expressed in dynamic creative writing that belied her 13, 14 years of maturity. All will remain in my family archives.

Early in the year, Rita found a job as a receptionist with a hair salon just around the corner from the apartment. We were getting along rather well, the aftermath Taraleigh turmoil not seriously affecting our new living relationship. Through February and March much of my time was spent in the legal support of expunging Seilor's fraud charge and advancing our suit against him. We continued to operate Conestoga Amusements, on a limited basis and we were developing an operating arrangement with a former Taraleigh customer, Grey-Bruce Amusements, whose offices were in Owen Sound Ontario. The principal of the company, Bob Cochrane, would soon serve as my employer in a totally different industry. My personal income with Conestoga was extremely limited resulting in my inability to keep the financial balls in the air and the surviving consequences towards two major commitments.

I had no alternative but to return my leased 1976 Cadillac, with lease terms only a son would receive from a father in the car business. I now did not have a car. I did manage the purchase of another sometime in April. More, on that subject later.

The second was a hard one. I just did not have the available resources to continue the heavy child support payments of near $1000 per month. The alternative was family welfare, which given the current circumstances Jane qualified. Of course she was angry and found it difficult to understand, but like always went along with my program, and once over the initial thoughts seemingly accepted it. I was just plain embarrassed and depressed.

In the midst of all these nasty, ugly decisions I received a call from Jane distraught that Julie had "ran away" and could not be located. She had done this on a few previous occasions, on what I termed "test runs" but always resurfaced shortly after leaving. She had gotten her nerve and this one was for real. After a dreadful two days contacting police and authorities and no available leads, I was awakened at my apartment by a phone call from the Toronto Police Department. Julie had been located hiding under an apartment stairwell and in the custody of the police. Unharmed and aside from being hungry and tired, ok. I called Jane to advise and Rita and I left immediately for Toronto and returned to my Waterloo apartment with my precious Julie by my side.

If you were to read any of her copious notes/letters to me you would clearly realized she most identified with her father. And truthfully, while my children demonstrate certain mannerisms/attitudes/methodology resembling those of their mother and father, none seem more evident than Julie's similarities to me. Don't misunderstand, there are rich qualities and faults of John found in each of them, from Connie to Jason. This was Julie's maverick way of dealing for her father's attention and want of his discipline and family management. She was and remains today a person with a tremendously brave heart, a will of commitment to herself and with the most devious, loving mind.

Well, here we were. A rebellious daughter, living with her father and his girlfriend, with the father fighting for his business life, struggling with an inadequate income and coping with a very troublesome legal position. While that is undoubtedly a recipe for family failure, you find a way to cope and overcome. It is true, at least in my mind, life does not always provide options fair for everyone but the bottom line is one plays with cards dealt and for me folding was not an option. For Julie, the only alternative was to move and reside with her father and learn to cope with his situation. Initially there were some problems between her and Rita, but not many and none that I recall as severe. Though that would change in later years. She had a few bumps with her schooling and a private tutor I had hired to assist her academically, but all went better than expected and most importantly, Julie was under control and functioning as a normal 14 year old.

During the April/May months I began working with Grey/Bruce

Amusements, contributing towards the co-venture of it and Conestoga. The details and purpose of that co-venture agreement escapes me and I find no notes to rekindle my memory. I do remember I disliked the almost daily 80mile ride to Owen Sound and return to Waterloo. I was fast loosing interest and enthusiasm in the amusement business. I needed a car and to facilitate the Grey/Bruce commitment I purchased a 77 Ford Ranchero. The Ranchero was a car with a front seat only and an open bed. The type of vehicle required for the continuous moving of equipment from one location to another. I enjoyed driving it, as it was fast and agile with a powerful 351 Cleveland engine.

Sometime in June I received a call from another past Taraleigh customer and friend at the time, asking my help setting up and running a Dune Buggy dirt track in of all places – the old Trails End western country complex just outside of London. I was totally familiar with Trails End having been a past customer attending Saturday night parties while living in London. More on this unique concept will follow.

I was intimately familiar with The Honda Dune Buggy, called a Honda Odyssey, as Frank & I had seriously studied the idea for a dirt track location in the Guelph area. There was another attraction for the Trails End concept. My doctor was real concerned with recent blood work. My triglycerides (type of cholesterol) were over the top. My blood tests indicated a count of near 800 and norm is 150>200. Getting away from the stress of the amusement business seemed like a good idea. So sometime in mid June, while minimizing my time with Conestoga I helped acquire the Dune Buggies and structured a 1mile dirt track. I actually dug the track with hills and turns using a tractor and bulldozer type blade. We were operational by the July1st weekend.

Trails End, was originally developed 20 years prior on a tract of raw land by a man from Tennessee, whose idea was to create a Western Country style mall complex reminiscent of the old West. The mall with 10-12 vendors, including a furniture store, a country style lounge and restaurant was totally built in wood with artifacts from the Old West Era. Adjacent to the lounge/restaurant was a gas bar. While the complex was very popular on weekends and holidays it remained sort of ghost like during the regular workweek. And that remained the reason Mr. Tennessee (who I actually met and talked to several times as a Trails End customer) and all subsequent owners lost the property, the cash flow not sufficient.

But now, Stewart Dom, a wealthy Cambridge Ontario businessman owned it, and was managed by a real estate company owned by Phillip Cassis – brother of my old friend and former employee, Ken Cassis. At another time in the future Phillip and I would become partners. It's a small world folks.

The tract had a successful season and ran through to late September giving way to the shorter hours and weather. Somehow, during the latter part of the summer the gentleman who operated the lounge and gas bar fell into disfavor with management and was told to leave which he did, as his lease contract expired. Someone took over the restaurant and I, looking for revenue, became interested in the lounge. The gas bar supplier and owner of the gas pumps was left with no other option but to operate the gas retail himself. He did so reluctantly because his business was distribution not retail. The lounge did not possess a liquor license, but somehow the former operator did sell beer/liquor – illegally. The lounge was not operating due to the vacancy and so, myself and a couple of guys involved with Trails End, decided to take a shot. Not doing so was viewed as a missed opportunity as the lounge was very busy on weekends. We soon realized that however the former operator managed to sell booze, we were not going to do so without being charged with bootlegging, a felony of course. But, before that eventuality we decided to test our current reasoning. If the former could sell "booze" and get away with it why couldn't we? Well we soon found out we were the exception. I as the "lounge operator" took the precaution to pay someone to take "the fall" (at the time I called it catastrophic insurance) in the event that the police found our reasoning faulty and visit us. Well, one Saturday night, this ill licit affair ended as the police did indeed charge "the fall guy" with bootlegging.

A lawyer visited me and thought he could help by forming a private club. To form a "private club" I had to retain a certain number of private members, and as such would permit selling liquor without the traditional LCBO license. It showed promise but then the fire marshal made the "members club" prohibitive. In the end I settled on continuing the Saturday night dances and Sunday Jamborees with live country bands all without the sale of booze but charged an admission fee and sold soft drinks, ice and snacks. Under this new policy (BYOB) the lounge became even more popular as customers learned it was less expensive.

As this was happening the gas distributor lost interest in operating the gas bar and approached me (I later learned that Phillip spoke well of me to the distributor) asking me to run the gas bar, as it did considerable volume. He was well aware of my financial disposition that I would be unable to front the $3000 - $4000 for the weekly gas/diesel deliveries. So, he said he would front the first load and that I would pay him after collecting the gas sales revenue for the sold product and remit payments after the fact.

Now I was back in business. I well knew the Trails End deal was temporary and that its sole purpose was to buy me time while I found something more to my interests.

Rita had landed a job with Clairol as a color consultant/technician and after spending a month at their Montreal offices training was now ready to assist local sales rep's selling Clairol products to hair salons.

With the changes involving the Trails End "ranch" we decided to move to London. In early December we rented a 3 bedroom, townhouse/condo. We would live there until our move to Michigan in 1984.

Meanwhile, back at the ranch, my weekend assistants, Rita, who covered the entrance collecting the admission fee and Julie who worked the mix/ice/snack counter. We all wore our western outfits, complete with boots and cowboy hats. I roamed the floor taking on a "sheriff" persona talking up the customers and selling Trails End. Actually, the revenues where reasonable and I began to see light in the past miserable financial tunnel. But, I well knew I would have a heavy challenge with past debtors and the latest, the GMC dealer repossessed the motor home at the banks direction. The list was growing.

In closing 1978 (the year the devil visited me) Dad entered a London Hospital having the first of his 7 surgeries, all within an unbelievable 15 months, and lived through all, including double leg amputations. Talk about strong! While that was the beginning of the end for Dad, the dreadful "78" for me was ending. Now, my only objective: repair and correct the past one and half years as revealed in chapters to follow.

The New Year began without any major mishaps. Julie was living with us and later in the year Penny moved in. Both of the girls had always seemingly been joined at the hip, so the move was in line with the past. Though the two together were subject to "trouble" and more "trouble" somehow finding them.

Trails End was doing ok with steady weekly income. I decided to punch up gas bar sales. If I remember correctly my margin was about ten cents per sold gallon. I began calling on local business's owning multiple trucks (fleet trucking) to acquire their gas business. To induce them I offered them a discount over a certain volume and I would open the gas bar earlier to afford them early access. That soon doubled my diesel fuel sales and of course increased gas revenue.

An interesting story involved the local musicians union, who suddenly were on my case for hiring non-union musicians. Trials End had always been a non-union hall. Alerting this fact to these dim wits was like water off a duck. They just kept hounding me to join the union and to hire "union musicians" only. Clearly, someone out there wanted me removed so they could take over the lounge.

Financially, I was doing a magical shuffling act managing to keep the balls in the air but fully knew I would be unable to continue keeping the wolves from the door. The time I bought by moving on the "Trails End" project would soon be over. The legal costs defending the fraud charges was a $2000 bill that I sure as hell could not afford, not to mention the on going effort with my debtors. Somehow, and I do not recall how, we sold Conestoga Amusements to a local amusement game operator, so I am sure some of that money helped. I am totally void of how that came about and who purchased our equipment and vending route, allocating the venue sites and revenue to the new operator.

As stated earlier, beginning in the New Year Rita was traveling with the Clairol sales reps and no longer using her car for work purposes and so we thought we could manage with only one car. Some time in late spring I sold the Ranchero resulting in lowering the monthly nut.

Near the end of the year we caught a break – a big break.

The condo we leased from a company, Anchor Homes, was in serious financial trouble. The owner, Wilf Erickson, approached me with the idea to take over the mortgage and title resulting in a purchase for Rita and I. For Wilf, the mortgage transfer would lower his obligations enhancing his "workout" position with the banks. I well knew given my financial position I would not be a successful candidate for a mortgage assumption. We succeeded in convincing Wilf and his banks, that Rita alone could manage the mortgage and association payments, as the combined payments were no more than the current monthly rent. So now, if you can believe it, we, and the bank owned our condo.

At a time yet to be realized, I would hire Wilf as a sales rep.

PICTORIAL BACKGROUND

Leonard Sarars, Dad and me, circa 1952, on the 14th Concession Farm

The Strato Tones (l-r) John, Wayne Muck, Marty Bechler, and Vic Denomy at the Imperial Hotel, Grand Bend, circa 1960

Medieval Times jousts in court with rival show

BY AMY PAVUK
Staff Writer

Medieval Times, the Central Florida attraction that treats guests to dinner while knights joust on horseback and duke it out with battle-axes, wants to stick a sword through what it calls a competitor's new copycat act.

And it wants to take the battle to the courtroom.

A longtime fixture in Central Florida, Medieval Times claims the new Camelot Knights Dinner Adventure & Battle at Pirate's Dinner Adventure has copied its concept and so closely resembles its show that it is likely to cause confusion.

Medieval Times says the image and appearance of its show are protected and wants a federal judge to intervene.

In an 18-page complaint recently filed in Orlando federal court, Medieval Times details all of the similarities between its show and the new show.

"Just like Medieval Times' show, Defendants new show takes the audience back in time and to faraway place, and treats them as royal guests to a period specific multicourse meal while watching, and participating in, an unfolding story involving costumed knights who perform on horseback and off for the royal family and the audience," the complaint said.

Medieval Times' dinner show involves six knights in unique costumes of six colors. So does the new show.

The costumes are similar, including the tunics worn by the knights. The horses even have similar accoutrements.

The Medieval Times story line involves a traitor or intruder. So does the new show.

Neither Medieval Times nor Pirate's Dinner Adventure responded to requests for comment about the legal complaint, which seeks relief for trade dress infringement, unfair competition and deceptive and unfair trade practices.

Medieval Times, which opened its Kissimmee location in 1983 and entertains about 265,000 guests a year, said it first became suspicious when officials learned an employee was moonlighting at Pirate's Dinner Adventure and helping train horses.

That employee has since left Medieval Times and now works for the Camelot Knights show.

In its legal complaint, Medieval Times also attacks the quality of Camelot Knights and details poor online reviews of the new show.

"These acts have caused and will cause significant damages, including lost sales and profits in an amount to be determined, and irreparable harm to Medieval Times," the complaint said. "Moreover, Defendants conduct has caused and will cause significant harm to Medieval Times' reputation and goodwill which Medieval Times has established through years of effort and expense."

Medieval Times wants a judge to block Pirate's Dinner Adventure from presenting, displaying or advertising Camelot Knights Dinner & Adventure.

The company is seeking unspecified damages.

apavuk@tribune.com or 407-420-5735

Medieval Times
Duplicated King Arthur's Court
To it's original concept
Article reports legal issues against
a duplicating competitor

Orlando Sentinel 1995

"Evidence the concept was a good one!"

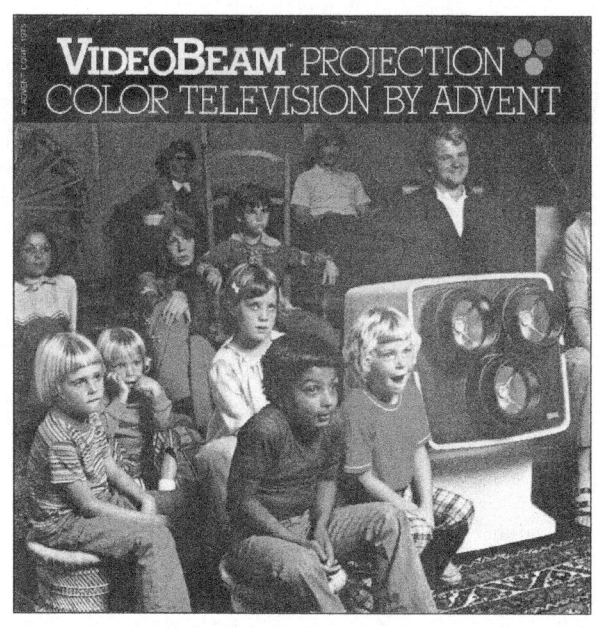

Taraleigh Investments held the Ontario Distribution rights to the Advents VideoBeam system from 1976-1978

Taraleigh Stables - "How to lose money" circa 1976/77

KALEIDOSCOPIC OF A ENTREPRENEUR

Me and my 1986 Corvette somewhere in north Michigan

CinemaKid
proudly presents
The Little People Pleaser

A Childrens Cartoon Theatre made in Canada by Canadians. Our coin operated theatre is easily operated by children & service backup is of the highest quality. Six major cartoon episodes on each cartridge with regular rotations of cassettes.

CinemaKid was a stand alone coin operated cartoon theatre that I designed and manufactured in the late 70's. Hundreds of the units were placed across Canada from 1977 to 1979

The Nu-Media Products Brochure circa 1990

KALEIDOSCOPIC OF A ENTREPRENEUR

Vern Watson and John, early 80's, in the London Nu-Media office

Phillip Cassis, early 80's, in the London Nu-Media office

John Masse early 80s Detroit Cobo Hall Trade Show

The first Nu-Media network electronic display installation, Chrysler Motor Company, 1986

KALEIDOSCOPIC OF A ENTREPRENEUR

CP Air

71 Yonge Street
Toronto, Ontario, M5E 1J7

December 16, 1983

Numedia Systems International Inc
148 York Street
London, Ontario

ATTENTION: MR PHILIP CASSIS

Dear Mr. Cassis:

I would like to express my satisfaction with the three Numedia electronic signs that we have installed in our downtown ticket office locations. The greatest advantage to us is the great ease with which we can change our sales message depending on what destinations have surplus seats- if we announce a seat sale to the media in the morning, we are in a position to advertise the details in our window by the afternoon- it is a great help.

It has been a pleasure dealing with Numedia Systems.

Best Regards,

Priscille LeBlanc

Supervisor, Ticket Offices

Canadian Pacific Air Lines Limited

One of many endorsement letters from Nu-Media's Customer base

ELECTRONIC DISPLAY NEWS EDITORIAL

STATE OF THE ART AT O'HARE AIRPORT

The new United Airlines terminal at O'Hare International Airport includes over 300 electronic signs supplied by Nu-Media Systems International, Inc., and Control-O-Mation. These signs are located throughout the new terminal—from the curbside canopy to the jetway doors. All signs are connected to a commuter network designed and implemented by United Airlines. Up to the moment messages based on current flight, gate and baggage information are generated automatically by the network and sent to the appropriate signs.

The 5016 series, a new state-of-the-art family of LED signs, was specifically designed to meet United's strict requirements. It provides a high quality, flexible, reliable display system. A modular approach allows each size sign to be built out of a common set of electronic modules. All signs contain identical software, providing the same functionality and interface throughout the system. The display sizes installed at O'Hare range from 16 rows of 150 dots to 96 rows of 200 dots. Flip-dot signs from Vultron, Inc. were adapted to use the 5016 controller, providing a totally compatible outdoor sign.

The 5016 series displays provide exceptionally consistent illumination with high contrast, wide viewing angles, and no flicker. The signs provide true dot matrix displays -- graphics and variable size characters can be displayed anywhere on a display, limited only by the overall number of dots. a wide variety of display modes and text attributes adds to the functional flexibility of the signs.

While the signs have been designed for a long, trouble free life, they have also been designed to be easy to repair. Built in diagnostics help identify problems -- the sign can even determine when an LED burns out. Since the diagnostics can be run remotely, the system can automatically check the signs and identify problems without human intervention. The modular design makes on-site repairs quick and easy while minimizing the spare part requirements.

Design of the 5016 series began in August 1986. The first units were shipped in March, 1987. All signs were installed and operational as required for the opening of the terminal in August 1987.

#	Location	Type	Face	Size (inches)
13	Curbside	Flip dot	Single	5.9x90
68	Main Lobby	LED	Single	9.6x45
10	Gate Concourse	LED	Single	4.8x45
51	Gate Concourse	LED	Double	4.8x45
54	Gate Backscreen	LED	Single	14.4x45
51	Gate Jetway	LED	Single	4.8x45
52	GateExit	LED	Single	4.8x60
14	Baggage Claim	LED	Single	25.8x60

DEC./JAN. 1988   Electronic Display News   31

The United Airlines contract was the largest single electronic display sale in the USA at the time (1987)

```
                         ASSIGNMENT
                         ----------

        WHEREAS, NU-MEDIA SYSTEMS INTERNATIONAL, INC., OF ROYAL
   OAK, MICHIGAN AND ABCOR PRODUCTS OF COOKEVILLE, TENNESSEE
   HAVE ENTERED INTO AN AGREEMENT FOR THE PURCHASE AND SALE OF
   VARIOUS NU-MEDIA ASSETS.

        WHEREAS, IT IS AGREED BETWEEN THE PARTIES THAT ALL TITLE
   AND RIGHT AND INTEREST IN AND TO ALL COMPUTER SOFTWARE
   EMBODIED IN UNITED AIRLINES PRODUCT AND SYSTEMS, A.C.D.
   SOFTWARE, PAGING SOFTWARE, AND ALL OTHER MISCELLANEOUS
   SOFTWARE OWNED AND DEVELOPED BY NU-MEDIA SYSTEMS
   INTERNATIONAL, INC., OF ROYAL OAK MICHIGAN, AND SUBJECT TO
   RESERVATION OF LICENSE RIGHTS BY CONTROL-O-MATION OR OTHERS,
   TOGETHER WITH THE RIGHT TO MARKET SAME, AND ALL CONTRACTS ON
   HAND FOR THE SALE OF PRODUCT FROM THIS DATE FORWARD.

        NOW, THEREFORE, IN CONSIDERATION OF THE FOREGOING
   PREMISES, AND OTHER CONSIDERATION GOOD AND VALUABLE INCLUDING
   1,000,000 SHARES OF ABCOR COMMON STOCK TO BE ISSUED FORTHWITH
   TO NU-MEDIA SYSTEMS INTERNATIONAL, INC. NU-MEDIA HEREBY
   ASSIGNS AND TRANSFERS TO ABCOR PRODUCTS INC., ITS ENTIRE
   RIGHT, TITLE, AND INTEREST IN AND TO ALL THE FORGOING ITEMS
   AS STATED.
                              NU-MEDIA SYSTEMS INTERNTIONAL INC.,

   _03-30-90_____           By_____
   DATE

                              Its_____


   SEE SCHEDULE:  A.  UAL DESCRIPTION
                  B.  UAL JOINT VENTURE AGREEMENT
                  C.  ALL OTHERS
```

The Assignment of Nu-Media public shares to Abcor Products, 1990

News from CCN Disclosure

Hydromet Environmental Recovery Ltd. Announces Issuance OF $815,000 OF Convertible Debentures
15:24 EST Wednesday, March 15, 2000

HAMILTON, ONTARIO--HYDROMET ENVIRONMENTAL RECOVERY LTD. ("Corporation") (CDN: HMEA.A) today announced the issuance subject to final regulatory acceptance, of $815,000 of 7% Convertible Debentures due on September 14, 2001 to three arms length subscribers. The debentures are convertible into Units of the Corporation at a conversion price of $0.04 per Unit resulting in the issuance of up to 20,375,000 Units. One Unit consists of one common share and one share purchase warrant. Each share purchase warrant shall entitle the holder to purchase one additional common share of the Corporation at a price of $0.045 per common share on or before 24 months from the date of issue of the debenture.

The resulting funds from the debenture issue will be used to reduce current debt and short term loans, and to provide capital and operating funds for the construction of a plant to process the slags at the leased Baha California smelter site.

Hydromet owns a 66,000 sq. ft. metallurgical waste recycling facility in Newman, Illinois and a lease on a former smelter site in Baha California, Mexico. The corporation has developed technologies to process the 2,000,000 tons of copper-cobalt tailings and 3,000,000 tons of cobalt copper slag at the Baha California site. These separate piles contain approximately $30 per ton of copper and cobalt mineral.

There are a total of 83,940,953 Hydromet Environmental Recovery Ltd. Convertible Class A Shares issued.

CCN Disclosure

The Hydromet project in Newman, IL, was a technology to extract copper and cobalt from hazardous materials

KALEIDOSCOPIC OF A ENTREPRENEUR

The Home Ownership Program and the Estate Tax Reduction Plan were two innovative mortgage products that John helped develop between 2003 and 2007

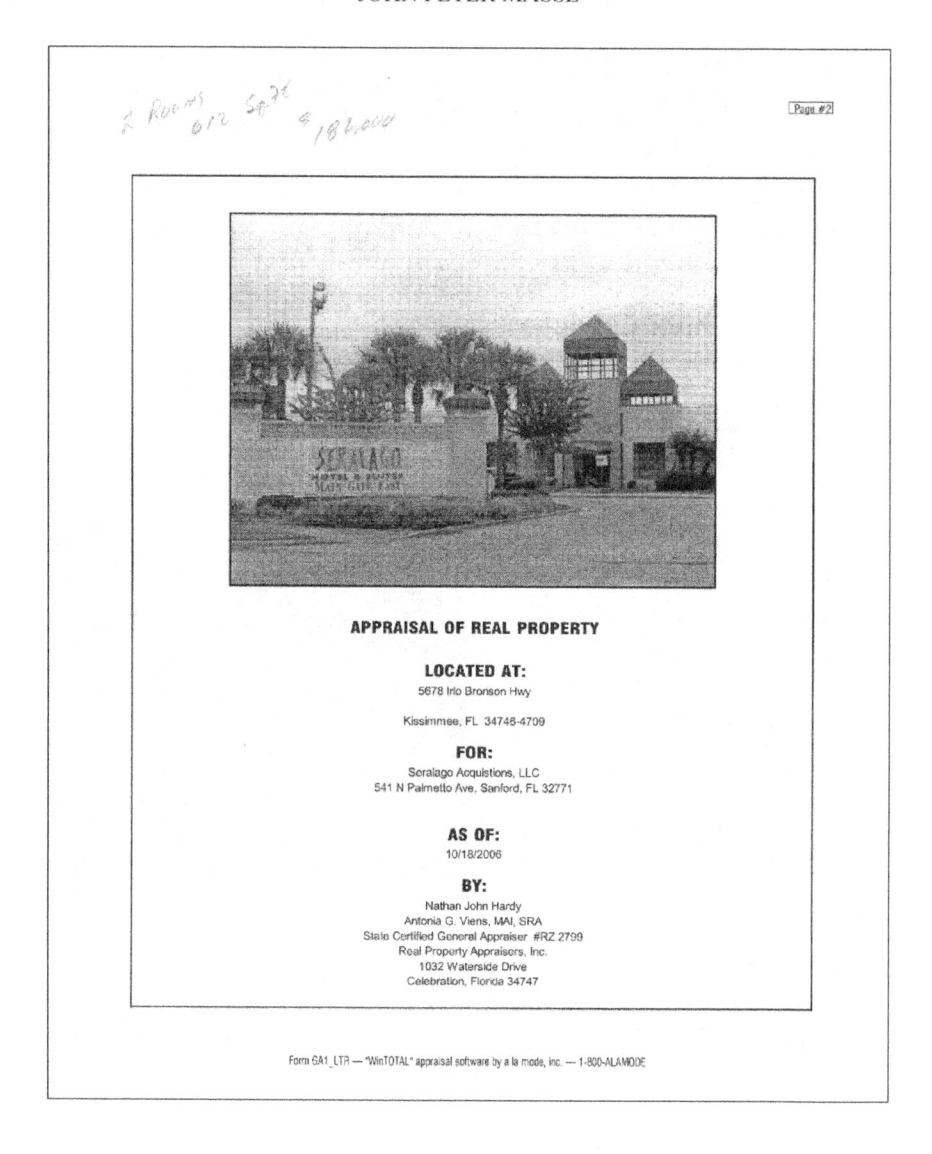

Seralago, a 750 unit Condotel project which John had the exclusive lending rights for mortgage financing

CHAPTER SEVEN

MOVIE HUT/CINEMA KID OF CANADA:

During mid summer Bob Cochrane began speaking with me about one of his companies. You will recall he was the owner of Grey/Bruce Amusements who Taraleigh formerly sold products to.

    A brief background on Cochrane: He was really an interesting guy and a true entrepreneur. In addition to the amusement company he owned The Fifth Season, a workout gym complete with 10 squash courts, a heated indoor pool, sauna spa, boxing rings and several real estate properties. His new endeavor was a coin operated cartoon theatre franchise out of Missouri called **Movie Hut**. The cartoon theatre's design was in the form of a colorful little house complete with a red roof, where kids would deposit .25 cents and watch a 3minute cartoon. "Huts" where placed in various venues, such as super markets, malls, department stores, any place children would congregate, alone or in attendance of a parent. Given a sufficient amount of quarters the huts would serve as a temporary baby sitter. The location received 50% of the gross revenue. At the time, Cochrane successfully operated about 100 movie huts throughout southern Ontario and east to Montreal.

    Further, Bob was afflicted with a disease called **Narcolepsy** – a condition of frequent and uncontrollable sleep patterns. One would be speaking with him and suddenly realize he was fast asleep. A deep handicap as this limited him to many activities including the inability to drive any type of mobile equipment.

    His interest towards me was to take over the management of the company and expand it across Canada. Back in the day we always got along well and deeply respected each other. Some time in mid August we held our last Sunday Jamboree, with the band bringing Julie, Rita and me on stage and presenting each of us with a white flag, signifying our surrender. It was really humorous.

I immediately started as Movie Huts general manager with a weekly salary, expense account and new company car! I don't recall the salary amount but know it was more than Trails End income, but not equal to Taraleigh days. I suspect it was an amount in the $3000 per month range.

My responsibilities were to promote new locations, see to their bi-weekly collections, report the locations revenue split and report any Tech Support requirements as required for any site location or venue.

I had the company convert the lower den in our condo to an office with all the necessary equipment. Not long after I began my new employment a legal disagreement erupted between the US parent company and Cochrane. The Missouri head office, objected to the planned expansion throughout all of Canada. They strenuously stressed the original terms limited the franchise to Ontario and Quebec. Endless lawyer meetings resulted without resolve. Consequently, Cochrane determined to scrap the franchise and build our own cartoon theatres. Hence, the name **Cinema Kid.** Not as embracing as the Movie Hut name but the best we could come up in the abbreviated time frame.

My job responsibilities quickly shifted to an area completely foreign to me. Working with design companies, seeking and securing all required parts, and sifting through competing entities to construct the new cartoon theatre. It represented a lot of work and made more challenging due to my lack of experience. Needless to say the original plans to grow the company was temporarily shelved. I would not return to the original management plans until late December. Just before the approaching Christmas holidays I took a 10day Newfoundland business trip. Working with the folks there was quite an experience. I did not place any theatres' as the trip was exploratory in scope only with the emphasis on developing a working business plan.

To expand and grow the new company I adopted a plan right out of the early Taraleigh Textbook. Seek new locations, sell the location owner/management on the concept, have the location sign an agreement agreeing to the terms, ship and place the units into the venue location, operate the site for a short period of time determining and recording the revenue history. Package 6 –10 theatres into a franchise representing a "operating route" and to complete the plan, find investors willing to accept a 100% investment return with-in a year to 18 months and upon full payment, title the equipment to the investor for the route and products, (i.e.) the franchise. Easy!

Over the Christmas/New Year Holidays I finally came to terms with a decision I was reluctant to make – file for personal Bankruptcy. In late January I initiated the beginning process that would not finalize until late 1981 – almost two years.

I hit the ground running in January arranging an appointment with Transport Canada in Ottawa, securing a confirmation letter presented to all major airport operation managers endorsing Movie Hut/Cinema Kid. This was major for us because not only were airports a profitable revenue source but also impressive to future investors. I followed that by a two-week trip to Western Canada beginning in Winnipeg and ending in Vancouver. In addition to the major airports (including Saskatoon for heavens sake) I met with Safeway Super Markets upper management for placement in their major stores.

I had the Owen Sound office place an advertisement in the Globe & Mail for Alberta and B C investors and sorted through initial discussions with those who responded. On my return to London I continued with the objective of securing local location venues with the likes of Dominion and Loblaw stores and numerous malls.

In March I returned to the West for another two weeks finalizing the location venues and secured the investors for Vancouver, Alberta and Regina/Saskatoon. Following the finalization of the West I concentrated on the huge Toronto market always spending 2-3 days per week within the city.

In late summer I again targeted Eastern Canada, including Montreal. Duplicating the recent successful business trip to Western Canada. Prior to my December trip I had never been to Atlantic Canada and immensely enjoyed the natural beauty, particularly at that time of year. The blueprint plan was identical to the west. Secure location agreements with airports, shopping malls and department stores. To help with initial collections and daily operations I hired an assistant. He resided near the Quebec/New Brunswick border, a perfect mid location for the entire "Eastern" operational area.

Speaking of help my working partner was a young man out of Owen Sound. Nelson Butcher, a black belt karate holder and I never, never argued with Nelson. We developed a great relationship. He was remarkable to work with, always on top of unit maintenance and tech support for the locations.

I took a July break. Rita and I took Patti, Jason, Kristal and Chad to Cedar Point, an Ohio amusement park for a 4 day weekend.

The remainder of the year was non eventful and I will not continue dwelling on what basically was a continuation of the first 6 months of 1981.

I finalized my final trip to Eastern Canada in October, driving, as I had multiple stops through Quebec (including up the St. Lawrence River to Rivier du Loop and Rimouski. I found the area dreadful and could not imagine why anyone would choose to live there) and east to Nova Scotia. As I was approaching the successful completion of initial company objectives I could easily envision the end was near. The chicken bones were increasingly becoming meatless!

By November I was mainly working the local Windsor to Toronto market. Very timely, I was routinely speaking with Joe Unk. He owned a successful auto parts distributorship company shipping maintenance auto parts everywhere. Jane, his significant other and Connie worked for the company. He had recently designed and built an attractive portable kiosk that was to be located in non-auto parts retail stores. The kiosks displayed numerous generally used auto maintenance supplies. A customer shopping in a lumber store for example, would notice the kiosk and select an item of interest to him/her and take it along with any other store merchandise to the counter for payment. Joe's company would service the kiosk regularly replacing the required merchandise. It was a true customer convenience. The retail store operation would account the collected sales revenue, remit a portion to Joe's company and retain their portion of the agreed revenue split. Brilliant idea! He named the concept **The Real McCoy**.

Joe knew I traveled the geographical area of interest to this application. The idea was to "piggy back" the Real McCoy concept, along with Cinema Kid. Cold call a retail store that I thought of interest to the Real McCoy concept and arrange for a kiosk placement. I don't recall the commission we agreed to, but I know that it was substantial and easy add on for me and lets face it – TIMELY as I well knew my days with Cinema kid were soon to end. Near the end of the year my longtime friend, Bob Broderick, introduced me to a Don Gent. The maverick and only son of a successful London Lawyer, who for defiant reasons chose not to adhere to simple employment rules, allowing him to work in his fathers legal business, and ultimately granting him the keys to a legal mint. Don was in his early 30's, single, obsessed with sex, had a degree in English Literature, and gifted with high intellect, very studious, meticulously organized who could not at any given time claim an ounce of common sense.

However, he was working on an astonishing product and wanted my help to market it. The new product: **Digital Programmable Signs.** This "Abbey Lane Road" story would represent a period fraught with long disappointments neither of us imagined during late 1980 and early 1981 era.

Much of the ensuing chapters of this narrative will dominate my writing and capture my interest into 1981 and well into the following 10 years.

CHAPTER EIGHT

COMPUTE-A-SIGN CANADA LTD:

Through out January and February my workload with Cinema Kid diminished to almost part time as the predetermined objectives were now near completed. I leaned on the Real McCoy to occupy my working hours and between these two part time jobs I generated sufficient income to pay living and debt expenses.

My mind was totally pre-occupied with the digital sign business as I was fascinated with what I conceived as its endless marketing potential. The following is brief description of the product and why I was so mesmerized with its potential.

The sign/display was housed in a wooden chassis containing electronic components including a microprocessor (small computer) that allowed a user to program messages to be displayed in a selected fashion and sequence. The face of the display was populated with LED's (light emitting diodes) Unlike other light emitting sources, LED's instantly light up permitting a scrolling message without a "trailing" light pattern. The face of Don Gent's product was a two-line display consisting of 16 characters per line. One-line display signs had been on the market (for about a year) consisting of 12 total characters and were limited to a "scrolling" message only, resulting in limited effective communication. Due to the sign's ability of "programming" a user need not be relegated to a static sign. One could change the message as often as required. An magnificent advantage.

Such was my thought preoccupation in March that I resigned my position with both Cinema Kid and the Real McCoy. With the resignation completed I formed a new company and called it "Compute-A- Sign" and asked Cochrane to consider investing, as a silent partner. He said he would and eventually did. He also agreed to lease me the 1979 Cougar company car on an open-ended lease.

In the early part of 1981 Rita resigned from Clairol and returned to her nursing career. Being a staff junior she primarily worked afternoon or evening shifts. The living relationship between Julie, Penny and Rita was rapidly deteriorating, caused in large part to my continued absence from home. Between my two-week trips to the West and East coasts along with weekly 2 & 3 nights in Toronto, I estimate I was away at least half of the time. As such my influence with my two teenage daughters was severely limited, and believe me it was needed. That, coupled with Rita being Rita (more on that later) I had a relationship problem on my hands. Truthfully, I could find fault with both sides but as much as I wanted to maintain my two daughters remaining with me and continue my relationship with Rita I knew I would be on the loosing end of one or the other or both. But what could I do? I knew I had to continue my travels to maintain income and as time evolved around Compute-A-Sign I felt compelled to further myself in that direction. Separating with Rita would mean leaving two teenage daughters alone and that certainly was not a realistic option.

Sometime in April and all within a week, Rita and I decided to separate and Penny served notice she wanted to return living with her mother. A side bar story: I had recently found a horrible letter written by Penny in the most disgusting unbecoming language of a16 year old. Within the past year I had my share of discipline issues with Penny's misconduct and defiant actions towards me. I chose to not take part in any of her attitudes and decided, given her past history, that "tough love" was the way I would handle this. (I will relate to the continuation of this later as it applies to a serious mistake on her part a year later) Anyway as Rita and I agree to separate, Penny moves to her mothers – this all in a week. A few weeks later Julie felt she should move back to Jane's as well. I suspect it was more in support of Penny, as Julie, Rita and I seemed to be on a more level playing field.

Rita was to find an apartment and I was to remain in the condo, pay the mortgage and receive the "first right of purchase" (effectively purchasing her share of the condo) that Rita agreed to provide by year-end. So now my new living arrangement would be one of living alone. An abrupt life style change to be sure.

In the midst of all this Cochrane agreed to my partnership proposal. He confessed he really did not want to get involved with any additional business's but he was so impressed with Cinema Kid's success he felt a justice in supporting me. What an ally and how often do you find the caliber of a person like Cochrane? His immediate contribution was an injection of $10,000 into the company account, followed with a $50,000 line of credit. I felt I was off the to the races. Not knowing, that in a few months everything would change once more.

Switching now to Don Gent.

He had less than 10 samples of the original product manufactured by an non-accountable engineering idiot, who could only dream of inventing new things that he imagined nightly and never bringing any one of his "night dreams" to a successful completion. Additionally, Gent had little money. I pulled some strings with some funding people I knew and eventually found investors who decided to invest with Gent's company, mainly due to my current marketing progress. I called the investors "the boys from Brazil" Why, I don't know because they were all Italians. A fellow by the name of Emilio Patani was the lead man and he was to correct the manufacturing problems getting production up to speed and most importantly correct the dreadful quality of this product.

I was enthused with the current marketing results as I had presentations with Transport Canada, hardware store chains, banks and an assortment of dealers interested in representing the product. I attended a sign trade show, as a vendor, in Philadelphia (where I had my first ever Bouillabaisse) drawing several enquiries from potential US dealers. If my notes are accurate I was in possession of 22 purchase orders (product yet to be delivered) with several additional interested enquiries.

Before moving to the next segment I should tell you preceding the registering of the company name and corporate papers, I was successful in obtaining an exclusive written international and national agreement with Gent for Canada and the USA.

May 17th. The day the world as I presently knew changed – forever.

Actually, it was May 18th, Mother passed away suddenly by way of an accident on May 17th. Her death is well documented and known by most who might be reading this so I won't pursue that further. I do wish to speak of the emotional pain one experiences with immediate family death. To set it right we must speak of the circumstances surrounding her death. First it was an incredible shock that she preceded Dad's death. Here was someone with both legs removed (yes double amputee) mobile by wheelchair only, in total care of Mother whose health was considered normal. As you observe your aging parents you give some thought to their death and how you will deal with it and how it affects you and family. Mother was never to die before Dad! How Dad was now going to manage was paramount with all our family. We all felt so sad and worrisome for him. Personally, I was devastated. Words are lost to express the inner pain I felt. I could not understand why God would want her when her purpose in life could not be understood as being finished or completed. You begin to understand, incorrectly, how some people come to question His choices and purposes toward life. I did not fault God. I so loved her, missed her and still do. I share no regrets of hers and my relationship together and cherish her lessons of life. Her kindness towards everyone is well remembered by all who knew her.

Rita and I of course had decided to separate prior to Mother's death and most of the planning decisions where complete but she still had not found an apartment and so we remained living together. Her decision to remove herself from the family and not attend the funeral was so disappointing to me. I never forgave her even into later years of marriage, and here is some irony for you.

Some three weeks into June, Rita had still not found an apartment. The girls of course were now living with Jane and when I would speak of the separation she was still "on the hunt for an apartment". Her moods were all over the place and while I was sticking with the separation agreement I still had feelings for her and disappointed that yet again I had failed another relationship. From out of the blue her mother, living in Tillsonburg, suddenly dies. I do not attend any funeral home visitations, abiding by what was demonstrated only a month previous. Returning home from a 3 day Toronto trip, the phone is ringing. It's a contrite Rita asking if I would attend her mother's memorial service and burial. My first answer was "no, under present circumstances I do not think it appropriate". Then you begin to think. "Your doing exactly what you condemned Rita for only a month ago". I called her back and said I would be there the next morning.

Almost immediately her attitude did a 180. Her aggravations no longer evident She no longer had the insistent "me" attitude. She pleaded that we should give ourselves another chance reciting over and over again that she "believed in us" and of course we did. We married a year later. The regrettable lessons of learning the true meaning of what life should be somehow does not come to many of us until years later when experience teaches you how to connect the dots. Looking back, the messages, loud and soft, should have resonated within me —but they did not. My heart closed off my brain.

I had 6 unbelievable children who I adored and respected. But for a few exceptions their lives mirrored how their mother and I taught them – against the many odds of a separated family. No crimes, no drug addiction, all were employed, none were on the government dole and apart of education money none asked for money handouts. How was this marriage to work given the ingredients? Like Mohammed Ali (who I adored) use to say "you have to listen to your body" One can also say "you have to learn from life's messages". One gets many of them.

Right around Mother's death, Bob Cochrane suffered a major heart attack. Due to my absence from the office I was not aware of this until 10 days after his admission to the hospital. I drove to Owen Sound to visit him and while he had recovered to the point of conversation he experienced great difficulty in remembering past and current. I knew his presence with Compute-A-Sign would be short and I no longer could count on his partnership. No question, a disastrous and untimely event for me. I could only hope to be able to collect cash flow by delivering some signs to any of my logged purchase orders. Shortly following that meeting we met again and if anything his memory had worsened. I advised him I would seek to replace him and return his investment.

On the lighter side Jason & Patti attended their first vacation camp enjoying a change they were un-accustom to. A side bar story now somewhat humorous but was not at the time. Kelly got a summer job at a mall selling raffle tickets for luxury cars. I mean these cars were in the $100K+. At the close of the day she was to lock up securing the keys. Well, she took it upon herself to drive home a $90,000 Mercedes. Not only was that irresponsible but guess what? No drivers license! I learned of this the following day and went nuts. To make matters worse she had great difficulty in understanding the wrong in her negligent actions. I instructed her, without any other options, to approach her superiors acknowledging her lack of judgment and to apologize. Of which she did. That example of honesty allowed her to keep her job and I suspect a valuable lesson guiding her through other life situations.

I continued getting sign orders but could not complete any due to non-available working product. Throughout mid July to mid August I was without any money – period. I remember walking back to our condo from a jewelry store just down the street that I had taken my wristwatch for repair. The jeweler told me the watch was not repairable. I was so despondent. I could not even purchase a cheap replacement.

Devine intervention again visits me.

I had prepared final papers outlining the intended partnership release of Cochrane from the company and was couriering the finalized paper work to him via a greyhound bus. I was in the process of leaving the bus station when Ken Cassis spotted me from his brother's office just across the street. He approached me and said his brother, Phil, wanted to see me. Phil, at the time, ran a investment funding company for several clients. Here comes my Guardian Angel again.

Shortening the series of events I agreed to a partnership with one of his clients on a 75%-25% basis – this would later become an equal 50%-50% due to unforeseen additional funds required to keep the company solvent. More on that as the story unfolds. The partner's name was Sam Mancuso. Retired Italian who loved life, was fun to be with, married to Phyllis, 15 years his junior, loved entertaining and cooking. He was what I call "old Italian" and his word was his bond. Not bad.

In the mean time Gent had engaged another electronics company, **Electronic Controlled Innovations**, a small firm in East Toronto. Their contracted assignment was to reverse engineer the existing software and manufacture it on their site. The new sign was called Mediatron 2001. The contracted time line for a finished prototype was October 1 with production of 40 to 50 units per month.

The UK dealer that Cochrane and I met in New York several months prior, met me in Toronto and finalized a dealer contract with an order for 100 units to be shipped on a staggered basis beginning in late December early January. Additionally, Phil put me in touch with a Chatham client who came on board as a dealer and they ordered 5 signs. Things were looking up.

I could go through a myriad of rescheduled dates for the prototype but it is really a boring read. The date was reset to November, then December. No sign no production. We were fast loosing credibility with our customers and no end in sight. The situation was acerbated with the notice from the two ECI principals that with the continued production delays and cost overruns ECI would need an additional $25,000 to finish the software debugging and start production. That was it for Sam! His Italian blood boiled. We set out that Compute-A-Sign would buy controlling interest in ECI removing the two principals and keeping the engineering staff.

That is how 1981 ended business wise. But the wheel of business ironies and surprises were far from over. The reader needs to store this name. Jim Pollard.

Before continuing with 1982, Kelly (20 yrs. old) served notice and wanted my permission, to move to Banff, Alberta, seeking a job and experience life in Western Canada. I could not fault her reasoning and said "yes". She left in mid January. I later came to refer to Banff as "teenage wasteland".

In October Jane and I finalized our marriage in an uncontested divorce. It was an amicable ending and we met for a couple of drinks following the proceeding.

Finally, in early January the much-delayed prototype was completed. And it actually worked. Production was limited but at least we had product to deliver, although, many of the past purchase orders had now cancelled as product confidence had seriously eroded, after all, we began promising delivery as far back as September.

Vic Brisson, brother-in-law, had long expressed dealer status interest with us and now with production available signed an agreement for Michigan. He and a partner, Gerry Cooper, formed a company, Branco Corporation. They took possession of 22 units in February – sadly a few of these were returned for failure. Obviously, ECI still had problems. The 22 sign purchase order contained a payment schedule of 30 and 60 days. The order and financing was accepted by Sam (he was the financier) and would later serve as a huge financing detriment. Compute-A-Sign held it's first product seminar attended by 18 people counting dealers and sales reps.

Back in October Cochrane had to liquidate 2 company cars and a truck due to severe company finances due to his illness. One of the cars of course was my leased Cougar. I could not arrange to purchase it due to my incomplete B/K discharge and so I arranged, through Phil, to lease a 1972 Ford from his brother in law. We came to call it "the corporate tank". I detested the car and for some reason in late winter left it at the Toronto plant, returning back to London with either Phil or Sam. I ended selling it to one of the ECI workers. Fortuitously for me, the worker told me two months later it caught fire at a stoplight. However, that decision caused Rita and I to share her car for almost the remainder of the year. Not easy when both of us worked and I did a lot of traveling.

The relationship with Sam began to unravel in early spring. The company was in severe financial difficulties. The bank would not extend a credit line without securing a mortgage on Sam & Phyllis's home and as often as Sam stated he would do it Phyllis prevailed. The situation worsened with the breakup of Vic Brisson's partner, Gerry Cooper (although they later patched things together) and Branco was unable pay the $25,000 for the 22 previously delivered product. We were learning that while many dealers saw the marketing of this product as very promising, many discovered that it was much more difficult than previously imagined. On the flip side of that Phil and I were always able to move the product on a consistent basis. In addition to this fiasco the first shipment to the UK dealer was completed but the transfer of funds did not materialize until much later. The lion's share of the $200,000 that Sam had now invested was primarily into ECI, the acquisition of the shares and the cost overruns due primarily to faulty manufacturing. Indeed much more than the original $25,000 Sam agreed in funding Compute-A-Sign as the marketing company for Gent's signs.

In April the business relationship with Sam & Phyllis deteriorated to a level no longer manageable. The strange part of this was not product marketing but the inability of solving the manufacturing problems. Much time was spent with meetings discussing the same subject over and over "financing". I was sick of it and welcomed Sam's decision to spin-off the marketing from Compute-A-Sign, assigning Phil and I company distributors for Ontario only. That left dealers I had appointed outside of Ontario, now under the company directed by Sam & Phyllis. This decision removed the expenses of Phil and I, the company office at 148 York Street and it's operating costs from Sam's monthly operating expenses. The office/operating expenses, and our personal income became our own costs. The company lawyer prepared the agreements and after several late night meetings, some until midnight, we all agreed to the terms which included money to bring certain payables current and 8 or 10 samples for Phil & I, and a 30 day account for new purchases. Meaning we had 30 days to pay for our new product purchases. Our negotiated unit purchase cost was $780. The established selling price for each unit sold was $1780. Therefore each completed sale on our part netted us $1000 gross profit. In simple terms we had to sell 6 units to equal the previous profit structure of 5 units. Given all the ups and downs of past financing discussions I liked the new math.

The company I formed, a little more than a year previous, was no longer mine. I signed all my shares to Sam and was absolved of any future financial company burdens. The separation and the distributor decision became another splendid, provident gift, as you will soon discover as this story continues.

The day after the completion of all the legal paper work, Phil and I were walking to our bank to complete banking arrangements for our new company. Phil turned and asked, "What do you want to call the company" In the hectic and sudden discussions neither of us had given a single moments thought to a name. Without missing a step I replied, "New Media spelled with a U. It just popped into my head.

CHAPTER NINE

NU-MEDIA SYSTEMS INC:

Our first month resulted in the sale of 3 signs and a signed purchase order for an additional 6 units. This was not sufficient to keep the balls in the air. But we both could see and feel that without the negative effect of daily problematic financing discussions we could concentrate on sales and marketing. Our target market at the time was hotels, banks and large retail stores.

Rita and I had set July 31st as our wedding date and so in May we began the search for an affordable reception hall.

The family kept a vigilant eye on Dad, with each of us calling and visiting on a regular basis. Jason often accompanied me to GB assisting me in jobs around the house and yard. Even at his tender age he proved to be a tireless worker. As I reread past notes and diaries researching this story we spent much time together, almost every weekend doing boy/dad things. He was and has been a wonderful asset to the family who is loved by everyone who knows him.

July saw *Nu*-Media enjoying a successful month. Information reached us that our main Toronto competitor had folded; it's backer, Hewlett-Packard, withdrawing financial support.

Kelly returned home, in part, in preparation for our wedding.

Several friends gave Rita and I "doe" and "stag" parties and finally the day arrived. Brother Doug was my best man and a friend of both Rita and I, Lynn Watt, was Rita's bride's maid. Chad and Jason were ushers. They were so concerned about their duties each going over and over with me the routine asked of them. Doug gave an awesome, over the top toast to his brother, having most attending wiping away tears. He is a wonderful speaker. Rita and I left our hotel the next morning at 7:30 for the drive to Toronto to catch our flight to Prince Edward Island, our destination for the next 9 days, vacationing on that wonderful little island. We toured it in its entirety and did the lobster church suppers the island is renowned for, on a seemingly almost daily basis. We canoed lakes and rivers, rode horseback, ate and drank excessively, saw live plays and acted like most couples honeymooning. I must say we were a happy married couple enjoying each other and the uncertainties of the new company did not seem to effect us in the remotest ways.

Back at the office, Stu Brister the company lawyer and Mancuso's lawyer, served notice to Phil and I, that Sam was not long for the sign business. The bug in my ear, my mind returns to a stored mental thought – Jim Pollard. More later on an exercise I undertook removing one of his digital signs from a customers location, on the pretense of regular company maintainence, to explore the advantages of his product over ours.

Labor Day afternoon found me at my office desk working on some product pricing. I was preparing to leave for home when Stu Brister entered my office and casually announced that the RCMP would be charging him the following day with grand theft of $550,000 stolen from his trust fund. He said he was relieved that it was finally over and that he had lived a nightmare for the past 2 years secretly hiding this illegal mess. He would be found guilty in December and sentenced to 7 years in prison.

I immediately knew this would soon be the final nail for Sam & Phyllis. From past discussions I was aware that Sam had $76,000 in Bristers trust fund. That too would now be gone. This along with the temporary Branco hit would, in the end, prove to be too much and eventually fatal to my old company, Compute-A-Sign.

I held both sadness and fortunate emotions, but for an earlier decision, I would be part of the company's demise. The company separation and reorganization separated Phil and I from the ordeal that was surely to follow and allow us to continue, unhindered, to doing what we did best, marketing these programmable digital display signs.

Knowing it wouldn't be long before our supplier would be unable to remain in business my mind returns to that stored thought. In mid October I reach out to Jim Pollard. Like we knew of him, he too knew of us, although not in the same affable manner. I made a brief pitch over the phone that we would better serve ourselves than compete with each other. Never known to be weak of mind, he agreed. We arranged a meeting, which would be one of several over the ensuing weeks.

A brief profile on Jim Pollard:

Jim was married to Barbara with their two children, and had recently moved from London to Mississauga to better manage his new sign venture. He originated from Harrow Ontario, the son of a prominent major trucking family, a degree in accounting and for all his small personal idiosyncrasies a prince of a man, very principled and honest. One could do no better choosing an associate partner. A deal was a deal. Our future business was founded on our mutual respect and if my recollection is correct, without written agreements. Hard to find in today's business environment.

Jim manufactured a product, which he called "Electromedia". It was vastly superior to Compute-A-Sign and the finished product was quality. There were four major differences though both shared a two- line display.

1. The display face was continuously populated with LED's, without space separation between characters, called a "full matrix" which permitted among other features – graphics. And due to the full matrix a two-line display could be programmed to a large one line.
2. The display itself was at least twice as bright in enhancing the viewable message.
3. The interface design was more advanced featuring "serial interface" versus "parallel interface". This allowed connecting other signs on location to be networked together, under what was then referred to as "master – slave" configuration. A huge advantage.
4. The housing was made of metal, not wood, lighter in weight and much more attractive in its flat black design.

Negotiations completed we permitted Pollard to register our name (he loved the name) selling it under our name with our logo attached to the finished product. We had the exclusive rights to all of Canada, except Quebec, where he had an existing distributor and all of the USA. Our purchase per unit cost was a little more than we were paying for Sam's Compute-A-Sign. We later determined we could retail this product for $3,160. And we did, very successfully. Our profit margin increased by almost $400 per single unit.

Until late December we sold our remaining inventory of Compute-A-Sign and the *Nu*-Media product, not serving notice to Sam that we were severing our agreement with him. More on that ugly scene will follow. As we demonstrated the new *Nu*-Media System we experienced sensational product acceptance by dealers and customers alike.

A fortuitous merger resulted and respected for the next 15 or more years. Our business relationship was simplistic in design. Where the manufacturing/software was our weakness, Pollard was our strength. Where the marketing was Pollards weakness, marketing was our strength.

In late October, I got our bank to kick in some personal loan money and I was able to purchase a used Datson station wagon for $1750. It was in reasonable shape, needing little in repairs and thus ended the past 7-8 months of car sharing.

November 17.

Late that evening I received a call from my brother saying he had just found Dad in bed, dead, Dad had passed away during his usual after dinner nap. I had spoken with him earlier in the evening, learned he had been playing the organ and said he was feeling just fine. By this time Brenda and her two boys had moved in with Dad, so along with Doug and Marilyn home there was plenty of weekend activity. Brenda arrived on the family scene by way of a "living assistant" Dad required due to his incapacities. She would be the last of previous assistants he hired to help him with his daily living routines. She like the others found themselves "in love" with his charm and flirtatious nature. However, Brenda was deemed dangerous due to her devious agenda. Over the course of the short time Brenda was on the scene I had several confrontations with her leaving little doubt I distrusted her and she definitely knew where I was coming from. Her dubious schemes ended at the funeral home during an open visitation time when Vic Brisson and I confronted her requesting a lesser presence and to remove herself from the "front and center" role she appointed herself resulting in the appearance she was now "part of family." This self-appointed position did not sit well with my sisters and it fell on Vic and me to inform dear precious Brenda. I relished it! When confronted with our request to take a lesser role than one of a "grieving family member" and respect the family wishes she vigorously objected making a terrible distraught full scene. To me this only confirmed my suspicions of her true intent and that was when I asked her to remove all of her belongings that now had found there way into the family home and she did the day following the funeral service.

By the time Rita and I arrived in Grand Bend, the ambulance had removed Dad's body and in speaking with the present funeral home personnel they reported he had most likely died of a heart attack while asleep. What a peaceful way to depart, particularly considering the intense suffering this man endured during the last few years of life. I notified the sisters in Michigan and met them the following day in Grand Bend. Poor Doug had now been present for both Mom and Dad's death. He and Joanne in particular took his passing very hard.

As I write this it is hard to appropriately place words into describing the immense respect I had of my Father. I cannot begin to describe his work ethics, his stamina, his positive attitude and his ability to find a way to succeed. To me, he was the epitome of a Father and someone to look up to for leadership and lessons learned. He was some guy! I wrote in one of my journals following the funeral, "the end of a most beautiful time and era".

Next for the family, was to settle our parent's estate, which we did in the following months in a most amicable way, an immense tribute to our family. Unfortunately many families fight and argue and engaged in family wars that continue for eternity.

Back to business: December was deemed to be the time to sever our business relationship with Compute-A-Sign. There were some not so pleasant scenes with Sam and it really was not formally resolved until January. Why there were such theatrics I don't know as the agreement was explicit in its termination terms. Either party had the expressed right to terminate without cause. It's called a "shot gun clause".

Our receivables to December 15 were $23,000 and we were beginning to hum!

My last diary entry for the year, "Thank you 1982 for what started out cloudy closed with sunshine".

Throughout the first part of the following year we continued to increase the number of agents and dealer networks. Vern Watson, a boyfriend of Rita's close friend and nursing buddy, moved to London from Windsor where he was employed in the insurance and investment business, joined *Nu*-Media as a London dealer. He would gain fame and notoriety bringing a financial investor on board for his dealership and targeted an advertising market, selling advertising time on a network of *Nu*-Media products placed in high traffic locations. The attraction for a business seeking to advertise was the ability to target specific locations for their product/services at a fraction found in traditional advertising costs. He coined the term "heavy signs", as a product description meaning they required large memory capacity to support the high degree of advertising graphics. Everyone in our business giggled at the product description and many would refer to him as "heavy sign Vern". At a later period he moved to Florida, continuing as a

US dealer.

12 to 15 hour days were not uncommon during the early years of company growth. I sometimes wonder if this work commitment was due to the desire to succeed or from fear of failure. We sometimes are lack for knowing the difference.

Our ability to include graphics in our corporate presentations, displaying their company logos, the single most important image to any company, greatly enhanced the success of present and future orders. Plus now we had the advantage of improved products, larger display viewing area, more characters per page, remote telephone programming and soon the ability to interface with desktop computers.

July was punctuated with Doug and Marilyn's wedding on a very hot July day. Many of us imbibed in way too much alcohol celebrating the youngest of the family's marriage. We all knew this was an event that would happen as they had been together for some time. I recall I became real upset with some party crashers who took it upon themselves ordering drinks from the open bar and aggressively accosting these "crashers" to leave or they would find themselves in grisly circumstances. Of course I was much worse with alcohol consumption then any of the accused. The bravado of drunks! Anyway they did find the exit and it became unnecessary for me to display my "fighting superiority"?

In the latter part of the year we participated in our first US trade show at Cobo Hall in Detroit. During the show, we somehow heard of a Brett Lincoln out of Iowa Nebraska. We would eventually hire him as "product technical support" when we started the US division. To initiate operations under the new US Company, *Nu*-Media Systems International Inc., Philip began spending 2-3 days a week in Pontiac MI, hiring 3 industrial reps calling on the auto industry, which would eventually become a huge market for us.

We were making a name for ourselves. Trans Lux, a giant in the digital sign industry, serving the financial stock markets, called us requesting a meeting. They were located in Connecticut and listed on the New York Stock Exchange. More will follow on this subject.

On the home front Kelly moved to Toronto working for a support company in the stock and financial industry. I hire my daughter, the ever-adaptable Julie as an office administrator. Phil and I were out of the office on a more regular basis and as the business grew the office work did too. She assisted Philip with invoicing, receivables and accounting procedures, and me with cataloguing, endorsement letters, letter writing and managing the office in our absence. I have a hundred Julie stories to relate, all of you would giggle at how she, true to her youth (she was 19 at the time) continued to push the envelope, always assuming that she was one step ahead of being caught in any misdeeds and of course she always got nailed. One example: during the later stage of company growth she was left alone at the office. Mysteriously, incoming phone calls were not answered or, the office would be closed, prior to closing time. I would fire her and Phil would rehire her. But let me say I could always count on her and she always practiced a principal important to me – loyalty! I have always admired her down to earth "no bull shit attitude" when it came to business or matters of importance. The exception being the "envelope pushing".

The export division of the Canadian Commerce Department sponsored a "Trade Mart" show in London England, scheduled for the late part of January. We were honored to be one of 12 Canadian companies invited to participate. A portion of the show's cost was deferred by the government agency but most was borne by the company. A sizeable expense, but afforded us a tremendous opportunity. Dave Dixon would spend 6 months in Scotland and England, as tech support for the dealers we eventually appointed, left first with Philip to set up the show. Jim Pollard and I followed a couple of days later. Everyone, except Philip and I, returned after the trade exposition closed as we interviewed and signed on new dealers. Philip left following the interviews and I remained for another 2 weeks training the four new appointees (my notes are void as to what happened to the dealer that joined Compute-A- Sign in the Mancuso days).

During our Scotland travels Phil and I stayed in a 300 year old castle owned by one of the Scotland dealers. We learned a few years later it burned to near total destruction. I spent more than a week in Scotland, working with the newly acquired dealers located in Glasgow and Edinburgh. Both are historical, ancient cities.

A side bar story: As mentioned earlier, Dave Dixon (and a friend of his) and Philip arrived ahead of Jim and I. On the first night the three of them decided to go to a bar in Soho. They ordered wine and looking very much like tourists, were joined by a couple of hostess. (I guess that is what they call them there) In the course of the evening Dave ordered some cigarettes. The bill arrived near the close of the night and to their amazement it was over $900. The wine was $75 a bottle, the cigarettes were $50 and of course there was an enormous amount for the ladies. There was an insufficient balance on Phil's A/E card. Before paying the bill with almost all the cash they possessed they tried to escape through a bathroom window (shades of the Pink Panther) but were prevented by the bouncers who were constantly watching the current version of the "three stooges". The next day Phil found me at the London office and ask that I pay some money on his A/E account, that it was very expensive in England and that I should bring a couple of thousand dollars with me. I expressed to Phil that he must of done something pretty stupid to be out of money in one day! At the time he did not elaborate to the cause of his distress and I did advance money to his A/E account.

I return home in mid February, exhausted and subsequently join Rita visiting her father in Florida. I spent much of my time on the beach – sleeping. In my Florida absence Phil signs a high profile dealer, Joe Orrechio for the Tampa Bay area. We spent a lot time with Joe and I visited him in Tampa several times discussing various market applications he was interested in, including a major client, Florida Power and Light.

It was late winter when Phil began spending weekly time in Michigan. By now Branco had ceased operations. Vic Brisson's sign staff had left and he was too busy with the Silverdome Parking to spend any meaningful time away from his parking duties. Phil hired the chap from Iowa and 3 industrial sales reps and we rented the main floor office of a converted Victorian home that Vic used for his business ventures. He moved his parking operation to the upstairs portion and we paid our monthly rent to him. A year or so later we converted the outside porch to a large conference office adding at least 300 square feet to the facilities. As part of negotiations with Brisson we agree to sell his existing digital sign inventory at slightly above his cost leaving him with a minor profit per sold unit.

This expansion dictated that I spend more time out of the office, mostly in the Toronto office, thereby using the talents of Julie maintaining the London office. She had been using the Datson for an increasing amount of driving, some for her personal use and for company business. Such was the reason I added her to the insurance policy. Very prudent, one Saturday night in late May, driving down a city street she some how lost control and hit a large tree. She and her companion were not hurt but old reliable Datsun was totaled. I collected the insurance payoff and if I remembered correctly, more than I had paid for the car, so Julie pretty much got off without serious repremand. This set into motion the hunt for a replacement. I convinced, the company's bank, to chip in some money and I purchased my first BMW. I loved driving that car!

In Canada I basically kept developing the same markets. Product presentations to large corporations and expanding our dealer network that represented markets geographically in distance to our home marketing base. Pollard and I flew to Rhode Island, working with an entity (a character by the name of Philip Kenny) who had significant influence with the local banking community and Chamber Of Commerce. Cassis completed a Western Canada trip setting up a dealer in Saskatoon and Vancouver.

Rita and I arranged to rent a cottage in Grand Bend for 2 weeks. I don't recall how but she had a lot of vacation time and spent it at the cottage, entertaining family and friends. I was not so lucky, as I was restricted to long 3-4 day weekends. But it was great and we all enjoyed the time remembering the good old "Grand Bend" days.

During the remainder of the year Phil had expanded existing Pontiac staff to include 2 retail reps (we decided to give females a shot) a tech support person, a sign maintenance person and a part time girl who had an art degree. She designed message display copy providing a "professional presentation touch" for our reps and any US dealers, along with designing brochures and mailers. Later in the year Phil hired a redneck bookkeeper named "Bobbie Lee". She would remain with us until I replaced her two years later hiring Marcella who was from Mexico and married to an American accountant. She proved to be much more competent than "Bobbie Lee". Business at the Pontiac Office was increasing to the point that I joined Phil for 2 to 3 days weekly.

Earlier in the year we had hired a Marketing guy, Ross Blaine, for the Toronto area, who was very capable and afforded Phil and I to be away from the Toronto and Canadian market while we tried to break into the Detroit and surrounding area markets.

A note in my time planner suggests that October sales for the two companies was just south of $50,000 and business from newly appointed dealers were still to be realized. We were beginning to learn that dealers, regardless of support time given them, were not as successful as the corporate corps in generating business.

Beginning 1985 Philip and I spent most of our working week in Pontiac staying in a motel only a mile or so from the office. For the past 5 years I had been jogging off and on never getting it all together. Watching my Father suffer from cardiovascular disease had a distinct motivating effect on me. I was determined that I would do all I could to prevent this disease from finding me and running was something I viewed as a means of increasing blood flow to the extremities. Staying in a motel resulted in less distractions and I began running every 7:30 morning, increasing my running time and distance. This routine would remain with me for the next 25 years when I eventually had to quit blowing a knee and the doctor's advice "park the running shoes". I still miss the running routine and the resulting endorphins, a natural high.

I do not recall how it came to be, but in March it was determined that Rita and I were to move to the US. I completed a L1 application. It is a 2year work visa, which I did not receive did not receive until a year later. Crossing the border on a repetitive basis without the actual "L1" drove Rita nuts. We looked at different places in the Detroit/Pontiac area and settled on a lake front ranch condo, in a community called Port Cove. We moved in April 1985 selling the London condo one week after listing it.

We elected to do a restaurant service show in North Carolina and another in the Detroit area with a sale of only one system. We learn the US food service industry was not as lucrative as the Toronto area and we never did another U.S. restaurant show.

"Retail" customers always seemed to suffer from the lack of solid, creative message programming, limiting the maximum potential the LED programmable signs provided. This was compounded by the era prior to readily available desktop computers. The brilliance at Pollard Manufacturing figured a way to load a predetermined message program, complete with graphics, onto a cassette tape that could then be loaded into a sign. We now sold programming enhancing the effectiveness of the product.

Aided by software that allowed us to tap into the automobile plants PLC's, a version of their operating software, we were able to meet a critical area of limiting "down time" during periods when the plant assembly line would shut down due to a malfunction some where along the assembly line. Down time was very costly to them as production was literally stopped. By providing "fault diagnostic information" our system displays saved the plant thousands and thousands of dollars. This new application increased our participation in the auto industry to the point that it represented the lion's share of business. That would change in the future but for now it was huge for us. In May we did a major presentation to EDS, formerly Hughes Electronics, along with a major sale to a GM plant in Kokomo IN. We were constantly taking pictures of these installations to add to our photo gallery, presentation books and user list. One current exception to the auto industry market, I hired Tom Buck, a hardware store manufactures rep and we did one of our first hardware shows at the Hoosier Dome in Indianapolis.

While working commercial trade shows I was amazed at our Japanese competition for their never ending nerve coming up to our booth displays, camera in hand, never asking permission or engaging in conversation, just endlessly snapping away like it was their inherited right. It was little consolation that the "want" of duplication was the best compliment.

Earlier, I mentioned a company by the name of Trans Lux, huge in the field of financial reader boards supporting the stock market industry. They had made previous overtures to Phil and me and now meetings with Ron Turcotte, senior executive, continued through the summer in both Toronto and Detroit. The Toronto Dominion Bank was an existing customer of ours and during the early part of 1985 they had contacted Phil enquiring about a stock quotation reader board for their stock trading division. This, of course was an industry previously served exclusively by Trans Lux. The news of this enquiry greatly infuriated them. It took little persuasion on our part to get Pollard (he actually loved the idea) to do the software and thus become a direct competitor to this current giant in this industry. The overtures culminated in September with an invitation from their president to meet him in Norwalk. Phil and I were met at the airport by the company chauffer and taken to their corporate offices. I no longer have notes to this effect but according to Phil, who has the memory clarity of an "Einstein", not to mislead you into thinking he is an Einstein, I refer only to his memory. The initial proposal was tabled in December and amendments continued for several months. My notes indicate the final agreement basis:

- They would purchase Pollard Manufacturing for an amount not noted in my notes.
- Would pay Phil and I $100,000 each as "goodwill" and $60,000 annual US salary.
- Phil would close the Toronto Office, move to the Pontiac Office, and would head up Industrial Sales and would hold the executive position of Vice President of the Canadian Company. We would also receive 2.5% - 3% of all gross sales as a performance bonus.
- I would continue to work out of the US assuming all facets of the sign operation as general manger. We would receive all company benefits They would buy the existing company inventory and fixed assets at our costs We were to sign a 3-year non-compete agreement.

As for the UAL sale (more details on this giant sale to follow) we would both receive "cash out" for existing company inventory and for any existing purchases not delivered. Unknown in all in these negotiations was the true $$ amount of the UAL contract and future extended orders. We all underestimated the eventual contract value. Not until late in 1986 did we realize the total UAL sale was 3.5 million and after United decided to add to the total order with outdoor signage at O'Hare Airport for incoming flights increasing the contract by another million. In 1988 we learned of another additional order by UAL for their other "hub" airport – Denver Colorado, adding another near $1 million.

The UAL technology and software would transfer to Trans Lux. The Joint Venture Agreement between COM/COM2 and *Nu*-Media specifically stated the aforementioned technology and software was the property of *Nu*-Media

Early in 1987 the deal unraveled when the Canadian Government deleted or, at least modified the current version of the "capital gains tax".

This major tax amendment changed Pollards advantage in a sale and he rightfully declined the deal. It may have been an act of divine intervention as this company later went through large realignments with many of their staff leaving the company. It is difficult to determine if we would have been subject to the future changes or, if the deal had consummated it might have kept this large International Public Company intact. I don't recall their eventual status, but for sure, Phil and I would have gained an enviable cash position with realized bonus money from the UAL contracts alone.

We were all extremely busy with bi-weekly 2&3day meetings in Toronto. To help curb this time demand Phil and I hire a maverick sales person, Chris Wyman, for the Pontiac office. He was extremely talented but a loose "cannon ball" requiring a tight tethered leash and that was not always sufficient. In the midst of selling signs Chris wanted to form a car leasing company with *Nu*-Media. Little money was required to infuse into the proposed company and so *Nu*-Dominion Leasing was formed. Philip and I served as directors only and were not involved in day-to-day operations. The new company served as a broker between lending banks and Chris's customers. *Nu*-Dominion Leasing became a subsidiary of *Nu*-Media Systems.

We were really doing great business wise. A notation in my day planner states December U.S. receivables at $95,386.

Following up on the previous mention of the United Airlines contract and to maintain continuity with this narrative I should mention how the contract came to be. In late 1985 I somehow learned that a major airline, United Airlines, had expressed interest in electronic signage for their new designed airline terminal at O'Hare Airport in Chicago. I chase this lead down ending up talking to a Dan Michaelson, for 2 hours, on a cold early December day. It was one of those times when you are in a "zone" and everything your mind perceives is the right one. Michaelson was duly impressed with our conversation and ask that I summarize our conversation in letterform and could I please remit it soon. When a salesman receives this type of a request following a two-hour phone conversation it receives enormous priority. The letter went out that day! To this day I know not how I managed this intellectual discussion with one of their top engineers about a market/industry I knew absolutely nothing about. Sometimes, when you are in one of those zones you just have to let your creative mind go.

I called Pollard and told him of my United Airlines contact and that it had the potential to be a huge project. I don't know if he was having a bad day or just did not want to be involved in a major U.S. airport project. Maybe the word "project" did not resonate in a positive way with him. But he clearly was not interested and declined any participation.

I was really disappointed. Now what? I could not accept letting this important opportunity slip away. In discussions and beers with Wyman, I met and had several conversations with an engineering friend of his by the name of Bill Kittle. He worked for a small electronic manufacturing firm in Dexter MI, near Ann Arbor. Out of desperation I called Bill and without mentioning names and too many specifics I outlined the United Airlines situation. He was helpful and did not discount or dissuade me from forming any provocative thoughts indicating his interest in working together.

A week later I received a phone call from Michaelson asking if I would be able to meet his people at UAL's corporate offices just outside of Chicago. One week before Christmas I meet a host of engineers and their project planning personnel. I don't recall the number in attendance but remember the large conference room was full. Remarkably I answered technical questions and ask some of my own and the 3hour meeting broke up without any commitments toward the future, but something within me was bubbling and I couldn't wipe the smile off my face. Merry Christmas 1985!

We continued contacting automobile plants and receiving orders. I recall one large purchase order from the Dodge assembly plant for 91 signs. It became obvious our competition was beginning to compete in this industrial market place. Previously, we seemed to be the only company providing 'fault diagnostic information' products and as such had little in competition. More, on this subject later. We began making inroads with the U.S. banking institutions. Though it never matched the success we enjoyed with the Canadian Banking Market.

This is a good time to reflect on my relationship with a local bank we initially began banking with - Pontiac State Bank. Compared to Canadian Banks, they were totally inept leaving me with little or no respect for their management and did not hide it. I cared less how they felt about me. Such was the case when the branch manager would call Phil in Canada and complain that "Mr. Maaassssee" will not return my calls. Phil, hardly able to cover his giggles, would eagerly patronize her while working hard to limit his laughs.

While waiting for additional UAL response we do 3trade shows within a 5week period.

- National Electronic Sign Association   Hollywood FL

- Tri State Industrial Show   Cincinnati
- Detroit Business Show   Cobo Hall

The following United Airlines segment will be much of what 1986 was about.

I finally hear from UAL requesting a meeting to discuss the 'working perimeter' of our product design to their specifications. Other than ideas I had gleaned from Bill Kettle and Chris Wyman, all theory and speculation, I had no product to show and as it turned out I was the better for it, as I later learned they wanted a product design that was theirs.

Discussion now elevated to a level way beyond my expertise and knowledge. I did have the presence of mind, earlier, to have Bill Kittle introduce me to Control-O-Mation's president, Dick Lundy – he too an engineer. I had briefed him on my past meetings with UAL and advised that I thought we had a shot at a big project. He did not appear to be in any level of "high alert" but did engage in light conversation. That changed dramatically, when I informed him that UAL called requesting a meeting to discuss product design as it applied to their specifications. After several meetings with Lundy in attendance, it was now quite obvious we were in a "primary position" as far as other competitors. A few weeks later we were advised that we were to begin drafting design and specifications, as we determined, to meet their product demands.

This triggered many, many meetings discussing designs and software. My expertise was clearly not in this field but felt I had to attend, as no one around the table I was sitting at knew diddly-diddly about the field I had been engaged in for the previous five years. My job, as I saw it, was to keep these engineers on practical electronic sign matters as it applied to the industry and in particular to this market.

By May we had the semblance of a design and a model we named the NM 5016. The name was derived by a clever design based around an LED module (think of it as a "block" of LED's) consisting of 16 rows of LEDs, each row containing 50 dots (LEDs)

This design permitted one to build a display sign of varing sizes by just adding modules (think like Lagos) to the desired size. To meet UAL signage needs our unique design allowed us to configure modules to meet the required display sign size. 16 rows of 150 dots for the smaller size signs and upwards to 96 rows of 200 dots for the larger size displays. All displays were adopted to use the NM 5016 controller. Sometime in July the completed blue prints and specifications, were submitted to UAL. Yet to be defined was the required outdoor display signs – something other than non-readable LEDs in an outdoor environment.

Within a week they ask to meet to finalize "a few questions" of what represented our final design. In August they gave us the "go ahead" advancing some money, I do not recall the amount, to produce the first proto-type. About two months later the proto-type was sent to UAL. They signed off on it and issued a commitment letter but, before issuing the Purchase Order and Contract they requested an "on site' visit of the manufacturing facilities at Contol-O-Mation.

I will never forget this. We proceed to prepare a "staged" work pattern simulating production of signs for the on site revue. Additional workers are brought in, fake assembly lines were in place, and even Phil was present to take the entourage to lunch. It reminded me of the old Compute-A-Sign days. Living it again was an absolute hoot. It worked with flying colors. During this time it was made clear the P/O and contract would be issued to COM2, the subsidiary company that Lundy had formed for the UAL project. Endless meetings were required to complete the 'Joint Venture Agreement' acceptable to both COM2 and *Nu*-Media. I would not budge off my preexisting position the UAL software and hardware design would belong to *Nu*-Media and it would be in total control of its ownership.

In December, almost to the day of my first contact, the contract and purchase order is issued. By the way, I learned some time later that we were 1 of 3 on the short list.

I have thought often of this: I firmly believe it was the unique modular design that went a long way awarding us this contract. Other competing companies would be inclined to meet UAL's sign requirements using their existing hardware and adverse to expend the time and money designing new hardware/software competing against their existing hardware/software. If I am correct in this assumption, Pollard would have been in the same predicament as our competing competition and as such, had he agreed to join the project we too, would likely not have won the contract. Weather or not it was the politics of "United" or that the "whiz" boys at "United" had to provide cause and reason to the "United Airlines Brass" it was clear to me, from the early beginning, they wanted their own type of electronic signage to add to the pleasure of the Board Of Directors and Upper Management.

Because the contract included curbside outdoor-signs I engaged Voltron, an existing outdoor sign company, neighbors to our Pontiac offices, as our source to meet the outdoor application. With contract in hand, I bring Voltron to the table, having their software people engage with

COM2 engineering. Their technology used "digi-dots" a series of luminescent round dots, easily read in bright sunlight, in place of LED'S. Before engaging and inviting Voltron to the table, I inform them that a preliminary Joint Venture Agreement would be necessary to protect existing JVA participants and with that agreement in place all participants would be protected with each other. They sign without hesitation.

Voltron's Digi Dot would later result in an additional purchase order for large display signs attached to the exterior of the terminal, facing the tarmac, providing " gate information" to incoming flights taxing in on the tarmac toward the terminal. It proved to be another near 1 million to the existing contract.

The initial contract was for 313 signs and with required spare parts United insisted on, brought the sale value to just south of 3.5 million. With added purchases for the outdoor terminal and the then unknown Denver airport purchase we now had a contract of almost $5,500,000. "Ya f------ Yahoo!!

To my understanding, the original O'Hare order was the largest single LED electronic sign order ever issued up to 1987.

Before continuing with the UAL project I wish to add that I was concerned with the display "brightness" of the 5016 modules. In the many meetings that followed the presentation of the prototype sample, I voiced these concerns and eventually shipped a NM 640 (Pollards product) to them for comparison purposes. Easily, the 640 was twice as bright as the 5016. I was sure the comparison would result in utilizing the brighter LEDs that Pollard used for his product. I prefaced my suggestion for the brighter LED's stating the traveling customer would find it easier to read and a decided advantage. "No" they chose to remain with the original design not even enquiring about the obvious additional cost.

On a personal note:

The Grand Prix, Rita's car, now had near 100,000 miles so we sold it and leased a new Corvette from N*u*-Dominion Leasing on a "preferred lease", meaning it was cheaper than the folks paid and Rita drove the BMW. I buy our first boat a pre-owned 17ft in board.

Throughout all of the UAL negotiations, verbiage and contract content required constant attention and time to its specifications and joint venture agreements, which caused an absence from our everyday business. I had a growing concern for a diminishing "cash flow". There were times were I did not know how to meet payroll and other operating expenses. Fortunately, early in the New Year we landed a large purchase order from Jarvis Webb, who had a contract with a GM project and another PO for the Ford Dearborn Fabrication plant. And further into 1987 we received 2 large orders: Chrysler Belvedere, IL plant and John Deere's large plant in Wisconsin. Combined, the orders were in excess of $750,000.

In Canada, we had worked for what seemed forever on two accounts that neither resulted favorably. A Canadian company hired us to provide electronic displays for a "on bus" information application for all Toronto City buses, and a network of our displays providing stock information at TD Bank branches quoting stock market pricing. Disappointingly, neither one came through.

The growth of business in the U.S. dictated that we have our own company accountant to work with our bookkeeper and company auditors, Coopers & Lybrand. I hired Ed Malinowski, a local accountant and was an excellent addition in keeping the U.S. firm correctly reported, particularly when Phil began taking the companies public.

With the advent of the major installation at O'Hare airport, I thought opening a Chicago branch sales office would be beneficial. So I hired Glen Gray, a Chicago native and transferred Bret Lincoln there, to form the "Chicago" team. I replaced Brett with an engineer, named Dave Evennau. He and Wyman would later prove to be adversaries. I would eventually regret the Chicago decision closing it some 18 months later due simply to the lack of sales and leadership. All of which was ultimately my fault though more available time was a lacking ingredient.

Regular meetings with COM2 continued in preparation for product delivery beginning in March 1987 and the final August delivery. All 313 systems were delivered on time and all worked without a hitch.

For reasons I no longer recall, Phil and I decide I would meet the Toronto-London sales reps at the St. Thomas office every two weeks. I suspect it was to help support lagging sales. The US market was basically financially supporting both companies.

As the year closed we did a major electronic sign trade show in San Francisco, attended by Pollard, Cassis, the Chicago sales staff and me. The show proved to be only so-so, but we all enjoyed the area and visited the Napa wine valley for a day. I ended the tour buying a case of very vintage wine that cost a small mint. Dick Coffey, the supposed wine critic of the family, always positioned himself for regular wine tasting events.

We receive notice from UAL's corporate office they intend to place another order for their other "hub" airport – Denver, CO. This airport too, had recently been expanded and remodeled. The order would not ship until 1988 and not as significant as Chicago, but added another million to the existing UAL contract.

Some personal notations:

Kelly calls in a panic. It seems a close friend advocated buying a certain stock that could "not miss and be very profitable". How many times have we heard those sorry words? Of course following predictive history - it tanked. She had purchased the stock on margin and now received the obligatory "margin call". Unable to make the full margin call she calls for "HELP". She repaid every cent of the loan.

- Rita and I take a 8 day Caribbean cruise out of Miami visiting several islands including St. Thomas.
- The Corvette lease is up and buy a 88 Lincoln Mark 7.
- This next part is the Patti and Carlos event.

Sometime during the year, Patti (youngest daughter) and a couple of her sisters decided on an Acapulco vacation primarily to join the revelry afforded by that party city. While there she met a very handsome young man of Mexican extraction and returned home blindly in love. Her first. This was definitely out of character, as past relationships were simply dating, nothing serious, almost platonic. Not long after her return home she called and asked to visit – just her and no one else. This in it self was unusual as past visits where always with an entourage. I agreed of course and arranged to pick her up on one of my returning Toronto business trips. On the same returning business trip, while in London as part of the planned trip, I got a call from Connie asking that while I was in London, she and Kevin would like to meet for a end of the week, Friday afternoon drink. If I haven't mentioned it Connie and Kevin Workman worked at the same TD Bank Branch and the one and same where N*u*-Media had it's accounts. Connie and Kevin had been an "item" for 2 or 3 years. The family was proud of this relationship as both where what I would refer to as "sterling persons". We met and after a couple of drinks Kevin stated that they would like to "advance their relationship" and begin living together, and, that they would only do so with my permission. You always find it amusing when your "mid 20s" children state "only with your permission" and in reality it is only a formality as the objective will remain unchanged.

The first thing that crosses my mind is the "no". But then I begin to consider the very mature and considerate approach and of course the "put it on the dad thing" quickly reduces ones options. In my attempt to recover and act Fatherly, I ask, "what are your intentions?" An appropriate answer is given and I hug both of them and we take our leave. Their mission accomplished.

In the land of parenthood this brief encounter should have triggered some warning as a harbinger of the "Patti's only" requested visit. We were late arriving in Pontiac and decided to have dinner at one of the local restaurants where Patti chooses to introduce the subject of the weekend visit. She has met Prince Charming and she is asking my permission to move to Acapulco and move in with this Carlos guy, where his family own and operate several restaurants and bars in this Mexican "play city". She is 20 and he is 26 something. My immediate answer is something along the line of "remove your head out of your ass and shake whatever drugs he has induced into you and get a grip on reality". NO, NO, and NO.

As the weekend transpired with more and more discussions on the subject one begins to move emotions aside and evaluate the entirety of her stated intentions. Patti and I always had a clear, honest, and strong communication line. We rarely disagreed and trusted each other immensely, both respecting each other's quick minds. I began to reason a simple straight "no" was not a correct or the best response. An extensive plan began to form and seemed to favor more to my side as I truly thought she would be unable to meet all listed qualifications. The plan? Formulate a 'qualification list' that if accomplished would set aside most of my concerns for her "well being" and security. It also had the potential of squashing this illegal alien's intentions of an easy ticket to Canada and who else knows what.

The list contained 10 or 12 items including acquiring health insurance, taking Spanish lessons, having sufficient money to return home in any required event. It was a very comprehensive and detailed list (Patti still has the list) and my expectations were that she would be unable to complete it to a satisfactory acceptance and thus disqualify herself. It was made clear that 100% completion was required. "no tickee – no laundry". A small reminder: Never short sell a resourceful and committed person.

Well, the longer story continues but the short version for now is all items were checked off, with supporting evidence. She dedicated and committed herself to its total completion. She did go to Acapulco and Carlos and Patti remained an item for several years and experienced a loving and caring relationship. He was a graduate of an American University, was industrious and abhorred hand out entitlements. He was a real stand up guy. Once again, the lesson a book cover is just a book cover! Reading the book is what the book is about. How many times must one relearn that lesson of wisdom? Patti chose well and I have no hesitation when I say the relationship would have prospered into permanent status but for the long distance between families and seemingly impossible work visas.

1988 began much the way of 1987. However, the winds of change were blowing. Our main focus continued in industrial sales and our continuing effort to establish a further presence with the airline/airport industries. Our reputation within the auto industry continued to serve us well but there were looming signs the auto industry was into the early stages of decline. They were subtle but we noticed a few warning shots. These observations prompted us to explore other markets in the electronic display industry and even business outside the industry itself. More, on this subject later.

Philip continued to move forward with his stock market passion seeking to take the company public. His main motivation towards a *Nu*-Media public company was fueled through the UAL contract and our industrial automotive success. Much more on this will be written, covering several years.

Joanne, Dick, Rita and I celebrated New Year's Eve with dinner down town and attending the traditional New Years Eve Red Wing hockey game followed by more celebration at the Joe Lewis arena. This is a good time to mention that as a lifetime hockey fan, Coffey and I purchased Red Wing seasons tickets and continued to do so right up to my eventual Michigan departure. During these 6-7 years we were afforded the period when the Red Wings dominated the league and some really awesome hockey.

Another1988 event. My sister, Joanne cast aside her 40 some years of single life and married Richard H Coffey on July 25 in 105degree heat. Coffee was employed as a real estate agent and became, to this day, a strong friend. He rarely took advantage of his older brother-in-law, except on the golf course. The wedding was a grand production with sumptuous food and drink, a litany of speeches and plenty of merriment. I recently saw an old picture from that same wedding day of me reciting "the duck" story as told by my all time favorite funny guy, Buddy Hackett, complete with rolling on the floor, while dressed in a tux.

Combined with the intentions of diversifying through the late part of 1987 and the first part of 1988, our accrued cash flow became a growing concern towards US Corporate Taxes. The Canadian Company was not suffering from that particular concern and in working with the accountants on both sides of the border they advised that the US Company declare a bonus to its parent Canadian Company. Canada was not in a financial position of paying any serious, if any, corporate tax and had bank credit notes to pay. In turn, completing the "bonus," lessened our US corporate tax burden.

In line with the above, Philip learned of an attractive, Lake Erie (near Windsor) Recreational Trailer Park that was listed for sale. The park had 30 fully serviced trailer lots, which most were rented or leased and an additional 4 acres that were not of any particular use other than a recreational area. We placed a purchase offer and while waiting for the offer to go through its process we received notice that the property and sale was "on hold" due to the discovery of an American Bald Eagle nest located in one of the many trees on the property. I no longer remember why the Government decreed the sale be officially listed as "pending" but absolutely nothing was to move on or off the site. We waited and waited for a decision and held to the possibility the "Eagles" just might decide to move. They loved their home and as far as I know may still be residing off the shores of Lake Erie. Our $5000 deposit was eventually returned and I lost track as to what may have resulted with the Trailer Park.

In trying to further good stewardship of our cash position we determined that reversing the notion of rent payments to mortgage payments would advance us in a positive direction. I explored buying the Pontiac office, as it was well known had been available for some time. Again, it was an old Victorian private home, at least 75 + years old, with antiquated electrical and plumbing. While it had much character it really did not meet our future plans. Unless we could purchase for a substantial bargain it was not right for us. The selling price combined with revealed financing data that electrical and plumbing upgrades were required, killed that option. I then turned to Coffey for assistance and in turn he arranged several locations for our revue. We settled on an industrial property in Royal Oak. It sat on a acre of land, with a fenced in compound, about 7500 sq. ft under roof, consisting of 4 private offices, with the remaining floor space as an industrial plant. The owner seeking to downsize, operated a precision grinding and tool & die business. In the end we agreed to a purchase price, $122,500 and exacted we would require turning some of the plant space to office space. The previous owner requested we rent the remaining plant space to him, affording him time to relocate. Everyone agreed and before moving into the new location we expended $15,000 in renovations. Adding 2 more offices, board room, small repair/tech space and warehousing.

Continuing with diversification growth, we had discussed over the previous months to try, on a trial basis, distributing electronic components and circuit boards. You may question why even the discussion as neither Philip or, I had any prior experience or any substantial knowledge towards this industry. The link to the equation rested with both Chris and Lisa as both worked in this business prior to their employment with N.M. I was encouraged with this change as both were becoming non productive in the day in and day out course of the sign business. Philip and I both knew some type of change with one or both would soon be necessary.

The final agreed test plan was they would pre sell product 5-10% below current market prices and then purchase the product for delivery and invoicing. Normal industry margins were 40% of cost so the above formula stood to render the company 30% / 35% gross profit. Remuneration to both Chris and Lisa was commission based and purchases would be completed by a NM line of credit. No purchases permitted with out an existing pre sold order or purchase order and invoicing was a firm net 30 days.

The first order was to COM, our UAL co-partner for $20,000 and another order that Chris initiated through past contacts. With the test successfully completed we approved the plan and incorporate it into our company business plan with the intentions of continuing foreword into 1989. Additionally, with the advent of the above Philip and I resign our positions, financial support and facilities with N*u*-Dominion Leasing.

We continued trying to diversify, but remained in the electronic display industry in two separate areas. At one of the many trade shows we participated in I became friends with an Asian competitor whose product line was not anywhere as sophisticated as ours but much, much less expensive. I had known him for 3 years and he remained in business, advancing his product line to better quality and expanding it. He well knew our product, as he was one of the earlier persons who took pictures after pictures of our display booths and products. He called one day and announced he was bringing out a new two line sign like N*u*-Media, and would sell to me for "weely, weely cheap". He met me at our offices and we eventually agreed to terms and pricing. This cheaper product allowed us to pursue a prior opportunity that we would never be able to crack with our original NM product and certainly not the UAL 5016. Now we could take a run at the 7-11 chain, as this product allowed us to present our concept of their on site advertising idea with 2 line signs, providing more available characters for more effective messaging, versus what they were entertaining with a 1 line sign. Our price, $900, was just a fraction more than other competitors. The project was huge, something over 2000 signs with remote programming, an additional feature representing continued monthly cash flow. The discussions continued for almost a year. In the end we lost the bid proposal to another entity. I later learned the project froze and eventually cancelled due to the economy. Sadly, it resulted in waste of valuable time for many companies.

The second plan of "industry diversification" was with a unique electronic display company out of Australia. I will only introduce the idea now as the plan really takes shape in the next year and encompasses much of 1989.

The product in question was a 1-line sign only, but provided messages and information in multiple colors in 16 variations and shades. Its software was limited and programmed with a hand held keyboard. The product was called **Color Cell** and rumored to retail for under $200. I no longer remember, but somehow we connected with a Hank Smith who resided in San Jose, California, he may have called N*u*-Media as the company was by then well known. He had real connections with large wholesale clubs like Price Club and Costco, previously selling products, as a Manufactures Rep, to this growing club retail industry. It had gigantic potential and we were vastly excited with this new development.

On the regular business side of business we experienced an unusual product failure with a GM installation in Morrison IN. Eleven displays of a large existing network failed and the plants software engineers could not resolve the problem. I ended visiting the plant and arranged for the units to be removed and either fixed or replaced. I don't recall the final conclusion of this segment. I often wondered if this tarnished our golden GM reputation and if it played a part in any future GM orders.

This next segment is right out of Laurel and Hardy.

Jim Pollard had recently completed a brand new product line and to introduce it to all our staff I hit on the idea of "new product seminar" and we would hold the seminar in my favorite old haunt – Grand Bend, Ontario. It would take place in July/August, so I thought mixing some pleasure with the business side would work well together. We rented the upscale Oakwood Inn facilities for the seminar and the necessary lodging rooms for the Canadian and U.S. staff and scheduled a golf tournament, complete with trophies for the winning single score and team scores. We held the seminar on a Thursday, and concluded it Friday morning and then held the tournament in the afternoon followed by an evening dinner and drinks after which most of the attending staff left for home.

To make a weekend of it and thinking some might enjoy a boat cruise I trailer my new 23 foot Sea Ray to the event. I had also served notice to friends and family that I would be in the "Bend" for this particular weekend and several responded they would meet there. To trailer the boat the 100 miles I swapped cars with Dan Brisson, borrowing his van. To securely store the trailer I contacted a former employee, David Dixon, who now resided in Grand Bend, asking if I could store the trailer at his home. Arriving Wednesday to my old hometown I contacted Monroe Marina (I attended high school with Dick) and arranged for the necessary dock space and proceeded to moor my boat.

Sometime following the business meeting and golf game while using the van to run an errand I noticed some kind person had damaged the two rear doors of Dan's van. It was totally obvious and the damage extensive.

During Friday night and the pre-dawn hours of Saturday a real bad storm erupted over the lake forcing all marine traffic to seek shelter where possible. After a leisure Saturday morning breakfast I wandered down to the dock to prepare for what would surely be a thrilling afternoon of boating. But alas, I couldn't find my boat! It was gone. I notified the marina and they had no immediate answers but were sure there was an explanation. Much later I was notified they relocated my boat. It had been moved to the opposite side of the river making space for the much larger boats that arrived during the night seeking shelter. I sat around patiently waiting for family and friends to arrive and finally Patti is there hugging me and she is so glad to see me and excited about a boat cruise and "Oh, I can't stay too long as I have a dinner date." She proceeds to inform me that she is the only one to see me as everyone has called and served notice all had conflicting agendas. Even Rita cannot make it. Even Vic Brisson and Margie have begged off. I am alone. The abbreviated Patti cruse is cut short due to time. She leaves and I find my way to one of the bars and proceeded to get seriously drunk.

I decide to head home early the next day and summoned Dixon to help with loading the boat onto the trailer. I instruct him to move the van and trailer over to the other side of the river, where the loading dock is located, while I negotiate the boat in preparation of loading it unto the trailer. I carefully instruct him not to try backing the trailer to the loading dock, as it is too tricky, particularly if you haven't had any practice. He is to just park the van and meet me where I will be close to shore, sitting in my boat. He then is to replace me securing the towline while I back the trailer onto the loading dock. In horror I watch Dave attempting the dreaded trailer exercise. He tries and tries while I am shouting stop and he just continues trying. I can't let go of the towline, as the boat will surely drift away. Finally Dave gives up and I am now fully aware of the damage to the trailer as the tongue is twisted at least at a 15degree angle. He just gives me the familiar Dixon smile of "sorry I tried my best".

I leave glorious Grand Bend and en route to Sarnia/Port Huron I meet an OPP cruiser traveling in the opposite direction. Moments later I notice that the cruiser has turned around and is now following me with red swirling lights. I pull over, not able to imagine why and what for? He informs me that he pulled me over because when he passed me he notice a radar detector attached to the sun visor of the van???? What?? I explain to him that if he was driving the speed limit of 50 mph and I am driving 50 mph, combined is the equivalent 100 mph and the viewing time would be a microsecond to notice a tiny black item stuck to the sun visor behind a windshield. No matter, he says there is the radar detector. It is a prohibited device and since its sole purpose is to defy speeding limits I must have been spending! I can't believe this little red headed prick and he then insists I must hand over the detector. We spend the next half hour arguing, with me telling him that it is impossible for me to do as the detector is not mine and if I were to do as requested I would be committing a crime and he would become an accessory to said crime. At some point I ask him when he graduated from the OPP College in Aylmer. He is astonished that I knew of the college and how is it I am so informed? I lie and tell him I was a former "college volunteer". It did no good, however he now has reconsidered and thinks it would be poor judgment for a police officer to be an accessory to a crime and informs me that if he allows me to keep the detector it is only fair to charge me with speeding. "It's only fair" he states. I definitely was not speeding but I am tired of this whole shit weekend and want home. Incidentally, he had graduated a mere 2 months prior to ending this fiasco-empowered weekend.

Boat Cruise summary: Repair Dan's van: $650. Repair trailer tongue: $400 plus the speeding ticket fine (I no longer recall the amount) for a 30 minute boat ride. Sometimes it is just better staying home boat cruising on your own lake.

We received a RFQ (request for quotation) from American Airlines. I no longer remember the airport in question but notations indicate it was a large project. The bid specs were weird and difficult to comprehend as to meeting the scope and objectives. We tried to have them explain the project objectives and alter the specs to compatible product specifications of Pollards or UAL systems. They said they would consider but never did. I suspect the bid was written to a specific competitors product and that competitor had the job locked.

Further to another disappointment. We had successfully won a major bid with Morrison-Knudson, a third party Cadillac electronic provider. A few days after receiving the PO we received notice the project was "cancelled due to funding", additional warning signals. Beware automotive suppliers?

Phillip now was well submerged in taking the company public, spending much of his time in Vancouver, meeting with lawyers, accountants and individuals whose business were providing venture capital and taking private companies public. This network led to an individual who owned an existing "public shell company" called Sancono Ventures.

Sometime before our move to Royal Oak two Sancono persons and a tumbleweed cowboy from Texas, flew to Detroit and met Philip and me at our Pontiac office and made a presentation to take *Nu*-Media public. Phillip roars to remind me (I have long forgotten) of my famous coined question: "Do you mean to tell me you flew 2000 miles to tell us, with that piece of tumbleweed in your mouth, that your going to give 2 assholes in one pair of pants, $200,000 to go public with your shell company?"

The rest is history and we became a public company, *Nu*-Media Systems International Inc. Symbol: V NMD. They did pay the $200,000 and damn if can remember what I did with my share.

Quite an accomplishment when one thinks back to the difficult 1982 days. A reminder: Anything. Anything is possible in our free market system found in Canada and America. One of the things that severely bothers me as I watch and study today's political and cultural landscape that so much of our society leans to dependent entitlements and expected handouts, rather than engage in proper work ethics, trusting your instincts and giving your commitment a chance to succeed. In short believing in the entrepreneurial system that essentially built these two glorious countries. To be in a position to learn such a wealth of knowledge and to reflect on the experience is such a gift. We are moving to such a sad, sorry state.

We close 1988 with another UAL order for 23 large, 15 feet long, curbside signs and were shipped to COM2 by Vultron, to install the main CPU board.

Most of 1989 was dominated by the Color Cell sign venture and *Nu*-Media as a public company.

First: Incidentals pertaining to lesser business issues and life in general.

To facilitate the planned departure of Lisa Papp (Chris Wyman's significant other) Rita took over most of her duties, including secretary, receptionist, invoicing and in general assisting Marcella with company bookkeeping. Rita was not in possession of a US work visa so we devised a method where she was paid through the Canadian company and then Canada was reimbursed through regular inter office channels. She did as good job as could be expected.

I keep my previous promise to serve a year as president of the Port Cove Association. I can assure the reader a thankless duty to be sure. The association becomes marred by our townships boat permit division reversing a prior long standing decision, permitting Port Cove residents to moor their boats along the public lake shore and community canal. The reversal decision if left to stand, would surely have a negative effect on property values. The townships intentions happen on my watch and as such the prevailing negotiations are mostly on my shoulders. There are many meetings and discussions with our and their lawyers throughout the year and in the end we prevail allowing the association to continue the prior practice. Untold hours and hours of my time are of course unpaid and in the end "forgotten".

On the home front Connie and Kevin announce their engagement and wedding plans, validating their previous stated intentions. Connie is accepted into college, being one of only 20 out of 200 applications. Carlos, now living temporarily in Canada, and Patti spend many summer weekends visiting us he being one hell of a water skier. Julie completes her studies obtaining her private pilots license and Vic Brisson and I celebrate our 50th birthdays at a party brother Doug orchestrates.

After many broken repayment promises I have a "come to Jesus" meeting with Chris Wyman. (*Nu*-Media and Chris, as previously stated, began the electronic component part distribution) I inform him I will keep and not release any and all *Nu*-Dominion Leasing records, files and documentation until he repays the loan balance for parts purchased by way of a cancelled P/O – I often wondered if the "PO" was fraudulent. I knew he would need all the files and documentation to properly file taxes and satisfy the funding banks records or, face serious consequences. This announcement gets his attention and we eventually collect most of the loan balance. The continued non-payment of this receivable was a very heavy financial burden for the company during a substantial drop in industrial sales. (I reference the anemic economy and the now present cyclical downside in the automobile industry) I vividly remember receiving written notice during a short period, the cancellation of 7 in hand, purchase orders due to financing restrictions. Waiting 9 months for the eventual collection was troublesome, aggravated further by the continuous delays with the Color Cell venture. Obviously, the Wyman leash was not short enough.

A short side bar story: Karma eventually caught up with Chris. I learned a few years later he was arrested in downtown Detroit for running a prostitution ring – out of his van! He did receive prison time.

With Philip spending most of his time with the public company and residing much of the time in Vancouver, I now am also managing the Canadian operation – or at least most of it. I hire another sales rep, Bill Lochead, who previously worked for another Canadian sign company. As part of the Canadian Marketing team he joins a very steady and reliable Norm Passi, who reigns from London Ontario, My time affords meeting them only once a week. Not sufficient or fair to both. The results are evident. We do however complete some sales and they successfully crack a new market, Automatic Call Distribution or, ACD. Though we do so with software only partially completed, limiting our marketing to smaller operations. Any company employing "call centers" with perhaps 50 to 100 service agents accommodating incoming calls from new or existing customers are potential *Nu*-Media customers. We bleed that software technology to the US market place and successfully sell it to companies like Ford, Blue Cross Blue Shield, Michigan Bell, UPS. You get the idea. We open another sub industrial market, with the introduction of "Time Counters". Not a high end product but cash flow never the less.

I attend the companies first Public Share Holders Meeting in Vancouver. I spend the best part of a week in an environment I know little of, though finding it interesting meeting and speaking with people that make this industry tick. It is amazing, engaging in actual conversations with these professionals, their continual expectations of the imminent, immense wealth, begins to follow you and your expectations are not if – but when.

Later in the year Philip is successful in completing a private stock option – I believe in the amount of $100,000.

After many conversations with the Australian **Color Cell** principals we had the initial underpinnings securing the exclusive Color Cell distributorship for North America. The final draft would follow the fine-tuning of production numbers and our input into the software and operational functions of the new product. Key to finalizing the above was visiting the production facilities and management in Hong Kong.

Hank Smith and I met in Hong Kong where we were introduced to the Australian Engineer. After several meetings with Chinese manufacturing principals we finally agreed to the final product specifications, the Joint Partnership Agreement, inclusive of cost price, sale volumes, required spare parts and delivery schedules. The final draft will be signed on my return to Michigan. Hank and I spend 8 days in Hong Kong. The city is unlike anything I had ever experienced then and now. There are droves and droves of people, literally a wave of humanity. A two-mile cab ride is at least an hour exercise. Scores and scores of apartments/condos. Buildings 50-60 stories high, containing 1000+ units. Average unit size, 350-500 square feet. Most units are void of anything resembling a kitchen and the reason almost all residents eat in restaurants.

HK is primarily a "trade city" and so next to restaurants there are thousands of small retail stores. They sell everything imaginable. I buy a ton of gifts to return home for immediate family and sisters and brother and a couple of custom-made suits for a fraction of American costs. The travel time is a killer with a 4hour lay over in LA my return trip uses 28 hours of my life.

Scheduled March delivery for the first 10 samples to Price Club became May, they eventually issued a written "product approval" and that secured the Price Club agreement, containing the usual conditions including product sale volume and pricing. Price Club would retail $199 per unit against their cost of $169 leaving our gross profit at $46 per copy.

Philip arranged a letter of credit for the first 100 units followed by a 2nd LC in the amount of $61,500 to cover the following 2nd unit container of 500 units. The letters of credit was secured by the existing Price club purchase orders and contract. Container units were to be shipped beginning in July and continue on a bi-weekly or monthly basis. A couple of lessons about Chinese manufacturing and product quality. July becomes October before the initial partial 100-unit shipment clears our LA warehouse. Promise after promise was relayed to Price Club. We dangerously came close to contract cancellation with the customer twice citing poor product performance. Somehow Hank manages to keep the contract enforced. We are all over the Australians to do something about the inadequate and poor quality manufacturing.

A hastily called meeting is scheduled in Vancouver, where Philip will attend in conjunction with public company business and the Australians finally agreed to a new manufacture. However, due to set up and securing required parts by the new manufacture, actual production will not be in effect until early 1990 a further delay of 2months. Mean while we receive an opening order from another warehouse club, Sam's. We hold off in accepting the order for obvious reasons.

What follows is the beginning of a long nightmare.

Of the combined 100 October units and the following 500 units in November, 300 are returned to our Royal Oak facilities under the standard "RMA" (Return Merchandise Authorization) faulty product the stated reason. A 10% return is accepted as normal in the retail market. 50% is unheard of! I will never forget arriving at the Royal Oak office early one morning to find 3 UPS brown trucks lined up in front of the compound gate waiting to unload 298 returned Color Cell signs. I recall kneeling in the employee bathroom toilet trying to vomit.

For several months I have dialogue with the Australians and Hong

Kong for the delivery of the contracted spare parts. The company line is always " should be in the U.S. within 15 days. Right now all parts are needed to maintain a tight production delivery schedule".

The consequences of returned product is two fold.

Nu-Media is effectively financing half of the Australian Company commitment to HK, because when Price Club replaces the customer returned product, they reissue another purchase order to replace their current inventory. Two delivered signs for one sale, if you get my meaning. Returning the non-performing product to Royal Oak becomes our cost. Paying twice for the same one sold unit. Secondly, without the spare parts I have no recourse to repair the returned merchandise, allowing me to recycle the repaired product to the market place. Price Club or any other customer. If you do the math the company as nearly $40,000 tied up in product that we cannot sell. All things considered, disastrous, and will surely negatively effect our Nu-Media stock shares distribution to company principals, and part of the public company share structure. In simple language the new shares assured to Philip and me by way of company financial performance and as dictated by the stock exchange will be denied and the negative financial reward associated with the sale of that stock. It results in huge financial loss for all share holders.

I am livid with Australia. They portray that this performance for a new product should not be unexpected!! I begin to realize they are using the dismal product performance, delayed production and the un-available spare parts to their advantage. Meanwhile, Price Club places a hold on all issued purchase orders until a further product evaluation is completed. Effectively putting a hold on "2000 unit purchase order" of which some of that order is already "on the water" paid by our letters of credit. Eventually, in early January the hold is lifted. Given the entire situation and my inability to repair the returned products we cancel any and all new orders with the manufacture - beyond existing Price Club orders – something in the area of 2000 units. My inner instincts prove correct. By the spring of 1990, when the new manufacture is now manufacturing the Color Cell product, I receive written notice our North American exclusive distribution agreement is revoked and cancelled immediately due to our cancellation of new orders. Beginning with the cancelled distribution agreement Australia will ship directly to Price Club and any other pending wholesale clubs. You could see that Australian Kangaroo coming for a mile!

More on Color Cell later but Nu-Media will take great pleasure learning that the mighty Australians will be canned by the US market place within 6 months after taking over Nu-Media's distribution for **"inadequate product performance"**.

We receive another UAL order for additional Ramp signs to be installed facing the tarmac (used to communicate incoming taxing flights and tarmac employees) at O'Hare airport. The gift that keeps on giving!!

Speaking of UAL, I hope to include an article that appeared in one of the electronic sign magazines. The negative article written by the magazines editor, Alan Angrist, a former *Nu*-Media dealer who was excommunicated from our dealer network for trying to have one of our models copied and got caught doing it, and my written response to the magazine article. I received many comments from industry competitors, not only for the quality of the response but also for having the balls to do it.

Oh! The drama of small business.

1990 was not that eventful but did have a high degree of drama and from the business side centered much around a new player, ABCOR Products Inc. More on this part of this segment will be written later.

As to the usual run of business we participated in a electronic sign show in San Antonio - and yes I did visit the "The Alamo". We did major presentations to America West Airlines in Phoenix and American Airlines in San Jose – none of which materialized.

I worked (it seemed forever) with Chrysler Proving Grounds Racetrack and finally succeeded in installing two large outdoor signs.

On the down side we received an $87,000 purchase order from the Kentucky State Lottery only to receive notice, less than a week later, that they were forced to rescind the order because some board directors opposed the signage based on "religious grounds"??

I enquired as the how an electronic sign violated religious principals and was rewarded with the answer that the "board" would get back to me. Still waiting for that return call.

Our Canadian rep, now more involved in the US side than the Canadian Business, was forced to resign as "momma" learned that he had been messing with some Detroit stock and issued an ultimatum "Detroit or me". Momma usually wins in these circumstances.

To add to Color Cells contribution towards our financial difficulties, cancelled purchase orders and general market decline, the office/warehouse, owned by Philip and me and leased back to the company, required major roof repairs. From no-where suddenly the roof became a sieve, rain poured into the warehouse part of the building. Into each and everyone's life some rain must fall!

Color Cell continued to be a major disappointment, though we were able to deliver the 2000 Price Club sign order that carried over from the previous year. We finally received the long awaited electronic spare parts that enabled us to begin repairing the 600 returned signs and due to part replacements restrictions and the required repair time, we were only able to repair 25 units per week, but eventually did sell the remaining inventory. This concluded our Color Cell venture but not before being a major contribution to company losses that combined with the economic times, N*u*-Media would never fully recover.

The major personal highlight of the year took place on October 6th. Kevin and Connie were married in London, Ontario, on a bright, warm autumn day. Beautiful in every aspect and concluding with a night reception, attended by my estimate, close to 200 people, entertained by endless speeches, music and beverages a-plenty.

The last potential "deal to Utopia" for N*u*-Media involved another a US Public Company, **ABCOR PRODUCTS INC**, Peter Caughill, a resident of West Palm Beach, Fl. learned of N*u*-Media Industries Inc, the Canadian Public Company and contacted Philip. Peter, Philip, myself and others became engaged in real serious meetings in West Palm Beach, Orlando and Detroit for the better part of 3 months resulting in an signed agreement between the two public companies. The upshot of the deal was as follows:

ABCOR wanted to be listed on the NASDAQ stock exchange but did not have sufficient assets to meet NASDAQ qualifying requirements. By buying the Canadian Public Company, they would acquire the US subsidiary with its valuable reputation in the electronic industry, and its profile as a provider to the US industrial market, both equally impressionable to the stock exchange and press releases. Most important, the financial asset value of the UAL software and existing contracts. With the successful acquisition of the Canadian Public Company, ABCOR would have more than sufficient assets to qualify its upgrade to the NASDAQ exchange.

The agreement stated that the acquiring US Public Company (ABCOR) would pay Nu-Media Industries $80,000 plus 1,000,000 shares of the new NASDAQ listed company, ABCOR Products Inc.

The sign company, now owned by ABCOR, was to be called N*u*-Media Corp, would operate independently, have its own directors and officers, and an employee contract would be issued to me paying $70,000 per year plus car and expenses. Philip would receive some income from the US Company and both were obligated to sign non-compete contracts. The public press release stated the transaction value was $2,000,000.

Many more attendance meetings with lawyer/accountant were necessary to meet NASDAQ legal requirements. There was insufficient money to pay the legal beagles for their services, but all seemed willing to wait for their money as all involved expected the deal to close and receive post closing payment. Although in the end the legal invoices became incumbent on the relative companies to eventually pay the legal costs in this failed transaction.

The sale was scheduled to close prior to August 1 with the new operating period to be August to January 1991. By July the deal began to unravel due primarily to insufficient capital to complete the terms of the purchase agreement. It would lie in limbo for the remainder of the year until in February 1991 when a California company, QVC, under the direction of Dr. Lowell Nobel, would purchase ABCOR and ABCORS subsidiary company, N*u*-Media Corporation. The deal was back on. QVC had a working, signed contract with the Korean electronics giant "**Samsung**" to provide software, marginalizing the cost of the soon-to-be HD TV technology. QVC software was defined and completed, save some minor tweaks, to provide near HD quality reception at a fraction of the HD cost to both the consumer and television signal provider. A major shareholders meeting was conducted in West Palm Beach were Dr. Lowell announced "**Goldstar**" a competitor of Samsung, was sending two TV's for HD modifications and Samsung was sending one for the same purpose. A month later both were satisfied with the software and issue letters of intent to purchase 200,000 and 1,000,000 respectfully, at $5.00 per chip. Everyone, including the accountants, was flying high with excitement. It was deemed a major breakthrough as High Definition television was predicted to be unavailable until after the year 2000 and the cost for this modified software was a fraction of HD projected costs. QVC had worked on this software for two years. Everyone within the three companies had met several times, liked and respected the need for each other's contributions. The new deal was a definite "go". I clearly remember a private conversation I had with Dr. Lowell. He expressed how impressed he was with the "synergy" of the group. At the time I had only a vague idea what "synergy" actually meant but took it as a positive comment.

A month before the scheduled closing, Samsung abruptly cancelled their contract with QVC. It was some time before we learned why? Samsung was slow in explaining their cause. Eventually the truth became known. It seems Dr. Noble absconded with millions of corporate QVC $$$. California shareholders became very incensed with this type of conduct and formally complained to Samsung. Dr. Noble was indeed eventually arrested and as to his sentencing I do not know the consequences. But I do know this last episode would be the cause for the US side of N*u*-Media to kneel and eventually fall.

I had almost made the decision to abandon ship. While seeking to get serious about selling the company building I learned, with fatal doom, that an old fuel tank buried next to the building, would, by State Law, require complete excavation. The law passed state legislation prior to our purchase, but only went into effect 3 months after the purchase. The company bank, that provided the 15year purchase mortgage knew of this law but failed to advise. The mortgage papers were completely void of any language to the issue. Our lawyers advised that this was grounds for a legal suit – perhaps to cover their own ass, as the same law firm handled the closing. The bank became complicit in the required excavation when the company hired to excavate the old fuel tank, advised me that all work had to cease as the tank was environmentally contaminated. I could not believe my eyes. The tank, buried 6 feet in the ground looked like a huge piece of "Swiss Cheese".

A Special **Environmental Company** was called into the picture. The cost to remove this 50-gallon tank was $90,000!! I quickly told the excavation company I could not afford to pay this kind of money and that I would require working something out with the bank. In contacting our bank representative I advised that he had two choices.

Pay for the excavation and I would not consider a legal suit and that I would continue working towards an eventual discounted sale of the property. Or, not pay for the excavation and suffer the financial consequences of we, the owners, entering into a voluntary property foreclosure. I also advised the entire roof had to be replaced. It was not a pleasant phone call.

Three days later I received a call from the banks attorney and after a short discussion he asked that I have the excavation company call him and that the bank "would be good for the removal costs". I received notice that the excavation would take place within two weeks and that the property would be tied up for a week. Anyone with a reasonable amount of intelligence would have suffered mind-blowing experiences watching this next act take place. Not only the huge power shovel and bull dozer to excavate the dirt around the tank with an additional excavation 10 feet under the building, 3 specially equipped dump trucks to haul the "contaminated" dirt to a special dump and not only a little army of evacuation personnel but the somehow required 3 environmental State Inspectors. Prior to the start of the job, I had made very certain that John Masse or Philip Cassis or N*u*-Media Systems were not on any paper work connected with the excavation and several times made it known to the excavation company owners we would not, could not, pay any part of the costs. They acknowledge that understanding and reasserted the bank was covering the costs.

Here is the kicker. The bank never paid the excavation costs. Not a dime. The evacuation company owner was furious threatening to suit, even burn the building, but he was unsuccessful in any form of collection.

All of the above took place in late spring of 1991 and the above scenario removed any doubt of my staying with the US ship. The converging forces were too much to sustain. I made sales calls and we did close some industrial sales but not many, probably because it was impossible to erase all the negatives blurring through my mind. The hardship of that decision was informing Philip of my thought process and to a lesser extent, advising Jim Pollard. I found it difficult in preparing this disclosure as they had demonstrated many, many times to be outstanding partners never reneging on any agreement. Their word was their bond. Our North American *Nu*-Media distribution agreement was never assigned to a written contract. But never in question during the 25 years *Nu*-Media was the marketing arm of this product. Well after I resigned, Philip continued, on a part time basis, to market the product. He later sold the name to Pollard for $2.

Both were gracious in their understanding and Philip was certainly capable of managing whatever orders might surface from the industrial market.

In the center of all this was the ever apparent fact my marriage was in terrible distress and was past a state of repair. The main area of turmoil was Rita's inability to control her emotions and distrust towards my five daughters. I tried and tried the role of mediator only to have brief periods of harmony when everything would again reverse itself to the mindset of distrust and anger towards my daughters. I was unable to live and function in that poisonous environment. What is a father to do? The strange part and one that I know, by experience, stepparents can illicit good solid relationships with stepchildren. I continue to receive "greetings" from Rita's two children, Kristal and Chad. It eventually got to a point of surrender and admission that nothing would result in family harmony. I often remember the flooding state of emotions mixed with the uncertainty of the future. Never had I endured a period such as this. I had previously managed failed companies and a failed marriage but not together at the same time. I am not sure how I escaped a nervous breakdown.

Out of the blue a bird, sent by my angel, lands on my windowsill.

My old partner, Frank Zolnai calls and tells me our old music company, Ontario Conservatory of Music (OCOM) is for sale. My reaction is one of little interest. Been there done that. He somewhat alters my thinking by explaining it is the entire Corporation. The Big Cahuna! I tell him I don't believe I am interested but will think about it and remind him that much change on my part would be necessary to facilitate. A few days later I am driving to some meeting and the frigging lights go off in my head. The phone call is like divine intervention! A plan forms in my head. It could provide alternatives for both ugly issues. I call Frank back and tell him I have to be in Ontario the following week and we should talk.

We meet and meet again and are not far apart in agreement. He knows I am not anxious in returning to Canada on any permanent basis as I am near completion for a Green Card and agrees if we can come to some ideal purchase price our plans would include expanding the company to Michigan and Ohio. He informs me if I do not decide to do it, he won't either. So, it sits with me.

None of the above had been made known to Rita but with the continuation of meetings and a planned meeting with Stan Stoyle, the only one remaining "original" OCOM Corporate Partner, it was time for a sit down with Rita. She was in basic agreement with the direction of closing the company and did not disagree with the developing plans, but with regards to moving to Canada was not interested and disliked Frank. So the direction of the marriage was clear and pretty much the way I had planned and foreseen Rita's decision regarding any return to Canada.

I resolve that before going further, with what will certainly be emotionally draining marriage discussions, more conclusive decisions with Stan Stoyle would be necessary to arrive at any final conclusions. I will cut to the chaste and just say over the following two Cambridge meetings we came to a basic understanding on a closing date and price. I remember the three of us were sitting in OCOM conference room and Stan had to take a phone call and left the room. I said to Frank "lets low ball a figure and see if he takes it. I think he is more desperate than he lets on. Frank said how much? I answered $250,000." Which we both knew was not any where near previous discussions.

Stan reentered the conference room and Frank said "well Stan we have decided to make an offer. $250,000. Stan excused himself and went to the bathroom, came back in and asked is that cash". We said yes.

Now, the decision had been made and I had a huge undertaking. Implement a plan to close the office in a measured, unobtrusive manner, moving as much future business as possible to the Canadian Operation and of course the marriage separation issues.

I remove myself from permanent company payroll to part time, leaving the technician and Rita to operate the business. I was to return to the office every Thursday, Friday and Saturday, reviewing the week with Rita and Matt, handle any open issues, deal with payables/recieveables and any required sales calls.

My decision to leave my co-founded company was a nightmare of a decision. Reflecting on the *Nu*-Media period represented the "jewel" of my working career. Yes, their were many periods of high stress and worrisome times but- there was an abundance of marvelous episodes, huge success's for a couple of assholes in one pair of pants and easily a life altering period for the three principals involved. There is only one word that summarizes the partnership I enjoyed with Cassis and Pollard. Magnificent! I was truly blessed to be a part of this history and the learned business education was beyond description.

With Rita, I agreed to leave her the condo and realize the net proceeds of the required condo sale, retain the BMW and basically most of the furniture. She would continue to receive pay from Canada for her services at the office and I would provide her a green card at my cost. But there were two provisions. 1) sell the condo within one year and I would continue the mortgage payments, taxes and association fees but not beyond a year and 2) no alimony.

In concluding this part of the story, she played games with selling the condo as I previously suspected. She listed the condo with a real estate company but priced it above current market conditions. She would not listen to reason and refused a written purchase offer some $25,000 below her asking price – actually right on with prior sale comparables. Accepting the offer would have netted a profit close to $30,000. I again served notice I would pay the mortgage, taxes and insurance as agreed, but only to September of the following year. She thought I was bluffing and would not exercise that decision virtually damaging my sterling credit. The condo did not sell within the one-year period. I served notice to the lender of "voluntary foreclosure". A young hotshot lawyer learns of the legal proceedings and offers the bank a lowball figure which they accept. Rita ended with zero equity for the condo. Sadly, she was forced to take full responsibility for these misguided decisions.

Both of the above were not easy but in the end the agreed plans prevailed. Leaving and moving from our condo, leaving friends established over several years and my US family was very difficult. Moving to a dreaded city that I immensely disliked was ultra, ultra hard. But, you have to play with cards you are dealt and continue to believe you can make lemonade out of lemons. It's not that I was so enamored with the music deal or the business, but I was in a serious jam. It seemed to provide the best solution to all and at the time appeared as a lucky ace card. Sometimes, fewer choices are best.

Next: my second music career.

CHAPTER TEN

OCOM CORPORATION:

As negotiations with Stoyle were completed, I set out a plan to raise my portion of the required cash to satisfy the purchase price. I had oodles of N*u*-Media stock and at the time actively trading so it became my obvious source of purchase money. I started selling stock and was on my way to the desired amount when suddenly the Stock Exchange placed a "temporary trading halt". I no longer recall why? I then attempted swapping restricted ABCOR stock for N/M stock, on a 2 or 3 to one ratio, but that was only marginally successful. As previously stated, the stock exchange indicated that it was a temporary measure and trading would soon be back on. Not in an enviable waiting position I began liquidating by selling my boat, I reasoned I would not be boating for some time, and my car with 100,000 miles, replaced it with a leased Pontiac.

The closing was on schedule, September 4 and with the above, I was negative $50,000. I had kept Frank in the loop with regards to the stock exchange decision and he had agreed to go ahead with the closing and loan me the money on the basis of course, that as the stock sold I would repay him. It took much longer than anyone imagined but in the end it worked out. Although as his attitude changed from time to time, I some times think he resented the delay, along with my combined absence from the company due to the on-going attendance in concluding the N*u*-Media business and selling the Royal Oak office. I made certain he knew during our initial discussions, that I would be away, initially, for 2 & 3 days per week, gradually decreasing to one day and eventually none at all and that is exactly what eventually happened. I will speak more on his demeanor later in this segment.

In the course of the summer I had been working with Jason who now had an interest in attending college. I believe his choice was George Brown, just north of Toronto, living off campus in a shared apartment. I had agreed to help with the tuition and rent. Living in Ontario allowed more time with him. A feature I treasured.

On an interim basis I stayed 2 or 3 nights a week with Frank at his then girlfriends home in Guelph. Sometime in November he and I lease a nice two-bedroom, two bath condo in Cambridge.

As we worked into the bowels of the stressed, degenerated company we discovered we had many company issues that needed rebuilding and restructuring. Not least was the existing lower and middle management with horrible attitudes and an antiquated office that shared one old computer. Most every office procedure was manually conducted with all or most in a redundant basis. It was a shame as I remembered what a sterling operation it once was. It's management team in the 60s and 70s were tops operating a combined corporate and franchised studios measuring 70 plus studios. I am unable to estimate the then financial value but certainly our purchased price a fraction of its prior value.

The two upper management persons next to Stoyle were Paul Johnson and Glen Parker. Paul was in charge of sales. He was gifted with an abundance of talent not withstanding his high caliber in practicing company politics and a cause of distrust on my part. However, to give due credit, he did serve the company well. His knowledge of the business went back to the early days of Turner and the early beginning of Ontario Conservatory. He left the music business about the same time as I originally came on the scene, to form his own music business and then left the music business altogether to go into real estate and development. This led him to a fraud conviction and prison time. No doubt, this had negative aspirations on me and I always had "doubt" when it came to any business deals with him.

Glen Parker on the other hand, to my mind, a complete failure in management. He was one of those persons who took the least of any effort and a short cut out of anything to do with his management responsibilities. He was just plain lazy. In the days of my OCOM franchises, he was the music supervisor for the Woodstock area. I fired him for his ineptness back in the 70s. I found him unchanged and how Stoyle appointed him "music director" is completely lost on me. Anyway, aside of Stoyle, who agreed to remain with the company for a brief period, that was the inherited management representation.

When we purchased the company we took control of 7 corporate and 6 franchised studios. The total student volume, under corporate ownership was 1200 with an additional 1300 through the existing franchise program.

We wanted to carefully begin moving dead weight and non- producers but cautiously, as to not cause more or additional poor attitudes. I began hiring new sales staff, trying to increase student volume by enrolling new students that had been dreadfully abandoned for most of the previous years.

In November, with help from Vic Brisson and Jason, I moved my personal belongings from the Pontiac condo, including the bedroom and dining room suite, the only furniture deemed to be mine per the separation agreement. I also buy, or take the executive desk and credenza from the Royal Oak office. Moving the above across the border was walking a thin line, as I did not want to repatriate back to a Canada. I explain to the immigration authorities I am on a temporary assignment with the Canadian company and that my green card application is near complete. It is tricky and somewhat dicey but I prevailed without any encumbrances.

Apart from hiring new sales people we do little in changing the structure of personnel seeking to increase new student enrollment and not looking to rock the boat. Our instrument sales were dreadful, desperately in need of new product lines and we were committed to change that in the new year by attending the Electronic trade show in Las Vegas and the NAMM (National Association of Music Merchants) trade show in LA and we do, attending both in January 1992.

Along the way with the closing of the Royal Oak office and company I began dating Sandy Weston, an old friend of sister Pauline. We had previously met but how the dating started I no longer remember although I am quite sure it was not through any efforts of Pauline. It continued for the next three years. I was primarily an Ontario resident so most of our dating was on weekends with the occasional holiday/vacation trips. She was fun to be with and I truly liked her. She was a heavy smoker, which negatively affected her health. I don't know if I was over sensitive to cigarette smoking due to the illnesses of my father but I was always on her to "quit smoking" particularly at the demise of her own health. The beginning of the end came one weekend when I arrived at her condo earlier than expected. I found her using an oxygen tank to assist her breathing. I was furious with her and she agreed once more to quit. This too ended unsuccessfully as she was severely addicted. Not long after this incident I was doing some shopping in one of the stores in her neighborhood when turning an aisle corner, I ran into a lady pulling a oxygen cart and in that instant I envisioned Sandy pulling this cart. I freaked out and could never remove that scene from my mind. This incident continued to have a profound effect on me and I could not imagine the future being anything but medical catastrophic times. Shortly thereafter I broke up with her. She tried to resurrect the relationship and I often was tempted to reunite – but it was just too late. With the relationship over she chose to discontinue her friendship with Pauline and I learned a few years later that she died. Sadly, Sandy would have been no more than in her mid 50s.

Our West Coast business trip was successful picking up new instrument trade-lines, which we immediately placed into our instrument inventory. I was instrumental in designing a trade show booth and we began conducting weekly mall kiosk displays, trying to reenergize the OCOM name. Necessary, even though it was a fifty-year old company, the name recognition had slipped from public view and we thought this type of PR would have a positive impact towards increased student enrollment.

Kelly, my daughter, joined the company and began enrolling students in the Toronto area, under the supervision of Paul Johnson and Mike Mitchellson. Paul, had now moved to Cambridge from London and the Toronto area became his main focus. Kelly was with the company for 3 or 4 years eventually resigning for reasons I totally agreed with and more on that later. She always did a great job, was immensely liked and added a real sense of professionalism to the Registrar Department.

I was still working towards concluding the sign business and selling and closing the company office. It was beginning to wear on Frank but I had little choice and as I had previously served notice, this would take time. Finally, in July, I am able to close the office and no longer necessary spending time with the now firmly closed US Company. I am also successful in concluding the sale of the office property late in the year having cancelled the real estate listing and sold it directly to the buyer, bypassing the usual fees to agents. I was better able to conclude the sale, directly providing a better purchase price. Even with that consideration, the net proceeds still resulted in a negative balance towards paying the mortgage balance. Thankfully, prior negotiations during the period of the fuel tank removal and the banks agreement to cover those costs also included the consideration of a "non recourse position" towards a mortgage deficit.

The Port Cove condo is finally resolved. I knew her only interests was to remain in the condo for as long as possible and she doubted my conviction to cease payments, thinking I would not jeopardize my credit. She was wrong. I was well aware this action would seriously impact my life style but I had decided to not be held ransom. If left unchecked, the mortgage payments/taxes/association dues would continue for an undetermined amount of time. It is a period of tremendous stress and frustration. In December, after three months of no mortgage payments the bank issues a foreclosure notice and Rita is eventually forced to vacate and move to an apartment. Some time early the following year the condo closes with an enterprising lawyer doing a property search finding evidence of foreclosure procedures and throws out a ridiculous low figure, of which the bank accepts, resulting in negative equity. This was totally outside the bounds of the separation agreement and this greed and short cited thinking left her without any residual equity and zero in net sale proceeds. She could well have enjoyed thousands more in appreciation had she only considered reasonable selling price. I had filed a "distressed foreclosure" notice with the mortgage lender prior to the actual sale and after several meetings with them I prevailed resulting in the bank not seeking re-imbursement for the mortgage deficient.

In October I finally succeed in obtaining my Green Card and as agreed, Rita's too. Almost four years in the making. And in November, my Canadian attorney finalizes our uncontested divorce.

I now have closed the Michigan chapter of my life – sadly, as I enjoyed such wonderful, self appreciating and satisfying times. I will always have the fondest regards for the ten years living and working in that very likable area.

On the music side of life I hire a super hot keyboard player, Lorne Whitby and Frank hires an equally hot Dave Hinchburger, to demonstrate and promote our new keyboard and piano product lines selling to our own students, our franchisees, and we develop a small wholesale distribution.

To close out 1992 Frank decides to move back with his wife, Bridget, and family. I enjoy delicious peace and tranquility in the Cambridge condo, where I will remain until June the following year.

We again attend the NAMM trade show in Anaheim CA securing more product trade lines. While promoting Bachman digital products and the new digital keyboard lines secured at the NAMM trade show I take-over the management of the London operation. My old franchise I operated in the 70s. Eon Wallace had been the designated manager and it was in pitiful shape both in profits and staff morale. We had just turned down a purchase offer of $25,000 from Wallace (we almost accepted) so there may have been an ulterior motive to his management performance.

With the newly added management responsibilities I spend two/three days per week in London and in doing so I rekindle my past relationship with Bob and Debbie Broderich. Bob and I had been very close in previous years and when Rita and I moved to London, in 1978, we often visited with both Debbie and Bob. In late summer of that year they introduced me to Carol McCaw. I will comment more on that ridiculous affliction later.

After a year of trying to hire Bernie Lawler he finally accepted the position of Teaching Director, replacing the inept Parker. His reluctance to join the team was past memories of Frank Zolnai, who at one time were music franchise partners. This took a long time to finalize but was a fantastic coup as Lawler had a proven record in the music business and was highly respected by our teachers, our competition and franchisees.

About the same time Frank is successful in registering the name "Florida State Conservatory of Music". An impressive name to be sure. But I am surprised and mystified as to why Florida as an expansion to the US. Past discussions were always surrounding Michigan and possibly Ohio. Florida is a long way from Michigan. Anyway I didn't pay a whole lot of attention to this, letting it ride somewhere out there as I thought it was mostly smoke and mirrors. It was only later in the year I learn of the Florida motive.

In early July (14th) Connie gives birth to my first grand child. Owen John Workman is born and everyone in the family is over the top with excitement and totally glee. Mother and child are without complications and the next time I see Kevin it is impossible to wipe the smile off his face.

Everyday office business had become difficult with Frank miserable and unhappy with his marriage. His frustrations and want of domination was increasingly difficult to work with. He and Bridget were constantly at war with each other and I know to remain "out of it". For certain, I am unable to solve the many problems that union possesses and as such change his business/work demeanor. I hatch a plan to lessen my time spent at the corporate office where Frank reigns and table a plan to save London from further financial collapse and reverse the current direction by developing the one London studio and expand the "London Area" by developing additional new studios. The plan has indisputable merit and is adopted resulting in most of my time spent in London. In June I terminate the condo lease in Cambridge and rent a very nice 2 bedroom, 2bath apartment on the 12th floor in South London.

My first objective is to retrain the existing 3 sales people and begin making modest improvement in monthly productivity. I also hire 2 new registrars, one of them Matt Daudlin, the son of a Kent County Judicial Judge. The plan I develop with Daudlin is with the successful completion of an agreed upon business plan, he will have uncontested opportunity to purchase a new Chatham Franchise. The business plan states the development of this new studio area will not be a part of the London area – it will be a separate area. Additionally I move Lorne Whitby from the digital keyboard dealer department to London, joining the enrolling staff.

In August I secure space for a "sub studio" in Strathroy, a town 25 miles from London, splitting the London enrolling staff in two, sending Whitby and Maudlin to enroll 100 new students for this new sub studio. We are not quite successful, starting 85 new students in October.

In September, I contacted a Chatham Realtor and by November I have signed a lease for 2000 square feet in the old City Hall. A magnificent old building requiring little renovations which I hire Jane's brother, Bill McNaughton, who now resides in London and is in the home improvement business. By January we are ready for business and Matt begins developing his-own future in the institutional music industry.

During the same time I interview an excellent sales person, formerly in the insurance field. His name is Greg Murray, has an MBA degree, married to a pharmaceutical rep, they have no children and own their own home, free and clear. He is one of the best, if not the best, I have hired while in the music business.

Using Maudlin's business plan as a model, I present the plan that incorporates buying the London area franchise upon the successful completion of the plan's stepping-stones in learning the music business. Beginning with successfully enrolling students, graduating to the management of all staff, to controlling operating costs and completion of monthly statements for the Cambridge head office.

The London Area would include the present London studio, the newly developed Strathroy studio and the yet to be developed Sarnia studio. Murray is one charged up guy and as previously mentioned, a dream to train and coach.

While all this was developing I receive notice that a Florida Department of Commerce Delegation as requested a meeting, in Cambridge, to discuss their eager support of glorious opportunities in Florida. Never underestimate Franks expansionist mind. The first meeting takes place in November with additional meetings in early 1994 when they actually visit our studios in Central Ontario and Toronto area. They are diligent and convincing that their state is in need of our brand, that an un-served market exists and that Tallahassee would definitely support us. More of this in the 1994 segment but it appeared the Michigan plan was fast finding a new home in the clouds.

As previously mentioned Bob and Debbie had introduced me to a friend of Debbie's - Carol McCaw. She was in her forties, a widow with two grown children and lived in neighboring St. Thomas. She did part time work for Channel, the fragrance and fashion company, doing fashion shows and manning mall kiosks. She was independently wealthy, the recipient of a large insurance settlement, resulting from an unfortunate car accident, ten years earlier, that instantly killed her young husband and father. She dressed immaculately, had a decent figure and was quite intelligent. Sounds like a winner right? That's what I thought too when I first met her but not until after 6 months of dating did I begin to have "the right" Carol figured out, connecting all the dots with this multi personality person. She was well aware, from the beginning that I was not a "keeper" that through my employment I was destined to leave Ontario, the result of a business plan established several years earlier. Initially it was Michigan and then later of course it turned out to be Florida. I was always very clear with this position and she never indicated anything contrary to this until Florida became a certainty. We dated primarily on weekends enjoying the easiness of dating someone minutes from my residence. A different Carol picture began to form when she made known to me that she had a dysfunctional relationship with her Mother who, allegedly, always found fault with her and blamed her for almost everything negative in her life. She claimed her Mother was just a nasty person. I cannot comment further as I never met "Mother". As the relationship progressed, she would cry almost over the least incident, no matter how trivial and she was a horrible drunk.

Early in 1994 it became most probable, the London and Chatham franchise plans were going to successfully meet their objectives and as the Florida meetings with Florida State Representatives continued it seemed apparent my most likely future lay in the warm state of Florida. This apparent future only exacerbated Carol's fears that she conjured in her mind and further exposed the many personalities and frailties she possessed. I deemed to set these "idiosyncrasies" (as I titled them at the time) aside, dating a few other ladies and resolved that when the time came to leave London I would just say "goodbye and fade away" knowing the option of revisiting past discussions, clarifying I was not destined to remain in Ontario and not a "keeper" to use her phrasing. It was not the most gentleman form of departure but I had real fears the end could be something out of Hollywood movies. With that said, I had no idea how close the actual would play into this "Hollywood" scenario. This period of "understanding Carol" takes us right up to the fall of 1994 when in fact Florida was in definite play and that was were John Masse was headed. I will leave the conclusion of this subject and come back to it later.

By January 1994, I secured a mall/plaza location for the new Sarnia Studio. It too required some minor renovations and when completed gave us about 1800 sq. ft and we opened for business in February with a ribbon cutting ceremony attended by the Mayor and the customary photo op for the local paper. Greg moved in with some Sarnia friends and was now solely working the new studio promotion returning to London for weekends only. The original London sales staff remained there to continue the always-required student promotion. The support and teaching staff for the Sarnia studio were in place for our first week of teaching in March. By early summer we were teaching a 120 new students.

Except for an incident with Matt, where I threatened to terminate him and his business-plan, due to lack of production attributed solely to laziness (his Achilles heel). He asked for another chance and with that brought his production back to previous agreed objectives. This type of management is what worked best for Matt and I tried to convey this method to Cambridge Management when and if I was no longer managing Matt. By April, except for the above incident, it was apparent that the London-Sarnia franchise plans were going to be successful. And with the continuance of the Florida Delegation meetings, subject to necessary financing, the Florida expansion would become a reality.

Revenue Canada continued nagging me with yet another audit of my 1992 tax returns. They had previously requested all my expense receipts, which I submitted. They returned the receipts and accompanying documentation all loosely mixed together in a cardboard box. Totally pissed me off. After 5 months they notified me of their satisfaction and released me of any further obligations. Now, in the midst of all that was going on around me with the London expansion and the Florida stuff, they again serve notice of a required revue of all my declared expenses for the same year, 1992! I filed a registered letter stating that in view of the previous written "satisfaction" they lift the so-called "audit demand" or I will have my lawyer file suit for pronounced harassment and obstruction to my business life and fiduciary responsibilities. The issue just went away and died and it was not until 2005 before I heard from my continued nemeses, for yet another audit revue regarding the sale of a St. Thomas commercial property Phillip I co-owned.

By early summer I began preparing the sale of the London – Chatham studio areas. The preparation was extensive, requiring an agreed upon sale value inclusive of the business, inventory value, changes to the studio lease documentation, utilities and keeping the staff on side and in support of what would be their new management and owners. Additionally, a London profit and loss statement for 1993 was necessary along with an abbreviated Chatham P & L for the initial 6 month period of operation. The P & L's were required to support all previously agreed sale figures.

By late July, the purchase figures are in line with prior discussions and we proceed without any objections or delays. The London/Sarnia franchise was listed at $150,000 + $100,000 in an actual inventory.

The Chatham franchise was a cost of $50,000 + $10,000 in an actual inventory based on our costs.

A cash infusion of $310,000 and a far cry from the $25,000 offer back in March 1993. Not too shabby for a 15 month effort. Unlike when I was involved in several franchises in the 70's, one paid their franchise fees on a monthly basis, continuing for many years before you experienced relief by way of a paid for franchise. With the above franchises they were both "cash" deals. Matt, incorporated "Daudlin Holdings" and a business loan that I believe his father helped with and Greg incorporated " Allegretto Music" and obtained a home mortgage for the entire amount.

In both instances the franchises where based on a 4-5 year payback based on current P&L statements and both franchisees did not dispute the P& L statements or the franchise purchase figures.

We closed both deals in August and my plan when tabled, back in April 1993, was not favorably viewed by some, is now deemed a major success and I am hailed as a temporary hero. The combined sales and the $310,000 is extremely timely, as the corporation was in need of serious cash due to some very delinquent office reporting for payroll taxes and sales taxes. The two sales averted serious proceedings.

The one regret occurred only four weeks after closing. I attended the first management meeting Matt attended with Frank, who now Matt reported to. There were some specific numbers I laid down with Matt that centered on the enrollment objective concerning the Chatham studio, that were key to its projected profitability and that no expansion was permitted until those numbers were met. In that first meeting with Frank, Matt stated that he had gained permission from the Leamington Separate School Board, of which his Mother was a director, to distribute school sheet forms to the students through all their schools. Of course an excellent lead source. To my amazement Frank went along with Matt's request. I objected stating this was not part of the overall business plan and informed Matt that not only was he aware but that he formerly agreed to it. Frank, who could see only the dollars recently brought in, stated that he would "think about it". I objected, and by my previously stated regret, not enough. I learned a month later that Matt did get the authorization he was seeking and began enrolling new students for the new Leamington Studio, removing any effort to maintain the enrollment numbers necessary to maintain the profit integrity of the Chatham studio. In addition, the additional new studio increased the business's monthly operating costs. Sadly, Matt would loose his franchise within the next two years. For me, I had a great sense of satisfaction, took a two-week vacation and prepared for the next journey. Florida.

I am going to condense the following 4 months as most of it was centered on the Florida expansion. Beginning in September and ending in December I made 5 trips to Orlando. The trips were shared with Frank and Paul Johnston and focused on meetings at the state capital, Tallahassee, meeting with State Education Legislatures gaining their approval and sanction for the distribution of school sheet forms through all public schools as it applied to the Orlando areas. The school districts in question where Osceola, Orange and Seminole Counties. Approval was key as the inquiring school sheet forms would represent a major source of our lead system and certainly provided credence and credibility to Florida State Conservatory of Music. The challenge in doing so is the longstanding policy of not permitting commercial advertising through government public schools. So, the procedure and negotiations were not all met with glowing encouragement by all educational state officials. But the Commerce Delegation that met with us over the previous 6 months, pledging their help, did indeed stay with their commitment and in the end we did receive the approval.

The next obstacle was to convert the state approval at the local County level and that involved meeting public school administration staff for each county overcoming the obvious objections permitting distribution of advertising through their own courier systems. While they were eager to encourage music studies they were rightfully concerned that if they did it for us the gates would open to hundreds of other worthwhile entities and then become commercial servants within their own government schools. Eventually, we succeeded here too and did prevail.

In the course of these school level meetings was where I met a Fran Kemp, Music and Art Supervisor for Seminole County Schools. I met her several times during every Orlando trip through the fall of 1994. She was exceptionally helpful, more so than any other that I recall and she had recently separated from her lawyer husband, currently living with her Mother in Sanford. All through these meetings I sensed an attraction but refused to act on it as I had had enough of this to last me a long time and well knew the dangers of mixing pleasure with business. She too played it very coy and carried on as to show little or not interest. I felt I knew different, for a variety of reasons including the Sunday afternoon she invited Paul and I to a music concert held at the Bob Carr Auditorium. She had also invited her long time girlfriend, Kay Ivey, also separated. The invited group where to meet at hotel lounge following the concert for a little get together and drinks. Kay, upon being introduced to me, chose to sit next to me on one of the lounge sofas. Fran arriving late, noting the seating arrangement cast a very disparaging look at her long time girlfriend and served very definite verbiage as to Kay finding some other seating arrangement. Kay and I, to this day, still talk and laugh about the incident.

In addition to the political meetings we met regularly with real estate agents reviewing studio locations where we previously agreed with the Commerce Delegation our first studio would be in Orange County. I learned at a later time, this agreed upon request was a "payback" to some county officials by the Commerce folks for a past favor. The choice of the

Orange County location versus other locations, particularly Seminole County, a more cultural and financially advanced school district, would be the key element that would hound the operation for it's entire existence. By December we chose a strip mall location, known as "Rosemount" as our first studio.

With school sheet distribution confirmed by local school districts, meetings Frank Zolnai had with a selected investor came to a successful conclusion. Pat Forde (and his group of Irish investors) entered into a shareholders agreement to invest $100,000 in the new Florida Corporation entitling then to 25% of company shares.

With the above investor agreement, the support of the two major county schools, the studio location lease agreement in place and my availability, the reality of Florida State Conservatory of Music began January 1995.

It is fair to mention now that the selection of Orlando was not my first Florida choice. In review of demographics my first choice would have been Jacksonville and secondly, the Tampa-St. Petersburg-Sarasota areas. To me, they appeared superior to Orlando. How the decision to overlook the above, surfaced around the familiarity of Orlando from the days of King Arthur's Court and the circumstances of Frank owning property lots at Erroll Estates (going a long way back) In my opinion, the above listed factors became the determining factors. Sometimes history happens for different and unknown reasons.

To complete this segment I must return to the summer of 1994, just prior to the successful completion of the London and Chatham franchise sales.

With the knowledge that unless some unexpected negative event occurred, the Florida franchise plans would likely be successful and with that assumption in hand I did not renew my one-year apartment lease, reasoning that while the Florida plans may not materialize, certainly my music future was not in London. In view that "Florida" was not totally finalized I thought it best to buy time and requested a lease extension to September. My rational was that by then the future would be more definitive. Well, as we now know that was premature and so I asked for another thirty-day extension through to the end of October. By November we knew Florida would be a go but unknown to the effective date. So, with hat in hand, I approached apartment management and asked for another extension and was given the ok, but that would be the last as they had clients interested in firm leases. I was in a bind.

My options, until we could pinpoint Florida's effective date, were to live in a motel for an undetermined period of time or exercise Carol's invitation to stay with her until all was affirmative. As history teaches the easy quick answer is not always the best answer and this would prove to not be the exception. In mid November I had the company warehouse staff move me to St. Thomas. The move included my personal belongings, dining room table and chairs and television. Why the dining room table, I will never know the logic or sense of it. The rest of the furniture was stored in temporary storage.

As we now know the effective date for Florida was January. My six-week stay with Carol was pretty normal and not too out there, but as the departure date became closer she no longer talked about moving there with me but incessantly spoke of visiting. I tried to dissuade these inclinations by pointing out that I would be extremely busy and she would find it boring as she knew absolutely no one there. Still I could not be too forceful as lets face it, I was a living guest. As the end grew near, things became increasingly tense, particularly over the Christmas season.

Anyway it all came crashing down the night before New Years Eve. Brother Doug had arranged for a "farewell" dinner and drinks. After a few cocktails and Carol furiously kicking them back, I noticed she was working on what I now knew to be an alcohol induced, ugly-angry period. She refused the dinner invitation with Doug and I and on our return, Doug followed me into Carol's home to say "good bye". It was tearful for both of us and my tearful emotions did not sit well with her, seemingly to inflame her more. I had spent the day packing my car (to the brim I might add) with all my "stuff" for the Florida trip scheduled from Detroit, January 1, New Years day. The plan was I would celebrate New Years Eve with my sisters and Dick Coffey. As the party plans were being planned, not to my liking, Carol wanted to be included and I finally agreed that she would follow me to Detroit and drive back to St. Thomas on New Years Day coinciding with my Florida departure. Well, as the time approached she charged that it was rude of me to have her drive back to St. Thomas alone. I should drive her back to St. Thomas and then double back that very day and begin my two-day drive to Florida. I refused saying that was utterly a waste of time and somewhat stupid. She objected to that line of reasoning stating she was no longer sure of attending the party. I did not argue saying that was entirely up to her, which only made her disposition worse. Actually, I thought it was my guardian angel intervening once again.

Anyway, right after Doug left she started and clearly, desperately wanted an argument. I sat down in front of her and said I was not going to argue as it was senseless in her condition and beside I was leaving the next day. She would not be deterred and continued the same line of argument. I just looked at her and asked that she please stop and if not I would leave this very instant. Just like a tank she kept coming. I just got up off the floor where I was sitting and said "good bye Carol, this is not the way I had hoped for".

I drove to London where I rented a hotel room and left the next morning for Detroit. I did call her before leaving the hotel and all I heard when she answered was a loud shrieking animal scream. It was blood chilling.

It was a hideous and horrible ending and one that could have been averted. Mostly, I blame my poor judgment in moving in with her. It gave her false hope and a situation she was incapable of coping with. I must own up to the fact that most of this was my fault and could have been averted. By the way: I never did get my marble dining room table back. I even turned Kevin Workman onto her, telling Kevin and Connie they should retrieve it and take it to their Oakville home. No dice. She was a tough lady.

CHAPTER ELEVEN

FLORIDA STATE CONSERVATORY OF MUSIC:

I closed out 1994, attending the planned New Years Eve party at Dick and Joanne's and left Pauline's for Florida at 10:40 New Years day with a temperature of 34F and 2 inches of snow, arriving in Orlando on Monday at 5:30 pm, in 67F and no snow! 17 hours of driving and 1180 miles.

Throughout the entire Florida drive I was possessed with an uncanny sense of a powerful self-knowing, alternative purpose for this Florida adventure and it did not seem to focus entirely towards the music business. I can't explain it, as at the time I had absolutely no other reason for this Florida business journey. Yet, I was constantly reminded that there was another purpose or reason other than the business at hand. I did not fight it as I long ago learned to trust this instinct or whatever you wish to call it. And, as this journal evolves the reader will learn the why's of this powerful intuition.

Now is a good time to restate the Florida business plan.

It was to establish a network of educational music teaching studios, populate them with active participating weekly students, and of course a supporting staff consisting of teachers, sales staff, office personnel, inclusive of music instruments, teaching material, furniture and office equipment.

Having successfully completed the above, the plan, when suitable, was to package a series of studios into a franchise area and sell the franchise to a competent franchisee. In other words, model it exactly to the just completed London and Chatham franchises. From there I would duplicate this business model in another part of Florida, continuing to use the support of the Florida Commerce Division.

What I did not know at the time and would begin revealing itself very soon, this new company expansion would represent the most costly financial losses, the most frustrating period I am capable of ever remembering. It was 4 years of abstract failure. It seemed every step foreword ended in two steps back.

No one unfamiliar with this part of Florida would realize the difference in the culture and work ethics as compared to Ontario. This factor only heightened the glaring error in selecting the studio location, known as "Rosemont". The short list of suitable studio locations provided by the real estate company (partially selected by the Department of Commerce) had listed 3 site locations. I preferred the College Park location best but the property owners would not permit any of the needed renovations. So that cancelled that site. The second, had to many things against it including a high crime area, thus leaving the remaining site listed on the "short list". Rosemount. The one engaging factor for Rosemount and why it made the short list, was the high number of elementary and middle schools within the accepted 10 mile radius.

In the early days, Fran being well acquainted with the Orlando area, warned me many times about the prudence of our selection. Ignoring her advice and choosing what I deemed to be superior professional information, I chose the advice of the Realtors and the Department of Commerce demographics. In hind site it was a critical mistake.

Initially, my personal residence was a condo in Erroll Estate, sound familiar, owned by a Cambridge acquaintance. In early March I leased a very attractive 2 bedroom, 2-bath condo in an area called the "Springs", located in a wooded area along a small river and known for the constant 74-degree large fresh water pool. The area was beautiful and where I would reside for the next two and half years.

After finally coming to terms with the selection of the studio site and the 5year lease agreement, the first order of business was to select a construction company and finalize the studio renovations. The construction company estimated the completed renovations would take the better part of a month, which lined up with past renovations in Sarnia and Chatham, setting the opening of our first studio around mid February. I received my first lesson in dealing with Florida trade workers. Due to delays with the subcontractors, like the A/C, plumbing and electrical workers, the renovations were not completed until near the end of March. I was shocked and appalled at the unreliability of the trade subcontractors. It was not uncommon to watch them leave in mid-afternoon for the day and speaking to them about deadlines was useless, as they would display annoyance and "I could give a shit attitude". This delay of course prevented staff interviewing and employee hiring until the completion of renovations was in sight and not until March did I begin that exercise.

I will pickup on the April business after introducing Frances Stricklind Kemp. Just after my arrival, Frank flew in to assist with some legal and banking matters. While that took no more than a couple of days he remained with me for 7 or 10 days. In the course of this time there was ample time to relax and play. One evening he got on the phone and called the Executive Secretary for the Seminole County Superintdent, whom we had met in the course of lining up public school support back in the fall of the previous year. He invited her to a dinner date, where she wasted no time in expressing her agreement. In the course of conversation he asked her to have her good friend, Fran Kemp join us. I later learned Fran was in an unusual "low" frame of mind, having returned from a New Years weekend in New Orleans. Apparently the planned visit and date did not go well, and she expressed little interest in accepting our dinner invitation. The dinner date was planned for that Friday night and when Marcie called and told Frank of Fran's decision he asked Marcie to call her again and express that her attendance was important. Somehow that did the trick and later that evening the two ladies in question knocked on the condo door. Well of course we had several "loose them up drinks" before leaving for the local Italian restaurant, returning to the condo for more libations and soon Fran and I found ourselves sitting together talking and talking and really talking.

Not much happened between Fran and I until my return from Anaheim, CA later in the month. Again, the NAMM trade-show the reason for the California trip. How the next date originated I no longer remember and there were no notations in my day organizers to assist. I do remember I agreed to meet her at one of the local television stations where she was conducting a live televised art show. Meeting her at the near show completion we left for the restaurant Fran had prearranged. An upscale private club, called the Citrus Club. From the beginning Fran and I have never experienced any difficulty with personal conversations. This evening was no exception. We discussed our past and left absolutely nothing out of any subject matter and to the best of my knowledge all was honest. The end result of this seemingly "come to Jesus meeting" left me with a clean conscious and high level of respect for this Frances Kemp. I later learned Fran suffered the same prognosis. This level of honesty became the cornerstone of a fast developing relationship.

It must be noted that as a result of family discussion while attending the recent New Years party and the Carol McCaw situation, I issued myself a proclamation and legislated that there would be no more relationships with the finer sex for an undetermined period of time. Wouldn't you know, no more than a month or so following the Citrus Club dinner date and interspersed dates I was busted! Unbelievably, I was right back into it, up to my ears. In my defense, early on, I well knew, without a shadow of doubt, my future destiny rested with this marvelous woman, who knew no boundaries in giving and loving. More of course on this as this journal progresses but I will close for now with this statement, "I have never been with any other and she neither."

While waiting for the completed renovations I use this down time to purchase the office furniture, office equipment including a computer in readiness for the studio opening. During this "down time" and with Fran's help, I schmoozed the Orange and Seminole School Administrations to insure the distribution of our school forms remain on the radar and not suffer a "changed our mind" scenario. During the discussions with the Department of Commerce and the local school administrations, Paul Johnston and I organized and originated a "music scholarship" titled **AIME.** This private entity would be the vehicle permitting FSCM to work in unison with the local public schools advancing neglected music education – often unsupported due to public funding. That scholarship concept went a long way in cementing our required public school support.

In March, the "investigation committee" inclusive of Pauline, Joanne and Dick Coffey visit me and of course the prime item on the agenda was to meet Fran. Pauline in ever present "tell as it is and no bullshit attitude" informed Fran that her brother "comes this close to making a million and it just seems to slip away and of course he can't go longer than a week without a woman". All though this news flash should have caused a "pause" for Fran, it didn't seem to, but to this day Fran vividly recalls this conversation. In the course of the 3 or 4day visit they meet Fran's daughter Meade and her husband Gordon, along with Meade's Father, Tom Bowden. We all enjoyed each other's company and to this day Fran thinks of my glorious sisters as her sisters. The family thing carried on into May when Patti arrived for a two-week vacation. She and Fran became friends bonding quickly.

I began interviewing staff in March and hired our first Registrars (enrollment sales staff for those of you who may have forgot the term) along with a teacher and receptionist.

Michael Bernier was one of our first registrars, he lasted a long 6 weeks before leaving. Through the years and to this day we remain friends. I was instrumental in his joining the banks mortgage department years later when

I was in the mortgage business. Also during April Shawn Zolnai was sent by OCOM to assist with the new enrollments and training of new sales people. He proved to be not much of an asset and was a poor sales trainer. He returned to Ontario 6 weeks after his arrival. To follow that lead Cambridge sent Kelly Masse for the same reasons. Perhaps because of her family ties and her natural ability to lead, she proved to be immensely helpful with both the enrollments, training and solidified a sense of organization with our new staff. She remained assisting the operation well into August before returning to Ontario.

Throughout this period I continue to hire more sales staff but the back door was as large as the front door. It's a continuance of replacing those leaving. The exception are the teachers who give it their best. There are a few exceptions but most are diligent and do a very good job. New student registrations results are a major disappointment as the closing ratios are 20-25% of new student appointment interviews, as opposed to the 75% closure rate in Ontario. The result of course are very poor sales commissions and the primary reason the rapid sales staff exit. Families who completed the school forms do have an interest to participate but most cannot afford the enrollment cost and weekly lessons. Parents who do decide to enroll in our music program end in an unusual high discontinuation rate beyond the provided loaner instrument, resulting in excessive active student losses. Counter to developing and building a network of successful music-teaching studios.

We start our first new students in May, all 21 and continue adding more new students and by summers end we are teaching almost 100 students. Not enough but we keep plugging away and we now have 3 part time teachers in our employ.

Fran, who had been living with her mother since her marriage separation, decides to purchase a condo in the "Springs" and we become neighbors. Just like that. In that same summer I experience my first hurricane and learn how the local media are masters in pumping up the dangers of such a storm to increase readership and viewer ship. When the storm finally arrives, after 3 days of hype, it is located 150 miles to the east in the Atlantic Ocean and Orlando suffers wind of 30 miles an hour with a day of light rain. The media has managed to close all commerce. What a farce.

To help offset the poor enrollment closure rate and high student losses we continue to suffer in Rosemount I seek to locate another studio where student enrollments would be more successful. To that end, I find an interesting location in Winter Park, a much more affluent area. The space in question is a vacant former "Foot Locker" store located in the Winter Park mall. The mall is to be torn down within two years, and the reason Foot Locker declined to renew their lease. It would serve as an excellent sub studio, the 900 square feet, not sufficient for a traditional design but perfect for our immediate needs, monthly rent is way below market pricing and it is a reasonable distance from Rosemount. I am concerned mall management will only will enter into a one year lease, restating this is the only type of lease they will enter into due to their demolition plans and they restate the well advertised and public knowledge that the mall is to be torn down for a new larger commercial complex. The one-year lease is obviously short term but I am so in want of this studio location, ideal size as a sub studio, under $1000 in renovations, certainly a boost to our staff/corporate image in comparison to Rosemount and excellent profit potential. I decide the potential is worth the disadvantage of the short- term lease and I continue to hope the end term maybe the prior mentioned 2 years before demolition occurs.

New student enrollments immediately improved, staff all wanted to work out of the location and we began teaching new students in early November. Student volume grew exceeding Rosemount within 3 months and we were teaching to studio capacity by the first part of 1996. The studio was profitable, helping offset Rosemount's financial losses.

I spend the Christmas Holidays in Detroit enjoying family along with the continued graciousness of my sisters. I return to Florida in time for New Years.

From the inception of the company, the Board decided that the OCOM Bookkeeper would add the FSCM bookkeeping to her daily duties. Initially, I supported the plan as it eliminated Bookkeeper costs associated with FSCM, but now, entering our second year, it was obvious the plan was not working as the US Company was second to Anna's priorities or she just did not have sufficient time for the added responsibilities. Reporting reports to the state were never on time causing late reporting fees. I struggled to know our true monthly financial position, an even worse condition when one is operating in the red. It wasn't until mid 1996 that I finally received board approval to hire our own on-site Bookkeeper. To that end I hired Charly McCue who would double as our studio Rosemount Receptionist. She was quite unique, somewhat overweight, single mom in her early forties, could swear like a sailor and had a seemingly unlimited level of work energy. Her duties included reporting to Anna and from the beginning Charly had a problem with Anna, one that I could not entirely fault Charly as her only complaint was that whatever information Anna was to provide was never on time. An added problem was Anna never completely understood US reporting tax policies. It is important to mention Charly had 17 years of bookkeeping experience and in confirming her references during the hiring process, she checked out 100%. But the good news was I now had a much improved, though not perfect, knowledge of our financial position and state and federal reporting.

During the early part of 1996 I hired James Wayne, a seasoned salesperson and an antique guitar aficionado to join our Registrar Department. Even he had poor appointment closing ratios struggling to maintain sufficient income. He did stay with me for more than a year before leaving to get his state realtors license. Over the years we managed to stay in touch with each other. To his credit and to underline his sales abilities he was immensely successful in real estate, quickly forming his own realtor brokerage and became highly respected in the industry. Some three years after his departure he invited me to an "open house" of his newly purchased office building in Winter Park. A 3 story building with a purchase price of 2.5 million. Not bad and I made sure he knew I was proud of him. He remained in Real Estate for several years before cancer forced him to sell the business and his commercial building in 2008.

I managed to remain in touch with many of the departed personnel and particularly sales persons. Many went on to successful careers mostly within the sales field so the failures they experienced in the music industry reflected more on the difficulty of enrolling new students. We struggled to maintain proper sales personnel to help develop our overall student enrollment but in early 1996 my notations indicate Rosemount had a student count of 110 students (very poor after more than a year of operation) and Winter Park, a sub studio, had 132 students, after 6 months of operation, teaching to near capacity and we also began teaching violin along with piano and guitar programs.

To add to our overall image, Gary Girrourd the US General Manager of an Italian digital piano manufacture, assisted us introducing a new concept in music education. Music Technology. This new 8week program combined the use of keyboard instruments with computers. We received authorization to provide it to public school students in an after hours program. Fran was immensely helpful in making this happen and it proved to be very well received countywide. The motive for FSCM was to help funnel students to our studios following the initial 8week music technology program.

It was not the right time, financially, to expand another additional new studio location, but there seemed no other alternative. I am unable to continue enrolling new students in Winter Park due to the near max teaching program and I am not encouraged to continue concentrating on the Rosemount studio, as it is just a front door – back door situation. I learn of a location in a Seminole County Community called Tuskawilla. Almost as upscale as Winter Park and with a ton of potential students within the 10-mile accepted radius. It is located in a strip mall shopping center. The available 2000 square foot space is on the second floor in a modern office building. Rental lease calls for $2600 monthly, more than I want to pay but renovations are not required hence not the usual heavy expenditure before opening the doors. We need 225 active paying students to be profitable, the monthly rent weighs heavy on my mind and I well know Rosemont will bleed us to death if I do not expand to eventually subsidize it's monthly losses. So I sign the lease and by the summer 1996 begin enrolling new students and teaching.

In that same summer Fran and I spend a long weekend with friends, Brock and Polly Magruder at their sensational second home in the mountains of Vermont. The home, of 1760 vintage, has a storied history to it, physically moved in the mid 1800's from Massachusetts, to its present location in Vermont.

To help with the expansion I hire a gem of piano teacher, with a Masters degree in music and a part time college professor. I would later appoint her as our Teaching Supervisor.

In addition to our after school hours music technology program we began a new program teaching a "music introductory" program to a neighboring Kinder Care School just across the street from our Tuskawilla Studio. Again, the objective is to help kinder awareness to the new studio and channel new students to our own teaching programs.

In mid October a directors meeting is called and the main theme of discussion is to have more money invested into the loosing bottom line of FSCM. The main focus of additional funds is to meet Kawai payment obligations, now 3 months in arrears, for the 100-loaner keyboards we purchased in early 1995. Everyone reluctantly agrees to another infusion of $25,000 and we are all growing dubious and weary of the constant financial drain.

Through out the entire Florida expansion I receive total support from Ontario with bi-monthly visits from Frank, Bernie Lawler and Paul Johnston. It was not from support that FSCM struggled.

In mid November, I receive a most disturbing phone call from Detroit. Vic Brisson was taken to the hospital having suffered a brain aneurysm. Margie came home from running errands on a Saturday morning to find Vic sitting on a bench in their backyard, holding his head complaining of a major headache. She called the ambulance and he was rushed to the hospital. Subsquente phone calls advised of his deteriorating condition. The prognosis horrible, unable to breath without assistance of a ventilator and with its removal he would die. He passed away moments after the breathing apparatus was removed and the horror for everyone was made worse by occurring only 2 weeks after his daughter Nicole's wedding. Fran and I attended the funeral of course and the sadness was dreadful for the entire family. I had known Vic most of my life. His family lived in Detroit but were from St. Joseph, Ontario and continually visited the area and thus how our friendship continued through our teens and into our adult life and of course he not only was a friend but my brother in law. What a shocking loss.

It is with this sad chapter I close out this year's narrative.

Before writing further into 1997 I must relate the fate of the Winter Park studio that I loved so much. Just prior to the dreadful passing of Vic I received a registered letter from the Winter Park management office advising they were accelerating the mall demolition and our formal notice requiring us to leave the premises by November 1st. Drawing attention to management the notice was basically only 30 days I did negotiate a further 30 days but we were forced to leave a profitable location. We succeeded in transferring some of the student body to the new Tuskawilla studio, but not all, as it was too distant for some. Regretfully we did not complete the original plan of operating this studio for the planned 2year period but it did afford us excellent exposure and we did experience a profit – for a change.

Before continuing with the business aspects of 1997 I must relate a short sidebar story that occurred in early January. I had been working my way through personal debt, following the decline of Nu-Media and the divorce, not to mention the hit my credit report took with the voluntary condo foreclosure. I was making steadfast progress with debt payoff and I was achieving some breathing room. In the course of this remedial repair I discontinued use of certain credit cards after leaving the matrimonial home and moving to Cambridge. Alone in my condo sitting in my big red chasse lounge, on an early Friday evening contemplating my Saturday appointments and working my way through a cold beer when the phone rang. The caller asked for John Masse and introduced himself as "Barry Gold". Being smart I commented that a person with a name like that should be a "bill collector". He said I am. Shocked, feverishly racing through my memory trying to remember if I had not paid an old bill and came up without a clue. My response, "you must have the wrong person"! He asked if my social number was such and such and I confirmed that it was and then he asked if I ever lived at 3575 Port Cove Drive in Pontiac Michigan? And of course he had me. He was collecting a delinquent account for Master Card Gold in the amount of somewhere near $3000. The purchases were made during a period when I did not use the card and was one of the discarded and paid off, which is why I was sure this could not be my account. So with a full degree of certainty, they were not purchases I made. It seems someone had the correct and proper information on the account and charged a number of purchases through 1993 > 1995. Some payments had been made during that period – not by me – but then payments stop and none had been collected since. Mr. Barry Gold had been looking for me for 2 years. Yes, it would be unlikely that it was anyone than the person we all think it is but I could not prove it and if I could it would do little to repay the account. I set up a monthly repayment plan and paid it off a few months later with the sale of stock that abruptly found its way to me. More on that episode will follow.

I get to visit my favorite city for a long weekend, following Fran to New Orleans where she was attending an educational conference. It is a city everyone should visit at least once, rich in history, culture, great restaurants, bars and music.

On the business side I hire two more replacement registrars and we accelerate the "after hours" school programs into more schools and now do so as an "off shoot" of the now respected Tuskawilla studio. To offset the perception that public schools were engaged at a high a level with private enterprise we form a new public school category that classifies us as "outside agencies". These programs continue to be well received and are of great assistance with overall enrollments.

With the closing of the U.S. *Nu*-Media Company the Toronto branch of *Nu*-Media was conducting all product sales but insufficient volume to have an impact on the value of it's public stock. For Phillip and I to be in a legal position to sell any of our personal stock, share value had to hit certain profit levels permitting the sale of our company shares. Result: no share dividends for Phillip or John. In the course of this Philip learned of a Chinese company who owned a diamond mine in China, wanted to go public and through negotiations he, with the Chinese, transferred the public company, *Nu*-Media, to the diamond mine company. Previous *Nu-Media* Investors where accepted as part of the deal and at some future date share trading would be permitted. The new symbol was CSM. With the stock of the former *Nu*-Media transferred over to CSM I was able to convert stock I still owned to cash. I believe I had something like 15,000 shares and I began selling it in small amounts and eventually accumulated $55,000. Because I no longer lived in Canada I had to convert it to US funds so the net amount was of course less. But never the less it was an unexpected windfall, particularly with all the negative money surrounding me. Philip did very well and part of the negotiations included having an executive position with the new public company. It was very taxing for him and his family as his home remained in St. Thomas Ontario and with the public company in

Vancouver along with necessary visits to the China diamond mine, home visits were at a premium.

I invested most of the money and formed a leasing company to help provide financing for families unable to qualify for a piano loan. I organized loan guidelines, including a necessary 20% deposit, with monthly payments paid at the studio along with their student music lessons. I called the company, Nu-Co. It proved helpful to many parents/families and interestingly I collected all accounts without writing off a single dollar.

Carrying on with the now seemingly regular quarterly tradition, the Irish are not happy as they replenish the company with another $27,000. Nothing but storm clouds in the future!

In addition to that cash infusion some time during the latter part of the year (I think I choose to forget this part) all investors are required to loan personal money to FSCM. Me included. **$25,000.** I still get ill when think of this decision.

To continue augmenting student enrollments I begin a "summer music" introductory program at a Sanford Church hall, providing weekly lessons for a 8-week program along with the use of a loaner keyboard which students are allowed to take home. It is income helpful through the summer when many students temporary discontinue lessons taking their vacations with summer camps and the like. The church is impressed that FSCM is providing something positive for Sanford young people, viewing this as an excellent community exercise and decide not to charge rent for the entire program.

During the early summer Fran and I do a get a way weekend to Ft. Lauderdale where I propose to her and present her an engagement ring. She seems deliriously happy, as am I, and say's "yes and yes again"! Fran has been an enormous team player and can do nothing but provide encouragement and support towards the company's success. It has proven to be a fantastic relationship and I would be a fool to not make it permanent. We do not have a specific date for marriage but agree to do so soon.

Things move fast and in September Fran and I decide to purchase a home. We contact friends of Fran who are realtors and settle on a 3 bedroom, 2bath, on a corner lot in a real nice gated, golf community, called Timacuan. The development began in the late 80's early 90's and our homes previous owners built the home in 1991. It is a great starter home, we closed in October and move our humble belongings on November 3rd making this our new home and are now living together.

Within a few days of our move in, Minnie had a come to Jesus meeting with Fran. While it was common knowledge by Fran's family we all but lived together for the past year and half (recall Fran purchased a condo two doors from my rental) this in Minnie's mind was far different. There was no hiding behind the now lost fact that Fran had her own condo and we now were definitely co-habituating and in her words "living in sin". Readers must understand Minnie's background. She was a devout Christian, read her bible daily, was a member of the "Daughters of the Confederacy", long a staunch southern social butterfly and would be totally embarrassed when friends and associates learned her daughter lived with some guy from the North. Maybe even a Yankee. My o my! The meeting lasted only minutes and the directive was simple. Get married and get married **now!** I had no problems with the just released news bulletin and agreed immediately.

We were married two weeks later, in the late afternoon of November 22, in Orlando by a minister friend of Gordon & Meade's. The small wedding group of 10 adjourned to the neighboring Citrus Club for reception, dinner and a handful of congratulation speeches.

We both were quite calm about the event as we had plenty of distractions following the two-week home purchase. Fran had just completed a new annual fund raising event called "Arts Alive" - only days before November 22 and of course our physical home move just days prior. I was so moved by the wedding event that I found time to purchase a lawn mower that morning. It is not that we were not excited about our marriage date it was just that we had so much going on we took it all in stride. Not for a second have we ever regretted this remarkable union and have enriched ourselves with the fondest of memories and experiences. It has been a treasure trove and one that I still wonder at the happenstance of our meeting and continue to reflect on that eerie "feeling of purpose" driving from Detroit to Apopka Florida that New Years day in 1995. Prior to the actual wedding date we had decided to postpone the formal reception until the New Year, as it proved to difficult for family members to attend at that time of year particularly with such short notice.

On the business side I decide to make a video to assist with the constant "training" of the ever-revolving doors of new registrars. Videotaping was completed with people *acting* as would be parents and student, simulating an actual student enrollment in a family home. It proved really helpful saving me tons of time in training and interviewing.

One of our teachers came up with an idea to form a Parent Advisory Committee and we took it to parents to contribute ideas that would help improve a student's musical success. I thought it was a grand idea and we implement it but received only marginal acceptance.

We have favorable Christmas instrument sales results in Tuskawilla, selling $36,000 in new pianos. We continue to experience dismal instrument sales in Rosemount - zero Christmas sales.

I spent my first Christmas away from Michigan and Canada celebrating it at our new home, my new family and Kelly spent most of the holidays with us.

Quite a year 1997!!

The big social event at the beginning of 1998 (Feb 22) was our wedding reception held at our home. We added a large outdoor tent to accommodate approximate 100 guests, had it catered, with an open bar and live music. The invitees came from afar. In addition to the locals and the expected from Canada and Michigan even the Cayman Islands. (Kevin, Connie Owen and little Emma) Everyone enjoyed the celebration and Fran and I were blessed with many attending friends and family.

The evening following the reception, historical tornadoes, category 5, hit the area with winds up to 170 miles an hour causing massive destruction and deaths. Fortunately no one associated with the reception suffered casualties or personal loss.

On the business side we began promoting two-hour music workshops in public schools. They become highly receptive and provided a source of leads for our enrollment department. Sadly, financial losses continued even with successful Christmas instrument sales in Tuskawilla and another infusion of loan money from Canada was required to meet overdue payables. On the brighter side with a little over 200 students in Tuskawilla and the 80 in Rosemount we hit the highest volume of active students.

Adding to the operating financial difficulties, The IRS, notify me of negligent federal tax filings. I no longer recall why, but Anna not Charly, retained the responsibility of filing the quarterly reports. The late filings kick in late fees, penalties, interest and worse making the "red flag" ledger with the IRS. The dread of any US business is to have the IRS on their weekly/monthly radar. They will hassle me for the year and into 1999.

Toward the end of May Charly, the bookkeeper and Rosemount receptionist, tendered her resignation excepting another bookkeeping position paying an additional $250 per month. I couldn't think of countering the offer and wished her well. She continued to be a source of unpaid assistance well into the end of the year. I replaced her with a gem of person who was very loyal and responsible, she would be with us until the near drowning of the ship.

In June the existing Tuskawilla lease was scheduled for renewal. Colonial Properties, the management company, presented the renewal lease for the following two years. The new lease contains the existing monthly lease amount but carried an additional 1% of our gross sales – this includes all lesson and sale revenue. I am unsuccessful in negotiating a 60day extension of our current lease and finding a replacement location within the area. The replacement options are either too small, too large, too expensive or prohibitive renovation costs. I am forced, due to no alternatives, to enter into this new lease with full knowledge it will eventually terminate our only profitable location. The end is on the horizon. The continuing battle with the IRS and this latest Tuskawilla scenario wears heavy on my mind and I begin thought preparations to leave the music business.

We again provide a one-day "summer music program" at a church hall in Sanford. The revenue is not gigantic but helps offset the usual "temporary summer losses" with regular students away for summer vacations.

To add to the IRS difficulties Anna was to file both the 1996 Federal and State corporate tax fillings by August 1st and failed to do so- this in addition to above referenced late filings for previous years. I have had it with her and hire a local tax accountant. It is to little and to late! The ever-mindful IRS were jumping all over it and now threatening to issue a bank lien for the full amount. I manage to tender an acceptable repayment plan and they eventually withdraw the lien threat.

While I have a load of mixed emotions about the business future, there are few alternatives but to set the emotions aside and push foreword with keeping the business going. I enter into an agreement with Wall Mart allowing us to erect a booth, at no charge, promoting "music education" within their retail facilities. It proves successful but to reiterate, the new Tuskawilla lease is unattainable and will eventually force us to permanently close the studio or be evicted.

After more thought full deliberations I decide I must admit failure, deciding on a final basis to leave and put together a plan to close the entire business. I say close it because I could not realistically believe someone from Ontario would venture coming to Florida on a galloping white horse.

In the course of these deliberations I had several business meeting with a mortgage broker (Terry Christensen) educating me about the mortgage industry. I had previously met Terry two years prior and he was extremely helpful with what became my eventual decision and would represent the final segment in my business career. Sometime around Thanksgiving I spent a weekend at a Vero Beach condo that Fran somehow had access it to as a gift from a pencil corporation. The purpose of the getaway was to be undisturbed in preparation of attending mortgage school for two consecutive Friday, Saturday and Sunday's. The successful completion is necessary to write a State Exam permitting me to be employed as a "Mortgage Loan Officer". I would write the exam the following February.

And as 1998 closes so will FSCM and my final career in the music education field. The failure of FSCM was such a disappointing end to everyone involved, perceiving it to be a resounding success. Personally, based on the recent London/Chatham performance and support of Ontario, my expectations were equal to everyone else. In reflection, success eluded us due to a number of factors, minor in nature to the colossal error in selecting the Rosemount studio. It just ate every morsel of profit that the business could generate, leaving in its wake a huge financial loss and wasted spirit by everyone.

On the brighter side FSCM was responsible for bringing me to Florida and meeting my life-partner. At the time, I did not perceive Florida to be the "end all" nor had I considered it to be a final home within my life span. More on "my life partner" as I conclude this writing.

CHAPTER TWELVE

THE MORTGAGE BUSINESS:

Having made the decision to phase out of the music business and enter the mortgage industry, I began 1999 with new energy and enthusiasm. Having secured an employer (as you continue to read he must have had a world of faith in me) willing to employ a "rook" who would require learning the business on a practical working level, without valid license certification and void of any referral contacts or, "book of business" as it is known in the industry. Additionally, obligated to separating my time between FSCM and this new business, dictated my business plan to spend the early part of the day at the mortgage office and the latter part and evenings at the Conservatory.

My broker, **TEC MORTAGE** and I had a pre-employment understanding the above plan would be in play until I successfully closed out FSCM and then be fully employed in the mortgage field. To assist to that end he permitted me to work within the office marketing my services to perceived interested parties. However, I would not be allowed to accept loan applications, work on loan files, close and fund loans until I successfully wrote the state exam and of course passed, entitling me ownership of a state license. I used the marketing time successfully and had a number of potential clients lined up and client information in my "loan basket". In early February I take the 2-hour exam and near ace it with a passing mark of 95%. Done! Lets go!! Some 10 days later I close my first loan and I will address this particular loan in a moment.

In the mean time I am holding down the FSCM fort with my part time effort tending to administrative duties including fighting the IRS. I had a series of meetings "disputing" the cause of yet another intended bank lien. This effort would last to the near end of the business with me prevailing. They out of the blue dropped the entire flimsy issue citing a lack of "provable evidence" canceling the intended bank lien. What bullshit! To this day, on this particular case, I firmly believed the government agent and her team built the case around totally circumstantial evidence to show work lines to the agent's office and her management. All of which wasted a year of my time. To rub salt into a sensitive wound, I had removed myself from the administrative payroll, eliminating any issues with the FSCM Board, leaving my only FSCM income source to commissions derived from student enrollments and instrument sales. Yes, I was back enrolling students. No matter, the enrollment staff had all by now disappeared leaving incoming leads to be managed by me. This temporarily worked to my advantage as student enrollments were always a part of my wheelhouse and as such I enjoyed the easy commissions. Coupled with the Tuskawilla instrument sales and the soon to be realized mortgage commissions my personal income soon accelerated to levels I had not experienced for some time. This part time effort between the two businesses continued into early 2000. I tried to "spin off" the music business to some of the existing staff and for one reason or another none materialized. My thought at the time was to not throw existing students out the door without a teacher and possibly salvage some payment for the hard assets and cash flow. Everything in this regard just seemed to continue through negotiations after negotiations without any meaningful results, partly because the intended recipients wanted the plan without paying. Their attitude was one of we will just relieve the company of it's burdens. So it was not until March 2000 that the business closed it's doors in final fashion. More later.

The continuation of the mortgage plan that originally spoke of 6 months was now a contentious issue with my broker. Fortunately for me, my business could not be faulted for lack of production and to add to my position strength I successfully brought another loan officer to the brokerage and together we were the only loan officers other than the broker. Together we dramatically increased the Brokerage business volume. His name was Carl Bergman. A blue eyed, blond Dane originally from North Dakota (loved Canadians) a former line backer with the University of North Dakota, a former US Marine who for 4 years flew EVAC helicopter missions in Viet Nam. He would later attend the White House to receive his **Silver Medal** presented by President George W. Bush. He would eventually leave the Mortgage Business choosing the Real Estate field. We did a number of creative business deals together. As the reader reads this portion of writing I will be referencing Carl a number of times and the reason I noted his accomplishments. He was and is a stand up guy and we remain friends to this day.

A quick overview of the workings of the mortgage business as it pertains to the loan originators – persons like me - and the mortgage brokerage business.

My first loan netted me a whopping $850! Evidence I had some learning to do in pricing loans and working with clients. There is no allegiance by a brokerage business to any bank or lender. It operates independently and sources the Lenders Wholesale Division for the best loan rates on behalf of the brokerage's client. This procedure is called "pricing the loan". The loan rate that is finally determined is the "wholesale rate" and then priced to the client on a "retail" level. The net difference is called the "loan yield" or loan profit for the brokerage and this is often referred to as the margin the **selected lender** pays to the brokerage in owning the mortgage, access to the customer, and possibly servicing the loan for the next 30 years or whatever the term of the loan.

The second margin level is negotiated with the client during the loan application process. This amounts to what the applicant is willing or prepared to pay to the loan officer/mortgage brokerage for obtaining a funded mortgage loan permitting the eventual home purchase or home refinancing. The Mortgage Industry refers to this margin level as "Discount Points" or "Brokerage Fee". Depending on the difficulty in successfully completing the loan the above referenced fee can be anywhere from 1%-4% of the loan amount. The total "loan proceeds" are then shared between the Brokerage Company and the Loan Officer (me) on a prearranged agreement. For beginners like me it was 50/50. As I became a more experienced L/O the split increased to 60/40 in my favor. And of course if the loan does not close, for a multiple number of reasons, no one receives any money.

I successfully complete and finalize loans in my initial months and I learn how to price a loan and the process of "loan negotiations" with the client. Now armed with this new- found wisdom, my commissions are now in line with industry standards averaging $1500 - $3000 per funded loan. A slight improvement over my original loan commission of $850!! I am really getting into this new business, actually becoming good at it, or so my broker advises, and I wonder why it took me so long to arrive at this decision.

Earlier in the history of FSCM with the constant arrival of Board Members arriving from Ontario the Board decided it would be a good investment to purchase a "standing car in waiting" eliminating the procedure and expense of a car rental. I never understood the wisdom of this but the board ruled. I arranged for a friend of mine who was in the used car business to meet Frank and I. On his car lot was 1995 Lincoln

Town Car, white with a red interior. The transaction took no longer than 5 minutes before we drove away with this "Pimp Mobile" that Fran later took credit for this inauspicious name.

With fewer incoming visits from Ontario the use of the gorgeous looking "P/M" grew less and less. The decision was finally made to sell it and use the badly needed sale money to pay a host of bills. None of the sale enquiries, over a period of 3 or 4 months, ever materialized. Around this time the lease on my SUV was at "term end" and scheduled for return to the dealership. I could not believe I was thinking this, but the company could certainly use the money generated from this supposed sale. I ended up suggesting I purchase it and entered into a purchase price and terms. I seem to remember the price was $8,000 – a good price for me – with monthly payments of $500. The car was in excellent condition with low mileage. My dislike was the appearance and I never have liked big, fat cars. No one will ever know how I hated this car and it refused to ever give up, I drove it for 3 years and as a side bar story, for reasons that were crystal clear to me at the time, although I no longer remember precisely why, I never fully finished paying for it and some how over time the debt was now owed to Ontario. Punctuation on a number of things I guess.

In July I celebrate my 60th birthday. The sisters 3 from Michigan, Patti and a boyfriend at the time, Gordon, Meade and Minnie join Fran and I with the celebration, capped by a splendid dinner at Wolfgang Puck and a day at St. Augustine – one of favorite cities.

A crown to the big 6 0, Fran buys a dog, who continues to be the finest family friend. He is a Bichon Fries, 2 months old and we name him "Mozart" after my sojourn in the music business. He has a personality that everyone adores, knows no strangers, loves all and is a "peoples" dog. What a marvelous giving gift.

I attend my first mortgage convention, Fran joining me, a 4 day weekend event in South Beach FL. I continue sharing my time between the mortgage and music business and manage to close 2 to 3 loans per month. My broker is happy and so am I.

In September the media is abuzz with a hurricane that they say is going to center punch Orlando. How this is to happen is curious on my part as the hurricane is situated in the Atlantic Ocean, 150 miles away, but like everyone I buy into the hype and follow the geese to Home Depot, standing inline to purchase plywood to board up a large window that encompasses an entire wall of our home. By the time I am able to make my purchase all available plywood has sold-out and all that remains is particleboard. I know that drilling a hole to secure screws or nails is near impossible with this type of material. There are no alternatives forcing me to purchase several 4 x 8 panels that are dreadful to work with. I have several friends assist me with the 5hour project, temporary securing the large wall window, burning drill bits to the point they are smoking, we finally finish. We all congregate in our now secured home breaking open the bar and indulge in the customary "hurricane party" awaiting this massive storm and enjoy watching our hard work protect us against a massive 30 mile an hour wind. Never again will I fall for the media hype all engineered to elevate viewer ship under the guise of community protection. Exceptions permitted!

I found my efforts and time contacting real estate agents/brokers not very rewarding as I discovered most had existing, long term relationships with banks and lenders. One could eventually breakthrough but it endured a long process and much time. One day as I was cold calling for referrals I came across a Log Home Builder. I knew absolutely nothing about this type of home other than the finished product looked very comfy and country. But I thought nothing ventured nothing gained, went into the office and introduced myself and asked to speak to the owner/ manager. The manager and shareholder in the manufacturing operation, Tony Koenig, and I hit it off immediately and resulted in a business relationship lasting until I began my mortgage-banking career. Most banks, refused to do Construction-Perm loans for log homeowners. It would turn to be a lucrative account for me because not many lenders where willing to enter into a C/P loan for a number of reasons, too technical to get into right now. That meant there was virtually little competition. Through research I managed to find obscure lenders willing to do these loans resulting in a new market for me. Because these loans were difficult to do and little alternative loan resources for persons in love with log homes I was allowed to charge the maximum the state allowed for loan yield and loan discounts, 5.00 % of the loan amount. Log Homes were costly to build and of course the mortgage included the land or lot so a $300,000 loan was not un-common. For those not acquainted with a C/P mortgage it is a construction loan allowing the owner to pay for the construction of the home and land and then at construction completion the mortgage converts to a "permanent" loan similar to that of one buying an existing home and the conversion is seamless. Securing two different loans was unnecessary with a C/P Loan.

It was sometime in September that I was rushed to the hospital for emergency gallbladder surgery. For several years I would get these attacks I had self-diagnosed as a "hietal hernia" and in recent times they were more frequent and much more severe. Now attacks were longer and left me wrought with stomach pain and exhausted. One Saturday I was at the office attending to piano sales attempting to liquidate our product inventory. Near the end of my day I was struck with severe abdominal pain to the point that

I had to end a sale discussion giving the customer a huge discount just to complete it allowing me to leave and go home. I barley made it home and when Fran found me in bed bent in pain and barely able to speak she called her Doctor who arranged to meet at his office. His examination and tests completed he immediately admitted me to the hospital across the street from his office. His concern was my white blood count was off the charts and he rightfully concluded that I had an acute gallbladder infection. I was operated the following morning (a Sunday) without complications and released two days later where I attended a Disney Anniversary Celebration that Fran had complimentary tickets, which included free booze and food. Following surgery the Doctor told Fran had the surgery not been performed the gall bladder was so deteriorated it would have ruptured within days and potentially death threatening. He went on to say the attending nurses and doctors could barely cope with the rotten odors evident throughout the surgery. Close call.

During our Thanksgiving holiday Fran and I travel to the Cayman Islands to visit Kevin and Connie and Jason, who had moved there 6 months prior. We have a wonderful time with the family, enjoying the Workman's ocean side condo and I believe met little Ava for the first time. Age: 6 months.

Continuing our traveling mode we spend Christmas in Detroit returning to Orlando on a near empty New Years Eve flight. World wide humanity were certain we would experience global hysteria due to all major computers not recognizing the new millennium and computers world wide would crash.

As this narrative now enters the new millennium I choose to write the final chapter pertaining to FSCM. Sometime close to 1999 year's end we were evicted from the Tuskawilla studio due of course to our nonperformance of the company's lease. In trying to resolve the rent arrears I had submitted a series of post dated checks that would have brought the company current but the mall management company returned them. That pretty much nailed the coffin closed. In hind site, it was a desperate attempt by a desperate man attempting to continue this loosing battle and all the postdated checks would have accomplished was more purgatory time with little or no difference to the resulting end.

In February 2000, I arranged closing the Rosemount studio adhering strictly to the company lawyer's directives. Unlike Tuskawilla, we did not have any rent issues, as our lease was only a month from expiration. There were a number of company accounts that required legal notice of closure including our creditors. To simplify the obligation of the remaining students, rather than leaving them without their own recourse, I served notice that the studio was closing and their current teacher would continue teaching students and that the teacher would work with parents/students as to a location, possibly there own home. I believe the final count of students was less than 60.

The move out date was set for February 24th with remaining unsold inventory turned over to OCOM who arranged for the company truck to complete that part of the exercise. I experienced no sadness in this final chapter, ending initial high expectations by persons and investors that possessed extensive experience within this industry. My emotions were of relief and my shoulders felt like I had just completed a major diet shedding 100 pounds. There were many factors in this failure but the Rosemount location clearly stands as the lead contributor. I was now fully employed in the mortgage business and I was thoroughly engrossed in it and enjoying it to the fullest.

Earlier in my deliberations to close the Florida Company I decided it was best to make a clean and final break with the entire institutional music business and sell my 750,000 shares in the parent company that owned OCOM. The final agreed selling price was $150,000 paid over a 2 year period in equal monthly installments. In the course of closing the Rosemount office I learned of a looming investment opportunity that most of the OCOM shareholders and other investors I had met during my residence in Ontario, were contemplating investing in this new company. This new entity would involve a RTO (Reverse Take Over) of an existing US public company trading on the NASDAG Exchange and would be named UNIQRIPT. It would manufacture and market a fax security system to corporations in need of "fax security" within their corporate offices and branches. The "Canadian press releases" were extremely positive and all contained expectant performances.

The investors I spoke with expressed enthusiasm and an interest to invest in the new US Company. After considerable thought I decided to convert part of the $150,000 payment stream towards the purchase of UNIQRIPT shares. The obvious disadvantage for me was I would be unable to fully participate in the IPO (initial private offering) offered to the initial investors.

In March Frank Zolnai advised me he held a first mortgage for raw land adjacent to the main provincial highway, the 401, close value wise to the $150,000 receivable owing me and had 5 years remaining on the mortgage term. The mortgage was current and the mortgagor was a senior stockholder with the new company, UNIQRIPT. Future discussions resulted in Frank assigning the mortgage to me in exchange for the purchase agreement concerning my former OCOM shares. This represented an improvement in the payment stream of $30,000 over a 5 year period and less of payment burden for Frank. Seemed like a win-win. We agreed and that new amendment was put into place within a couple of weeks.

About a 2 months later Rob Kelly, the senior stockholder in the newly formed UNIQRIPT Company called advising that NASDAG agents required more investment dollars to meet Regulatory Rules permitting the intended IPO Listing. Noting my current plan of a graduated share purchase restricted me from participating in the IPO and now that I held his mortgage on the raw land we could work something out meeting the request of the listing agents for additional share purchases allowing me to participate in the IPO. This meant that I would elevate my share position for a lower stock cost and my shares would also elevate to "free standing" shares and would no longer have a trading restriction. I would be allowed to begin trading within a couple of months – July 23rd. The conclusion of the above equal swap, mortgage for stock weighed heavy on my mind, not able to decide what was best. In the end the little greedy gecko sitting on my shoulder won out and I signed the deal. Sad as you will all learn, but true.

Just a few days prior to July 23rd the IPO investors were advised that a "temporary trade hold" was in effect due to "stock listing" issues with NASDAG and the SEC. The temporary hold was extended yet again but to keep the originating investors pacified the company notified share members each would receive an additional 2% of the original stock purchase each month until the stock traded to a maximum of 6500 additional shares per shareholder. As the listing issues continued the new company suffered another setback when the listing agent terminated its services with the company.

The company Board of Directors issued a five-month reorganizing plan and in May 2001 the same Directors served notice that if UNIQRIPT's listing issues were not entirely settled by August 21 2001, shareholders would receive an equal exchange of each members stock to another established US Public Trading Company.

Was I sick with my decision? Almost every day! I turned away a payment stream of $180,000. What I could have done with that. All did not seem lost, as the consensus of the original investors was somewhat upbeat. Surely all of this would work out to our advantage, as all of our shares would be converted to an existing public trading company and in early 2002 investors learned we would join a company called **Hydramet**. More later.

Remarkably I was cooking with new marketing ideas. Earlier, I had completed a refinance loan for my neighbor and friend, Chuck Turner. (more to follow on the mind blowing conclusions with this individual as we near the end of this journal or book – I never know how to term it) It was a complicated loan with several "clear to close" conditions, all seemingly impossible to satisfy the loan under-writers demands. Somehow over what seemed forever I managed to find creative ways to rewrite the application restructuring the framework of the loan and closed and funded the loan for the original loan amount.

Chuck was a Senior Regional Vice President of his company, AIMCO, (knocking down $250,000 per year. You would wonder why refinance? Because he was one of those persons who had to buy, buy and more buy) a publicly traded company on the NYSE. In the course of our relationship I grew to learn much of his company's operations. They were a huge, and I mean huge, property management company, managing primarily apartment complexes throughout the nation, controlling over 400,000 units in well over 2000 apartment complexes.

Chuck and I spent many hours together absorbing countless cocktails with many discussions covering politics, religion, and AIMCO. Over time, my knowledge of his business grew and he developed respect for my creative mortgage sense. This combination led me to formulate a marketing plan that could be highly beneficial to John Peter.

With more discussions the plan began to take shape and eventually became known as the AIMCO/TEC HOME OWNERSHIP PROGRAM. To remind the reader, TEC was the name of my mortgage broker. The business plan was directed to apartment renters who served notice they would not be renewing their current lease for the expressed purpose to purchase a home. The potential new home owners were hand delivered an information form by the apartment manager, informing them of the Home Ownership Program advantages, discounts and the likely scenario their new home purchase payments could be within an amount equal or near equal to their current rental payments. If they expressed an interest and completed the information sheet, I would be informed and arrange a personal meeting held in the apartments on site social room. Purpose being to further advance information of the program and obtain sufficient information to pull a credit report and pre-qualify a mortgage loan. If the potential homebuyer qualified for a mortgage the pertinent information would be given to the real estate broker, my partner in the program, Carl Bergman. Sounds good right? Well it was good and it would serve a tremendous assistance to new buyers, often newly married with expectant families. The problem after making certain all completely understood the program was convincing AIMCO Corporate to sanction the program. Their concern cut across the fundamental purpose of their business. To some of the executives it discouraged their client from continuing to rent premises from AIMCO. I had to convince the non-believers that AIMCO stood to gain much from the program once incorporated. So now would be a good time to explain the program intricacies.

1. The borrower would receive a $300 New Home Appraisal refund at loan closing. This amount would be paid from my loan commissions. Additionally, a $500 - $700 loan closing cost credit administered at the closing table. This portion of the credit was to be equally shared by TEC Brokerage and me. Combined, this $800 to$1000 represented a substantial savings to the new buyer.
2. AIMCO would receive from the listing realtor (Carl Bergman) 1% referral of the collected 3% realtor commissions of the home sale amount. Legal by realtor standards as this portion of the transaction was a realtor - to - realtor action.

To advance the plans merits to the AIMCO Corporate office I convinced Chuck's offices to provide some vital information. Regional records indicated that the annual rental turnover was 33%. Of this amount, few reversed their decision to remain within the apartment complex and 55% of those leaving was for the expressed purpose of buying a home. I was able to "clinch" the Corporate Officers with an AIMCO income projection based on only 20% (in other words 2 of 10) of the 55% home buying non-renewals utilizing the AIMCO/TEC Home Ownership Program. The figures were staggering, even projecting a mere 20% participation into the program.

Using AIMCO numbers the average size complex consisted of 175 apartment units. 33% of departing-clients equals 58 in total and 55% leaving to purchase a home = 32 new home buyers. 20% breaks down to 6.4 former AIMCO clients participating in my program. Based on local real estate purchase figures the average new home sale for first time buyers was $131,000. Here is what turned the deal around:

- $131,000 x 6.4 = $838,400 x 1% = $8384 per apartment complex.
- AIMCO managed 44 properties in the Orlando, Tampa and Jacksonville area.

The above conservative projection would provide AIMCO Corporation **$386,896 of newfound profit!**

That got the high muckety mucks attention and I received their authorization to implement the program for the above referenced area on a "test basis" with monthly reports to be provided by me and confirmed by Chuck's regional people.

We spent several weeks designing brochures, renter's information forms and other supporting documentation, to control lead generation and the necessary corporate paper trail.

I began interviewing the departing renters in the Orlando area only, as the properties were the most accessible for both Carl and me. The beginning proved to be slower than expected but activity increased as we continued to work the plan and worked the program through out 2000 and well into 2001. As we continued to crank up the numbers the plan began to receive positive influence from the apartment managers and renters. With no adverse warning Chuck called a meeting where he informed me Corporate decided to end the program, until further notice, with no reason provided. We were all astounded and at a loss to figure why as the regional AIMCO staff considered it successful. Within weeks Chuck visited me with a bottle of single malt and laid the news on me. Corporate now saw the merit of the program and wanted to expand it to several national regions and mirroring the Orlando test in all the expanded areas would be too daunting and difficult for me to execute. Corporate believed that it was best accomplished "in house".

Done! Just like that! I was devastated because in my entrepreneurial mind I had begun an "expectant attitude" of generating thousands, if not millions of dollars through this AIMCO/TEC program. It has been my experience that if you let these business setbacks corner your mind you allow yourself to regress or go into a negative funk. Better to rationalize there had to be some reason, unknown at the time, that this type of thing happens and you have to trust your instincts that someone knows better so except it and move on. I did receive some satisfaction less than a year later, when Chuck reported that corporate were canceling the program entirely as it proved too difficult to manage and not worth the effort. Meaning in corporate code, "poor performance". Yea!!

When the AIMCO program kicked in I took the precaution to set an organizational schedule to also concentrate on other mortgage aspects, including a day of cold calling banks and real estate offices, introducing myself and informing these entities that I was not only capable of completing difficult mortgages but they were my specialty. In the course of these cold calls I called on a local bank, Crown Bank. (I did not know that I would eventually represent this bank)

Some 2 or 3 years earlier Fran introduced me to Jack and Shay Koegel, friends of hers for many years. Jack was the sitting president of Crown

Bank. In the banking industry it was known as a "regional" bank with 17 branches located in the Orlando area (their head offices) the Gulf side of the state and north to Jacksonville. The bank was very active within the mortgage business with particular emphasis in Construction Loans and was a favorite with new homebuilders. I had not a particular deep friendship with Jack, mostly only a casual relationship seeing each other during social events.

On one of the "cold calling days" I called on Crown Bank and was granted a meeting with Jack, the Bank President, primarily because we knew each other. He had heard that I no longer was in the music business and was now engaged in originating mortgages. I told him the reason for my call and made it clear that I was in a position to help his mortgage department with any mortgages in default or if they received applications that they were unable to process due to any number of denial reasons. He did not offer an immediate response and we parted amiably.

About a week later I received a call from Jack requesting a follow up meeting to our last discussion. I will cut to the chaste with this story and just say I was overwhelmed with what was presented. Several office boxes containing over 300 files of "default loans". Jack instructed his mortgage loan-servicing department to give me their full support assisting me in refinancing these troubled and under performing loans. Moving them to a new lender, or to be more correct, obtaining a new lender would result in Crown Bank paid off and would effectively remove the default loan from the banks portfolio or if the loan had been sold at time of funding, the negative potential of the Bank having to buy back the loan. I was literally given what could constitute a year or more of new loan applications. I notified all the sub prime wholesale lenders I knew and arranged for the selected lenders to revue the files and determine which of these had any merit of refinancing based on file information.

Well, again actual results did not equate to the anticipated potential, but I did manage to close a dozen or so loans over the next 4 to 6 months. No hysterical results! But, I did cause a major level of respect with Crown Banks Mortgage Department and with Jack as well. It would serve me well 2 years later when I would join the banks mortgage division and become one of their top 3 producers.

I now had a little more than a year of experience in the mortgage business and obligated to attend the annual state mandatory 3day school in continuing education along with the 3hour written exam.

On the lighter side I accompanied Fran on a "freebie" trip to Los Angeles paying only for my airfare. Speaking of "freebies" nothing compared to the 10day trip to Italy. I qualified for the trip selling digital pianos manufactured by the Italian Company, Viscount Pianos. The airfare, hotel accommodation, tours, meals and wine all paid and included Fran. How exceptional! We both enjoyed a very close relationship with the US Manager, Gary Gerriourd. He was instrumental in conducting the previously referred Music Technology Workshops we conducted in Orange and Seminole County Public Schools, resulting in enhancing the Viscount Piano product line and FSCM image, gaining needed public relations and lead potential.

We toured several cities located in the middle of the country and along the Adriatic Sea including San Marino, an independent country within Italy, located high up a mountain and a serious tourist attraction due to it's non tax status. The food and wine were outstanding and a word about their wine. Unlike wine in North America, theirs contain no sulfates, an ingredient added to preserve shelf life. I suppose the deduction from that is Italians do not require extended shelf life. The difference in the wine is remarkable. No matter the amount consumed there are no after effects, meaning hangovers and general issues of over consumption. Fran had been to Italy several times but this was my first, we did not know at the time but we would return in a couple of years under the auspiciousness of Fran who assisted the Italian Piano Company marketing digital pianos to her school district.

In October only a week or so upon my return from Italy, My Semper Fi (Semper FI –De –Lis, the motto of the US Marine Corp) friend and partner in the AIMCO program married Michelle and asked if I would be his best man in a small, quiet wedding ceremony and celebration. I was only too proud to do so.

Not more than a month later Chuck Turner decided to marry Amy and he too asked that I be his best man in an exorbitant and costly wedding celebration. I will write more on this marriage later. But now is a good time to mention a little side bar story during the post dinner speeches. I pull the old "apartment key" prank. Prior to the wedding I gathered as many old door lock keys possible and brought them with me to the wedding reception. When it was my turn to speak a few words I announced, "Chuck has requested that I inform all former girl friends to please return all door lock keys." Right on queue 10 or 12 really hot looking ladies, that I previously approached with the gag, began marching up to the head table some faked crying and lamenting did they really have to surrender keys to Chuck's home. The wedding guests roared and applauded like what seemed forever. As a photo shop glance at Amy's intellectual properties, while at the head table she pulled Chuck aside and wanted to know the meaning of this. Additional Amy stories to follow and Fran and I close the millennium year with another New Years trip to Michigan.

My mortgage production was humming along quite well but in May I suffer 7 loans lost due to what the industry refers to "Closing Table Blowups". About $10,000 in lost commissions for May and June. "Blow Ups" at time of loan closing can be anything from insufficient closing funds, to an assortment of issues with borrowers faulty documentation that they suddenly know nothing about or choosing to not provide, hoping to finalize the loan without having to explain negative information. Every one in the loan closing process, lawyers, title companies, closing agents and mortgage personnel are all involved when this happens and is particularly disappointing when it occurs at the closing table.

In March of 2001 Fran and I spent a long weekend at Pauline's ocean side condo in Pompano Beach and in June, following the death of Fran's mother, Minnie Strictland, we spent 5 days in Key West – just to get away.

Suffering form pancreatic cancer first diagnosed in March of that year she passed away on May 29 at 4:20 am. Fran moved her into our home in early April, took a leave of absence from work, attending to Minnie in her final days. She died with both Fran and I present and we both observed her last breath. The experience of death is quite extraordinary, humbling and one not ever forgotten.

Living most of her life in the local area, as a social butterfly and her entertaining nature afforded Minnie a huge funeral. The memorial service and cemetery eulogies continued for a near hour. A few days after the funeral, I wrote a eulogy, hoping it would serve as a marker on my relationship with Minnie. Fran as it filed in one of her mementos.

Minnie Strickland was an extraordinary Southern Women, raised, educated in Georgia, having lived 96 years with many experiences. One of my fondest memories of her is holding court at our dining room table recounting one of her thousand stories. Possessing a remarkable command of the English language, which only enhanced recounting past life passages. In addition to the former she had an unbelievable memory, recounting minute details and coupled with her delivery manner left anyone attending this dinner entertainment - spellbound. We all marveled when she would be forced into a temporary pause caused by some attendees temporarily leaving the table would, upon their return, pick up on the story right where she left off without repeating a single word.

She had doubts early on during Fran's and my relationship, fearing I would take Fran "away" and did not really trust my intentions. Early, she was rumored to think of me as "the wolf in sheep's clothing" syndrome. We grew to have a special relationship with her referencing me as her "angel sent from heaven". I loved her and liked her and miss her friendship.

In early September Meade, Fran and I fly to Toronto. Meade and Fran's interest was to attend the Toronto Film Festival. Mine was to attend an arranged meeting attempting to bring closure or at least some common ground to a two-year family feud. I won't spell out the details as that would appear as choosing sides and could become, at this time, counterproductive. I will say while it was not successful to the then hopeful expectations it did lay the groundwork for common ground that transformed over the ensuing years and today there exists partial harmony but complete family harmony remains an objective still to be gained. It is a sad commentary and difficult for a Dad to completely understand and accept, particularly when all I ever knew was total joy, fun and love in my own family. I continue to pray that someday common sense will prevail.

Our return flight home was scheduled for Monday, September 10th. We deliberated a little to stay for another day, but in the end chose to keep to the original schedule. Not, would have resulted in the almost certainty of being grounded for many days due to the senseless and horrendous 9/11 attack on the United States. December 7th 1942 was referred to as "a day of infamy" by then US President Roosevelt and it too was terribly horrific and devastating. But this seemed more dramatic perhaps because we were all able to watch in "real time". For sure history will remember 9/11 with equal contempt and the saddest of memories for both tyrannical events.

I was at my desk at the mortgage office when the attack took place and someone who heard of it on the radio on their way into work, turned on the television and of course everyone became glued to it, fixated on the horror that was unfolding before our very eyes. With the distraction and unbelievable event, absolutely no work was at hand here and everywhere. The office closed and remained closed the following day, as did almost all offices pertaining to banks and mortgage supporting offices. I went home and soon was joined by Fran as her office closed as well. I couldn't believe watching some of the people in the Mid East dancing in the streets celebrating this dreadful, sneaky, deceitful act, murdering innocent people who had nothing to do with the politics and policies of the US Government. Shameful.

Earlier in the year I made contact with another log manufacturing company near St. Augustine, FL and arranged for a meeting with the principals. In early October I asked for a Friday meeting with senior management and used that schedule for a long weekend in Savanna GA, as we both wanted and needed a "get away". What a charming old city flooded with history going back to the early 1700's. By the way, the Log Home (Suwannee Log Homes) meeting was successful and I did complete loans for their customers

I became more and more disenchanted with TEC Mortgage, slowly coming to the conclusion it was time for me to move on from the "mom & pop' mentality of this small brokerage. I was not in the least disappointed with the decision to begin my mortgage career with this small brokerage as at the time it was the right fit for me, but now a change seemed necessary. The office still completed loan applications by hand and anyone in the business could see the industry quickly moving to computer generated paper work. I had long asked the brokerage to apply for legal licensing permitting FHA loans, a popular Government Loan Program that offered certain qualified borrowers 97% loans for a home purchases. Meaning the borrower only required 3% of their money to purchase a home. I was told repeatedly it was only a matter of weeks before the license would be available. I learned, by accident, the broker would never be granted this license because of years of legal IRS proceedings against the owner, both personal and his business. That became the turning point and I determined in November to leave and signed on with Alliance Mortgage Banking Corp, who had a large office in Daytona Beach. Alliance was a branch office of a Correspondent Lender in NYC. The major difference between a direct lender and a Mortgage Broker is the direct lender closes the loan in their own name. The result is the lender has more control in closing the loan and often fewer closing conditions making the entire "loan process" smoother. It was an easy change as the owner's son use to call on me as a "wholesale" rep while I was with TEC.

I made certain before signing on that Alliance, as a Correspondent Lender, was able and allowed to do Log Home Construction loans, as this was and would continue to be a major part of my business. It is worthy to note not all lenders were able or even wanted to do log home construction loans. Another requested condition was allowing me to work from my home. In the course of negotiations, I was given the title of area manager. Which allowed me to hire loan officers that functioned under my direction. I purchased a computer, converting the 3rd bedroom to a functioning office. I had absolutely no prior experience with a desktop computer so believe me that became a large challenge. I had to learn, as the Daytona Office was fully computerized. With some help from my old buddy, Carl Bergman and Fran, who had slightly more experience, I slowly became sufficiently acquainted with the procedures and operations to complete loan applications and the ensuing supporting paperwork and mortgage forms. I learned to enjoy the process and it made many industry procedures much easier and efficient. As we closed 2001, I hired two loan officers to work under my supervision, receiving 20% of their commissions. The situation looked promising.

2002 proved to be quite eventful. As stated earlier I joined Alliance Bank (it was not a servicing bank but a mortgage lending bank only) in

November but the real beginning date was not until January. My career with Alliance would be short lived as I would resign in June, a mere 6 months later, made necessary due to the lack of operational support brought on by extreme difficulties the Daytona Branch experienced with it's parent NYC company. I never learned the specifics but clearly the relationship between NYC, the lending money source, became strained to the point that normal everyday operations became near impossible or at the very least difficult. Towards the end of my employment the strain and stress on the owners was ever present. However I did manage to close my first 2 loans in January and did ok up to about May when my branch working relationship failed to exist in any normal way. Following a heated meeting with my immediate supervisor I tabled my resignation and left with 5 loan files under my arms with the obligation to find a new loan source for customers who had entrusted me to be their loan source. Worse, the timing could not have been more untimely as it was just weeks before closing on our new home. For about a year Fran and I had been toying with the notion of expanding our starter home and adding a pool. After numerous contractor proposals we determined we would never realize a return of the constructions costs if we were to sell 471 Arrowmount. So with that realization we set out to purchase another home. We loved the Timacuan area and decided we would buy only in that community. We went through the usual process of looking and providing purchase offers for at least 4 or 5 months and by the way, our realtor was my old friend Carl Bergman. Finally in May we get the proverbial break and find our "dream home" and our offer is accepted at well under market conditions. At the time of the offer I could not have imagined I would be unemployed by the agreed closing date. To assist with netting the most net funds possible I chose to sell Arrowmount myself relieving us of any realtor fees and Carl advised he would not charge us any realtor fees for the new purchase. A win – win!

In the course of my "come to Jesus" meeting with Alliance I had them agree they would not report our terminated relationship and would continue the loan process through to loan closing as our loan application was already "approved". During the period of our 471 Arrowmount home ownership both Fran and I dramatically improved our credit scores and had necessary assets to successfully qualify for a new loan. But of course I needed to be employed and remain in the mortgage industry where I had been gainfully employed for the past 3 years. Well the short story is Alliance kept their word, and I managed to sell our home for our asking price and the new buyer was "pre approved" for a mortgage loan. We were good to go and we close on both properties on July 12, complete with the actual move-in.

448 Flora Creek Court was definitely an upgrade for both Fran and I. A

4 bedroom, 3 bath, L shaped floor plan, on a closed end street, complete with a large pool and patio. We loved the home from the very beginning. Because of the excellent purchase price and the escalating real estate market, it more than doubles in value until the real estate melt down in 2008, but again because of the purchase price, it continued to remain in a high equity position. Best of all due to lower interest rates the new 2002 mortgage resulted in lower mortgage payments than our former loan. In between phone calls to potential employers I was free to organize the unpacking and help arrange "living" conditions and remarkably Fran and I had 99% of everything completed within a week of move in.

I recall I interviewed with 3 major banks/lenders and in-sufficiently impressed to enter into a second or follow up interview – for a variety of reasons – like the distance in driving to what would be my working office or the compensation plan etc. While mulling the 3 past interviews over in my mind it suddenly hit me. Call Jack Koegel and I did – immediately. Jack explained that since our last conversation Crown Bank had been sold to a Puerto Rican Financial Institution and Crown's Mortgage Division had been taken over by a NYC lender, Continental Capital Corporation. He provided me with name and phone numbers of the operational manager, Tammy Powers, who I called and arranged a next day interview.

The interview went very well. I instantly bonded with Ms. Powers, appreciated the synergy of the bank/branch and she too indicated that their would be "no problem" finding Construction Loan money to close my 5 C/P loan files – providing the borrowers met the lending criteria of our New York Lender. She provided me with the compensation plan that was a little better than most. Specifically, a monthly draw of $2400 against a better than usual commission structure, equal bank contributions to a 401K, car allowance, excellent loan products and "in house" loan underwriting. Believe me "a biggie". When a loan officer is able to speak directly with loan underwriters, it is a different world when it comes to successfully funding and closing loans.

Two days later Tammy calls and wants me to join her "elite team" as she puts it and I agree to come on board. I began my employment on July 22 joining 2 other loan officers. I did not realize it at the time but this new venture would eventually represent my "swan song" in my near 50 year working career and absolutely enjoyed every hour through to the final one, when I would retire from full time employment (age 67) to semi retirement.

During my interview with CCC I fully apprised Tammy Powers of Fran's and my plans to enjoy another Italian Spaghetti Tour, compliments again of Viscount Pianos. The bank had no objections to the two weeks I would be away and gave their full permission.

In October Fran and I fly to Newark NJ for an overnight flight to Milan and then ground transportation to Ricconi, located on the Adriatic Sea. We spent 9 days touring cities and areas that we had not seen during the previous Italian trip. Rome, Naples, Pompeii, Bologna are some of the cities/areas visited. You maybe asking yourselves how would we qualify for another Viscount Piano sponsored trip when I was no longer engaged in the music business. Fran continued as the Arts and Music Supervisor for Seminole County Schools and assisted Gary Girrourd with many digital piano sales to several High Schools within the district. So this time I was the "carry on recipient". It was a grand vacation and of course other than personal purchases the trip cost us zero. We were and remain very grateful for such wondrous generosities. We would make one more visit to Italy in 1997 as part of our 10th anniversary Mediterranean Cruise.

Kelly and Patti are our first new home guests, followed by Margie and Pauline and all seemed thrilled with our new home.

From my initial week through to the end of August I attended endless loan product seminars and computer training to correctly navigate through the many software programs. I had definitely advanced my knowledge of "computer navigation" during my 6month employment with Alliance, but CCC operating software and loan products were more comprehensive to facilitate the loan application through to loan closing. A big challenge for my very lean computer knowledge/experience and my daily mantra was "learn John learn".

I close my first loan in September. Soon I would be closing 8 to 10 loans per month – a number I had never previously achieved – and would elevate to the title of "Mortgage Banker – Sr. Loan officer". Lost in the increase sales volume is the failure to close the 5 loan files I had carried to the initial interview with CCC and the promise that subject to approval loan criteria the bank would close and fund. Well there was nothing negative with any of their credit, loan history, employment or income. The bank (CCC) was not able to sell any of the loans to any of their established investors. My hands where tied and there were no other options. I even tried to "off" the files to outside and competitive entities without success. After almost 5 months of continuous delays I was obligated to notify the borrowers I could not assist with their financing. None were able to understand and I truly was to blame and frankly, who could argue with that rational.

This is as good a time as any to introduce my final attempt at getting rich with personal stock investments. Does anyone want to thank God? Hopefully the reader will recall the **UNIQRIPT** deal that was eventually de-listed from trading and the lead organizers commitment to transfer all of the investors stock to a currently trading stock. Well, the time finally came and the investors involved with the above stock were notified that a public trading company had been selected. The new company, **HYDROMET** operated plants in Newman Illinois and Baha CA. The plant in Newman was the focus of the new investors and where specifically attracted to it's function as a **hazardous waste plant.** Even a minor informed reader would recognize that in this day of an environment sensitive society this surely would have enormous potential. As the past statement suggests HYDROMETS business was to process hazardous waste material and sell the derived compounds.

The Newman plant, built at an original cost of $46 million was a state of the art plant designed by a Canadian, Dr. Robert Morgan, who had previously been involved in a similar Hamilton Ontario operation but not of hazardous nuclear variety. The new investors, with previous UNIQRIPT investors, agreed to the new proposal. The discounted purchase price of $6Million included the plant building. Investors were divided into "tiers" and my tier and investment (carried over from UNIQRIPT) would result in 1 million shares with an initial early scheduled payout of $200,000 and a payment stream formula to follow. I no longer recall the formula nor do I have any reference notes. But recall the "cash payout" plus the "payment stream" would at least triple the original $150,000 that Frank Zolnai and I had originally agreed to 3years prior.

The history that follows over the next 3years is extremely complex, convoluted and difficult for any reader to follow and understand. The investors all lost their investment, some approaching a million dollars. It is difficult for me to succinctly condense all the problems but the primary factor and most costly was an over regulated EPA. Time after time they would site a required procedure only to site another procedure replacing that procedure. Each time a specific test was cited the required lab work represented a direct cost to the investors measured in thousands of dollars. And there were many, many of these tests from dirty water to floor contamination to situations I no longer recall and of course the above prevented the plant from processing the contaminated waste and selling the derived components – the cash flow to sustain the company – not to mention eliminating very dangerous hazardous wastes. Regretfully, that ended my personal Public Investments as an "entrepreneur" and the zero financial gain in the Ontario Conservatory Investment back in 1991. I dwelled and dwelled on this for a long time knowing nothing I could now do would change history and "dwelling" only resulted in negative, unproductive time. So like previous occasions I concentrated on the present and tried to make the most of any opportunity.

As 2003 arrived I was totally familiar and comfortable with the various operating software programs and loan products where I did not have to consult loan documentation guidelines allowing me to be more effective while speaking to potential clients. This and the mortgage industry itself was "booming" with excellent loan rates and as mentioned previously, the fact that the bank had it's own "underwriting department" where I could walk to their office and quickly resolve any loan resistant issues.

All of the above permitted my first ever $1,000,000+ month in funded loans. This type of volume would continue through the year. I believe I missed that amount only once and achieved a couple of months approaching $2 million. I was humming and really enjoyed the business.

In January I finally sold the Lincoln Town Car and purchase an "off lease" 2001 Lexus SUV. You cannot imagine how I hated the Town Car and I will remind the reader Fran would casually refer to it as "the pimp mobile" so you can readily appreciate the un-love we shared for the car – and it was one of those cars that would just not give up. I swore the engine was bullet proof.

I enjoyed a pleasant surprise when Jim Pollard invited me to a game of golf while he was vacationing in the Orlando area. I say surprise because it had been 10 years since we had last seen each other.

Our new home was well occupied with Kevin, Connie, the grandchildren who spent another Easter Holiday with us and are joined by Kelly and Patti. This makes for a busy time particularly for both Fran and I, employed with a busy work schedule. But we seem to be able to cope with both and enjoy the fun of "family time".

Unbelievable the IRS re surfaced and rekindled their war with me regarding FSCM. Add to that scenario their Canadian Cousins, Revenue Canada, informed me I owe $4737 (Cassis also is informed) from the sale of the St. Thomas property 7 years prior. Property that Philip and I purchased going back to the days of N*u*-Media. Both our former US and Canadian CPA's vehemently argued there was no supporting evidence in the Tax Filing to substantiate Revenue Canada's agent claim and even informed the agent that this charge was "bogus". Still she holds to her position of pay the fine or ask the courts to rule a legal decision. We know from past experience the legal costs will most likely exceed the $4700 (of course the agent is well aware of this) and we take the lower road and pay what we now all refer to as the Ottawa Thieves.

The bank increases the loan officer staff to 7 and advances the idea that all L/O's must spend time at bank branches. I am allocated the Winter Park and Clermont branches – a brand new branch.

2004 personal notes:

Fran and I spent Thanksgiving with the Workman's in Jamaica. It was a glorious and joyful time and we got to spend a weekend at an "all inclusive" resort called "Sandals." in Montego Bay. Guests of Kevin and Connie no less! Kelly spent Christmas with us – always enjoyable. She is such a class act and Ken Cassis surprised us with an unannounced visit.

We spent a 4day weekend in Denver visiting Chuck and Amy Turner, enjoying a day in the mountains and interesting parts of a great city. I really enjoyed it and it was early April so weather was ideal.

The biggie was the Stanley Cup visited our home in early June. Tampa Bay and Calgary played the 6th play-off game in Calgary where almost everyone expected Calgary to close out the playoffs. Tampa won the game in overtime forcing the final game in Tampa. Florida, very much a Southern state, was abuzz with the game of hockey.

Unknown to me, Fran and Kelly conspired to surprise me for Fathers Day but with a major twist. I was told that Kelly was flying in for a Fathers Day Sunday visit and then would rent a car the following day for the final game in Tampa. It is always nice to visit with Kelly and I am pleased she will be with us for Fathers Day. She arrives with the normal "how do you do's" but I begin to get suspicious when I notice Fran has purchased a ton of food for the proposed BBQ steak dinner – and Kelly a non red meat eater. Plus suddenly Gordon, Meade, Caitlin and Parker are on the scene. I ask a few questions all with unsatisfactory answers. It is mid afternoon and most of us are sitting around the pool enjoying the beautiful day having a few pops when the back gate to the pool area un-expectantly opens and this strange man, wearing a black suit with white gloves and is helped by another similarly dressed person and carrying this shinny looking thing. After a few seconds it registers on me "it's the f------ **Stanley Cup!!** I just cannot believe it. How could this happen? Everyone is screaming and yelling and taking pictures and I slowly begin to follow the explanations of how this event came to be.

The plan began to take shape over several phone calls and it wasn't until the completion of the 6th game and knowledge a 7th Tampa game would be necessary that the dots could be put together in a structured sequence. Kelly convinced the curator of the cup - Phil Pritchard – that he along with Craig Campbell, would fly out of Calgary at midnight arriving in Tampa early on Sunday and then rent a van to drive to Lake Mary, presenting Lord Stanley's Cup to me for a Fathers Day surprise and return to Tampa so the Cup could be presented the following night. Can you believe this? It is over the top!

Well, we begin to party, cooking steaks and drinking plenty of cocktails and wine. I invite some people over to see the cup including Lyman Carter, a Florida resident Canadian who played semi professional hockey in Sacramento CA and a star center for Boston University. He sat in our living room for an hour cradling the cup and was in near tears in disbelief. To this day he speaks of it every time we see each other. It was quite a Fathers Day. By the way Tampa Bay won the Cup.

Sometime in late February I had a dream about Ken Cassis. Unusual because while I like Ken and consider him a close friend, having dreams about him is not the norm. I make a mental note to call him but before I get around to it he calls me. There is a truth that exists within me "if prayer is you speaking to God than your instincts is God speaking to you". The first thing out of his mouth after the usual salutations is "do you do Non Recourse Mortgages?" He went on to explain the requirement for this type of mortgage, how it would apply to his clients and if available how it would generate a tremendous amount of business for both my bank and his company. He and his partner, Mike Evers formed a company, **The Canadian Estate Planners**, whose sole market were Canadians owning 2nd homes or vacation homes in the USA and the introduction of a new program called **The Estate Tax Reduction Plan.**

While **NRC Mortgages** are common in Commercial Financing they are basically unavailable for residential properties or stated another way, retail mortgages. So now is good time to explain how, in point form, how the dots came together with this unusual financing project.

NON-RECOURSE MORTGAES: Is a specific type of financing that designates the subject property the only security available to the lender. To be clear: In the event a **Conforming Loan** defaults a lender is allowed to attach "other forms of assets" like other properties, stocks, bonds and cash to satisfy a loan balance deficiency. With an NRCM the subject property is the only asset available as security to the lender and will be unable to seek relief from other available assets. For these reasons the NRCM could never be sold in the secondary market and should a lender decide to fund this loan type there would be no other alternative other than carrying it as a "port folio" loan for the duration of the loan term. Banks/Lenders do not like to commit to any loan product resulting in a loan that is categorized as a "portfolio loan" and remains on their books for extended period.

Why this loan product: Canadians who own 2nd homes in the USA are subject to an enormous US Tax burden in the event of the principals death while owning the US property. A whopping 35% to 55% of the market value (by way of an independent appraisal) is due the US Government within a year of death of the principal owner. Ken's clients who qualified for his services were all very wealthy and many owned homes in the USA, specifically Florida. Vacation homes value ranged from $550,000 to $2,000,000. Simple math: $1,000,000 x 40% = $400,000 payable to the **IRS.**

However: If the Canadian owner could obtain a **NRCM** the entire loan amount could be deducted from the market value. An example: a 70% loan on a $1,000,000 property value would result in a mortgage value of $700,000 which by tax law was permitted to be deducted from the market value resulting in only $300,000 subject to the 40% estate tax. Now, the IRS could only claim $120,000. **$280,000** - quite a substantial savings.

While seeming to be an easy sell for Ken and Mike it proved to be a little tougher as all clients enjoyed mortgage free properties. Their mind set, culture and wealth where not tuned into property financing – particularly a US mortgage loan. But as this genius plan unfolds there would be more sizzle and benefits to sell.

<u>The Burden For Me:</u> Clearly, if I were to participate in this new game, I would have to find a Lender/Bank willing to carry the loan as a "portfolio loan. There was little point in chasing the norm in residential financing as no one investor would ever buy this loan from any lender, no matter the guarantee provided. I will cut to the chase limiting much mundane and boring reading. I engaged the Banks Mortgage Manager to introduce me to his son's real estate law firm resulting in several meetings, which in turn resulted in contacting a Boca Raton Fl attorney, Steve Garellek, who miraculously closed a NRCM a few years prior. He graciously provided my new lawyer friends a copy of the mortgage document spelling the necessary verbiage for any bank considering doing such a loan. I got away without paying legal fees assuring them they would do all the loan closings for this new loan program.

Next on the agenda was to engage my bank to do this unheard of loan program. Initially, that's how my superiors referred the NRCM program to. After many meetings I prevailed and we eventually arrived to the following agreement:

- Trial of 5 loans only before permission for any additional loans
- 70% loan to value only (meaning a 70% loan of the appraised property value.
- 5year term only and the conceded "interest only payments" (it was in the programs own interest to not lower the mortgage value)
- Borrower to open an account with the bank and deposit 6 months

payments and maintain the deposited amount

- Interest payments to be a minimum of 3% above banks regular loan rates.

POST LOAN CLOSING PROCEEDURE: Following the imposed "3day right of rescission" net loan funds were wired to the borrower(s) who in keeping with the plan would deposit the entire funds into an established Canadian **Segregated Fund**. Here is the deal sweetener referred to earlier. The mortgage was a US mortgage and as such the net loan funds was in US currency. At the time US currency was 125% greater in value than the Canadian dollar. Net proceeds of $650,000 US became $812,500 Canadian. The "coup de grace?" The Segregated Fund paid all mortgage payments and provided a year-end residual! How creative and a tribute to the Canadian Estate Planners **Estate Tax Reduction Plan.**

Our first loan followed a summer of putting the pieces together and proceeded through to mid 2005 when I made a "faulty decision" regarding my continuance with Crown bank. Details of how this came to be follow.

We close out the year with Fran and I attending, along with the Detroit troupe, the 2004 Player Induction to the Hockey Hall Of Fame. Kelly is the chief organizer of this major hockey event absorbing almost all her time from September through to the event, usually held in late November. She does a bang up job and is held in sterling esteem by the hockey player inductees and Hall Management. Upper Management recognized her qualities and promoted her to a **Director Position** and to this day remains the only person sitting on the Hall Directors Board not possessing large amounts of Testosterone found in abundance with remaining members.

While I am enjoying huge production months, my best ever, there is a growing unrest within the mortgage department, particularly with the loan originators. All are central to the ever-increasing influx of Puerto Rican personnel from the Puerto Rican parent company, **RG FINANCIAL**. The bank, prior to 2002 was called Crown Bank, but was now called **RG CROWN BANK,** reflecting the parent company's name. The concern of the mortgage personnel was the marked difference the new comers from Puerto Rico demonstrated through their culture and management style. Some barely spoke English. Communication in some instances was near impossible. The above coupled with "noise" from the Federal Regulators became worrisome to some of us in the sales department.

In mid April the 3 top producers, including me, interview as a group, with a leading Winter Park Bank. We are unimpressed with the "Bible Pumping" general manager and decline their employment offer. The unrest continuing I had a meeting with Charlie Dowd, the leading honcho with Royal Bank (the same Royal Bank of Canada) only in this instance their US subsidiary. He is fully aware of my involvement with the Canadian Estate Planners, Estate Tax Reduction Program and is committed to implementing it with his bank. The plan is not yet on board with RBC but Charlie is absolute to putting the pieces together and certainly when successful will be a major opposing funding entity to my resources. Mostly, because any Canadian will trust RBC much more so than an American Bank. Because this program as such potential and is so profitable I considered leaving RG Crown joining RBC once their required loan products were available and their Board of Directors approved the program. Dowd indicated he expected the plan to be approved by June. However, it was further delayed, their Board citing more unresolved legal issues.

Meanwhile my entire mortgage division is in a negative funk with growing dissatisfaction with upper management and the parent Puerto Rican Company. It just seemed their manner of management was "don't do anything until a crisis occurs" and seemingly demonstrated they were inoculated against any Federal Audit concerns. The issues were abundantly clear to all management with specific instructions to resolve the audit issues within a specified period.

In June my immediate supervisor served notice that a giant in the mortgage industry, Wells Fargo, made contact with him advising they were interested in making a "package" offer to the top 4 producers, including our supervisor. In the mortgage industry this is referred to as a "Corporate Raid". Several meetings followed with both Wells Fargo and the selected group of 5. When the "packaged" is tabled all involved agree to jump ship.

Before continuing with this part of the narrative I want to explain my supervisor and I had separate meetings with Wells Fargo upper management concerning the Estate Tax Reduction Program and the required NRM loan program and additionally, a growing **Condo/Tel** Development I had been working. I will elaborate more on this project. To a person, Wells Fargo indicated there would be no problem funding these potential loan programs either through "Wells" proper or, through one of their many "associated network lenders". I personally contacted the provided associated lender names and further explained the programs, types of required product and received written advisement their intended involvement with both programs.

The attraction to go with Wells Fargo were two fold:

First. The company name in the mortgage industry was huge, primarily through their loan products and general trust within the industry. Attracting more home builders and real estate agents to Wells Fargo versus RG Crown Bank was a given.

Two. The "package" was generous. Signing bonus of $7500 for each of the 4 sales originators and a salary through to the end of 2005. The salary was based on a "tier" basis relative to previous sales performance. My tier provided a salary of $2750 per month plus regular loan commissions. Taken with the intended usual monthly production, after a month of "Wells Orientation", commissions were expected to be at least what they were with Crown - $8000 to $12,000 per month. It was a general consideration amongst most of us, that in addition to the signing-bonus we would easily pull an income (salary/commissions) equal to $50,000 to $60,000 by years end. The agreed commencement date was August 1 and we were instructed to not advise RG Crown Bank of our resignation until the Friday afternoon prior to the August 1st start date. Agreed, not morally right but done all the time in the banking and corporate world. The resignations were tabled, while not unintentional, the same day that middle and upper management were all in Puerto Rico for management and family visits and did not learn of the 5 resignations until there arrival back in Orlando – well into weekend. Understandably they were furious and let it known to all that the deceitful ex-employees would never again work with RG Crown Bank. We all felt bad about the manner of departure but were certain this mortgage division would soon face serious consequences and as this narrative unfolds our assumptions proved correct.

Before writing about the actual August 1 start date a few notations leading up to it.

Received in early July were 3 large NRM loan applications on behalf of the Estate Tax Reduction Program and were in various form of loan processing but not near funding finalization and the loans would not close until <u>after</u> our group departure. To insure their successful completion while I began with Wells Fargo, I initiated a plan with an existing senior loan officer, who was not invited to participate with the Wells plan. The agreed plan was simple. He was to follow the applications loan underwriting procedure working to resolve any underwriting issues, assist with any additional required borrower documentation, consult with me for any further direction involving the loan process and we would split the commissions, 50/50 on the 3 specific loans. Further loan applications for that program I would do through Wells Fargo.

I previously mentioned the **Condo/Tel** project. For those not familiar with the name or its function, a Condo/Tel is a converted hotel to several

Condo units and purchased by individuals wanting a small inexpensive permanent vacation condo that are completely furnished including a functioning kitchen. When not in use by the owners the units could be rented with available hotel service amenities if desired. At the time Condo/Tel's were considered a prime investment. The concept had huge, giant profit potential for real estate developers, investors and lending institutions. I had begun work on it beginning in 2004 and it was progressing into a personal giant project. As it began to take shape I learned that it was a massive 750unit development near Disney. I became acquainted with the project through several meetings with their real estate attorney, Rick Larsen, a friend of Gordon Owen (Fran's son in law for those with a forgetful mind) To cement my bargaining position against other financing competitors during the course of these 2004/2005 meetings. I struck on the idea of forming another Joint Venture Agreement involving Gordon and Rick Larsen. In October I arrange a lunch meeting with Gordon, who represented Larsen and himself and my immediate Wells Fargo manager and his boss to discuss the proposed JVA. There were no stated objections from either side and we departed with a basic agreement to proceed with the proposed JVA, subject of course to the development finalization permitting unit sales/marketing.

For me, and any potential mortgage lender, the financial potential was mind-boggling. Here is simple math based on discussions I had with Larsen and the project developer:

- If only 50% of future buyers required purchase financing = 750 x 50% = 375 loans
- Average unit purchase price was $182,000 (see property appraisal) @ 60% loan value = $109,200 per unit loan
- $109,200 x 375 loans = $40,950,000
- $40,000,000 in loans and calculated at a conservative 4% loan yield = $1,600,000. Based on a 50/50 split between the Lender and the Loan Originating Team the profit potential was enormous for both parties.

Early in November I was advised of the sites name, **Seralago**, and the Developer and his team were scheduled to begin unit sales in January (2006) and the good news! I will be the lead source of any required unit financing. I am the man! Believe me, the Wells Fargo Branch Management were tripping over themselves and I temporarily, was like the Saddam

Hussein of the branch. Temporarily, because my friends, it would soon end.

Personal Notes:

With the knowledge of my new employment date and the planned family reunion celebration that brother Doug and Marilyn arranged for early July, Fran and I fly to Michigan and then drive to Tillsonburg and further to Grand Bend Ontario for an extended weekend. Already in Ontario, we included a week's vacation in Montreal. I was previously acquainted with the Montreal Jazz festival and always wanted to visit it – that along with the belief that Fran would enjoy this old French City. Kelly had pre-arranged for VIP train tickets, which were fabulous and so enjoyable.

After returning home and realizing it would be some time before another vacation time we strike on the idea of traveling to New Orleans with a 3day stop in Biloxi MS staying at the fabulous Beau Rivage hotel. So we added another week to our vacation time. It does sound excessive but I knew vacation time would be in short supply for the coming year.

While writing personal entries this is good time to write about Julie's decision to locate to Iraq accepting an employment position. In mid October she had called to inform me of her consideration to work as a private contractor for Haliburton, utilizing her training and education in water management. The family was deadly against the idea fearing the natural fears of living in a war zone. After learning more of the details as to where she would be posted and the security employed matched against the tremendous financial package I advised "I would do it" and went on to say that this would be a "life altering" event. In December she celebrated Christmas with us (Kelly and Patti included) and left shortly before New Years, for her Haliburton training and orientation in Houston. She was in Iraq less than a month later and returned home a year and half later. During this period she met Harry Cheek, who too was a Haliburton contractor. I met Harry through a surprise visit they both played on us showing up unannounced during Thanksgiving weekend in 2006, with Harry asking permission to marry my daughter. I was tremendously impressed with Harry and his attention to an old custom requesting permission to marry my daughter- it spoke volumes to his character. To this day Harry and I remain very close. They were married at our pool patio during a beautiful October day – 2007. Additionally not only did Harry gain a marriage partnership but also became a parent 6weeks later with the birth of Genevieve Josephine Cheek. For some reason when I first learned of her interests in Iraq I was immediately struck with the notion that this would be a life-altering event. Pretty good instincts I guess. They eventually returned to the USA first living in Louisiana and later relocating in Hot Springs AK where they remain today. Julie got her Green Card and both are currently employed with Harry involved in supervising the Electrical/Air Condition Departments on Oil Rigs located in the Gulf of Mexico.

I am getting ahead on the subject but not until early 2006 did it become evident to all former RG Crown Bank employees who became part of Wells Fargo that the transformation move would become an abject failure for everyone – including Wells Fargo. The first negative sign, while noted at the time, virtually past with only moderate concern. Part of the decision process of our group was the location of this new mortgage team's office. Early discussion was to join an existing office and mortgage team. That changed to a new main floor office in Winter Park. I, and other team members visited the proposed new office location and were delighted with the selection and aided our decision process, pleased that this would be our very own branch office.

Our training and orientation began, as scheduled August 1st, in an off site training facility near my home in Lake Mary. The initial daily training at the selected off site venue would continue for all of August. One day, during this period we learned the Winter Park office lease fell through and a different site would be necessary. In the rush to find an office, WF Management found an obscure 3rd floor office in a new area called Baldwin Park. While new and attractive it was not close to the potential of the Winter Park location. It was obscure, difficult to find, with little hope of any walk in traffic and void of any street visibility, not even a Wells Fargo Sign. The replacement office move took place on Labor Day weekend.

No one on the new mortgage team could believe our new employers training regimen. All of August, September and part of October was primarily daily training. We were virtually removed from any "loan acquisition" efforts due to unavailable work time and not until mid October did management permit any submissions of new applications. In addition to local daily training, mandatory attendance was required for two separate weeks in Atlanta and another week in early December.

I closed my first loan with W/F in early November and I would close a total of 2 loans during my entire tenure. Get ready for this shocker. The entire team of 5 closed a total of 9 loans from its inception through to my departure – March 2006. One would ask how was this possible at a time of rigorous demand for mortgage financing. The Banks insistence for continuous training negated the necessary time, or at least made it difficult to schedule time to market and conduct sales calls to realtors, developers and connect with past clients. Two: The office location resulted in zero walk-in traffic or any loan inquires. Three: The most serious of the 3 cited reasons was the inability of the entire team to have any direct counsel with Loan Underwriters. At the time there existed a battery of them, I estimate upwards to 20, all located in the "Underwriting Center" and the only source for underwriting loans for all of Central Florida. A personal appointment with the underwriter working the file was not permitted. Phone calls were allowed but speaking directly with the underwriter always ended with a v/m – I recall few return calls. The Corporate Advocated Procedure was emails. We all vastly missed the privilege of direct contact with Loan Underwriters working our loan files. Almost always, this lack of direct contact resulted in the inability to overcome loan issues the Underwriter was experiencing. This operational condition was at the central core of file after file returned to the L/O with the notation "UNDERWRITING DENIED". And to be fair a portion of this condition was our inability to successfully function by electronic means only. By June the entire staff resigned and W/F closed the office and never had cause to reopen a replacement. What a tremendous wasted expense and failure by a highly respected company. The chocking loan underwriting policies/procedure resulting in so few funded loans, coupled with the following, is the why I terminated my Wells Fargo career. In early January I learned the two separate associate lenders W/F had previously introduced me to, notified me they were unable to accept any NRC Mortgages supporting the Estate Tax Reduction program. The VP of the one lender that demonstrated the most interest either resigned or was discharged of his duties and his senior management position. The Lender now expressed this was not the time to consider "risk programs". The remaining Lender just stopped accepting my calls and v/m's were unreturned. Strike #2

    In early March, while again in Atlanta, training for the expressed purpose of getting "ramped up" on Condo Loans supporting the company's nation wide intentions in setting the industry lead for condo financing, I received a phone call from Rick Larsen (a reminder: the lawyer for the Seralago Condo/Tel project) stating the owners had received notice the state was satisfied the development project met State Regulations and they were permitted to proceed with the final approach to begin marketing units to interested buyers. I thought, "great, what timing" just when the company had expressed their punched up interest towards the condo market. During the mid afternoon break I notified my manager and his boss of my phone call from Larsen. Later, the Senior VP of Condo Lending asked to see me and proceeded to inform me the Company had now decided, along with their highly charged direction towards "Condo's" that Condo/Tel's would not be included in their loan programs, citing the catch-all for all Lender reasons to not provide loan products –"Loan Risk". Strike 3 and out!

I was totally devastated, angry and could not fathom another day with Wells Fargo. I left the seminar, called the airport arranging a flight back to Orlando and tendered my resignation that very afternoon, receiving only mild resistance from management as they were well aware of how important this project was, the amount of work I had put into it and their prior endorsement to be the Lender of Record.

Unknown to me at the time, a close co-worker, Jamie Corral, had been in discussion with our former employer and was negotiating a return to RG Crown Bank including a Management Position for himself. Days later, while at home, he called informing me of the above, asked that I not to do anything in so far as interviewing with another lender and informed me there was a new non Puerto Rican Bank President. While procrastinating my unemployment position and respecting Jamie's request to "stand still" I learn there were 3 new NRM applications for the Estate Tax Reduction Program submitted to RG Crown Bank and were in early stages of loan processing. I knew the person I appointed was NOT as program knowledgeable as I, further fueling the want of returning to my old lender – Federal concerns accepted.

In a matter of days Jamie called informing me he successfully negotiated our return to RG Crown and he would be my new manager and the mortgage staff eagerly await my return. What a wonderful, great full feeling! On Monday, March 13th I return to my old desk with many of the processing and underwriting staff standing applauding my return. I may even have been blushing. Adding to the excitement the new Bank President requests a meeting for that evening. I suspect the reason for the meeting is to discuss the 3 new NRM applications as this new loan program is completely foreign to him. So I study the details of the applications and decided to change the structure of the applications, in minor ways only, but the result was our new President would find them much easier to understand. I also had the loan officer I appointed during my absence, sign off on the loans leaving only me in charge of the files. The 3 applications total $4 million.

The meeting lasts about an hour with his welcoming me back comments and is pleased of my return. His revue of the NRM applications are positive and states that he sees them as "solid loans" and unless something unforeseen by the bank they will carry them as "portfolio loans".

This is as good as any to reflect on my return to RG Crown and why the reason to leave only 8 months prior seemed no longer as previously important.

    1. I knew I had 3 large loans in my pipeline that unlike the past with

Wells Fargo, I had the control to close and fund all three

2. I knew I could work with the Bank's Underwriters to close and fund loans.

3. The new President greatly influenced me with his positive-ness and knowledge of the mortgage industry. He did not totally endorse the Condo/Tel project but he did commit to assist me in "bank brokerage approval" of Condo/Tel Lenders allowing and permitting our bank to broker these loans. I could not ask for more.

While reservations remained regarding the Federal Agencies past audits, returning remained my best alternative – at least for the present. Proving this comment I close my first loan upon my return in early April and we close 2 of the 3 NRM by June/July, the 3rd applicant declined to proceed with the Estate Tax Reduction Program. I close $3.62 million with in 4 months – nine times more than the 8 months I was with Wells Fargo.

As a reminder of my advancing age, in June I complete the necessary documentation permitting me eligible for Social Security (I could have applied 3 years earlier) but chose not to commence monthly SSI until age 68. While I began receiving the Canadian equivalent 3 years prior, it did not penalize my employment-income as SSI would.

Also, by waiting the extra 3 years SSI monthly income increased considerably. A win-win if one is in a position of regular employment income.

Apart from working the arena of regular business my main focus was organizing the **SERALAGO** Condo/Tel project. Confirming and finalizing qualifying issues including developer's insurance coverage, property surveys, property appraisals and a host of other issues. With information arriving monthly and the dots beginning to connect my challenge now was to find Condo/Tel lenders who specialized in this particular real estate market.

Most traditional lenders considered Condo's and particularly Condo/Tel's fundable but definitely fall into a higher risk factor than conventional traditional real estate. For this reason there were selected lenders who specialized in Condo/Tel's because their investors where prepared to accept the higher risk in exchange for higher loan yields. Meaning loan rates and discount-points were considerable higher to the borrower resulting in higher lender/investor profits.

Be early October the initial "launch date" was targeted for late November, early December. The President of the Investment Group and

Marketing Team projected the Roll Out finalizing the sale of all or most of the Condo Units to be completed within 18 > 20 months, basically by mid 2008. My research for the type of lenders mentioned above, narrowed down to two major lenders, Magna Resource Financing, a division of Regions Bank and Allied Capital a major condo lender located in Pennsylvania. They both studied the requested documentation detailing the Seralago project and were satisfied that all state and loan requirements had been met or would be satisfactorily completed by the targeted launch date. For those questioning a "launch date" it is a real estate term referencing the beginning of project unit sales to the public.

The remaining financing hurdle was to have my bank approve the above lenders as **Broker Lenders.** Meaning the Seralago loans would be completed and approved by RG Crown with a "pass through" to either Magna or Allied, for funding with the loan proceeds sent to RG Crown. The mortgage would be held by either of the above referenced banks and the approved borrower owed the mortgage payments to either of the two funding lenders. True to his previous promise our Bank President did his due diligence and approved both Magna and Allied, as "Co-Lenders". I was basically good to go except for one rather dicey issue.

I had legitimate concerns of being capable of managing the shear volume of the loan applications as the marketing launch expanded to the anticipated developing apex. The loan application volume would be overbearing for one loan officer. Seeking relief from that scenario and assistance to keep pace with the expected loan volume I began investigating how I could legally incorporate staff that would not be RG Crown Bank employees but could assist with loan acquisition applications.

There were many twists and turns on the road to resolve the above and so I will just cite the bottom line. I had Rick Larsen (the projects attorney) form a Limited Liability Corporation, **ENCORE CONSULTING LLC** registered in my name with my home address as the companies registered legal address. The sole and only purpose, as stated in it's Company Corporate Articles, was to **procure real estate referrals** on behalf of buyers seeking mortgage loan assistance. Encore was not a licensed mortgage broker entitled to perform anything associated with completing a loan application, loan process, loan underwriting or fund a loan. Only to procure referral leads. Not unlike television advertisements advising the viewing public that if you need a licensed attorney for any legal matter call the listed number and your request will be forwarded to attorneys competing for your business. Mr. Larsen, and I use the Mr. out of respect because he completed and finalized all the legal paper work including registering it with the state for no charge. When I inquired about the charges he deferred stating "the office must have forgot". With the LLC in place I appointed a Florida State Licensed Mortgage Broker I previously had several conversations regarding Seralago. As a matter of fact in an earlier time, she was a "competing entity" so she was well acquainted with the project. The mechanics of participation with Encore was simple. Excess referrals would be passed to Encore and then Encore would advance the referral lead to the Licensed Mortgage Broker for usual initial processing, including loan application, negotiating the loan rates and discount points through to acquiring all required supporting documentation including credit reports, current income and past income tax filings. All of the above would be packaged and forwarded to RG Crown Bank to verify all documentation and upon "Underwriting Approval" issue a "pre- loan approval" subject to final acceptance by either Magna Corporation or Allied Capital. The Mortgage Broker would not be charged for the referred lead but was to receive 2.00% of the funded loan amount from Encore, only when the loan funded. The loan yield proceeds were to be an even split of the 4% loan yield or 2.5% if the loan-yield was 5.00%, which ever was greater. Encore would remit to RG Crown Bank their portion of the yield. I projected that I would be able to complete an estimated 65% of the referred Seralago loans leaving the remaining 35% for Encore to complete through the appointed Mortgage Broker.

The above projection was based on an estimated 131 loans completed by the Broker representing $14,300,000 in total funded loans. Their allotted 2% commission fees would net the Broker about $286,000. The remaining $286,000 yield balance represented RG Crowns portion sharing it equally with me - $143,000. The larger loan portion, 244 loans, completed by yours truly, would net me a commission total of $314,466. Combining both sources of commissions represented a grand total of **$457,496.** Undoubtedly, there would be some "fall out" for non-approved loans but at only a 70% or possibly even 65% loan to value the loan denial would be minimal. I will leave it to the reader to appreciate my enthusiasm for the **Seralago Condo Project!**

The original launch date originally set for November was rescheduled for late January as State Regulators requested further submissions of owner occupancy documentation, citing additional reviews by a separate Government Agency. We had no option but to comply with everyone waiting for the New Year to begin.

For reasons I no longer recall the Bank sent me and Jamie Corral to Puerto Rico to assist their local Mortgage Division of RG Financial explaining Condo Financing to a large group of their local clients interested in purchasing Condos. I questioned why they chose to send me when my ability to speak Spanish consisted of "Hola". Management explained it was because I best understood Condo Financing. Jamie consoled me by advocating that I treat this as a paid vacation. I spend 4 days attending many client meetings sitting alone at my designated table looking totally stupid.

The above should represent a quiet message to the reader that my banks management continued to remain in shallow form and almost all mortgage personnel were aware that Senior Management had not resolved any of the Feds Audit concerns and management had to know the Federal Regulators were becoming increasingly inpatient with the continued delays and un kept promises.

While waiting for the Seralago Marketing team to begin selling the condo units, our Mortgage President was transferred to the Banking Division and was replaced by a person from the "outside" as the Mortgage Sr. Vice President. He vacillated between supporting and not supporting the NRM and the related Estate Tax Reduction Program, causing new applications to be placed "on hold" until a firm decision could be concluded. In the mean time **RBC** (Royal Bank of Canada) Board of Directors resolved their compliance and legal issues and began funding loans for that tax saving program and rightfully the Cassis and Evers team began referring their interested clients to RBC. I waved "good bye" to a program I really believed in for both how it rightfully served their clients and the tremendous profit potential for both the Canadian Estate Tax partners and the lending institution.

Side bar story: Two years later the entire program came to a screeching halt as the US Real Estate Market began its dreadful decline followed by the collapsing American Banking Industry. Regrettably, all but killing an exciting very creative tax saving program, and as most of us remember the onslaught of a global economic recession, that contrary to government speeches continues, albeit to a lesser severity.

In March I close almost $2 million in loans, my best in nearly two years and would represent my final "biggie" within the mortgage industry – the beginning eve ending the largest mortgage boom in US history.

The Seralago Sales Team finally received the green light to market their Condo/Tel's units and they began their endeavors in Ireland and Scotland. The first reports indicated 80 sold units (in one weekend) purchased by an individual groups of 11 investors. Fifty of the orders were sold as self financed with the remaining 30 in need of US financing. At my end we were ready with the lead marketing team stating the required paper work would begin flowing through to my bank by early to mid April.

But by mid April the State and Federal Bank Regulators served notice to Bank Management they were unsatisfied with the Banks progress in resolving the Compliance issues, specifically "cash reserves" necessary to support the level of **Risk Loans** their audit had uncovered. Following usual loan resale procedures, the bank had sold these same loans to Fannie Mae and Freddie Mac - the Government Agencies who through their investors, purchased funded loans from bank lenders. Now the bank was in danger of being forced to "buy back" the above referenced "risk loans". Added to that was the Fed's dire concerns, revealed again through their audit, the banks inability to secure the necessary cash reserves to facilitate a "loan buy back" This worrisome information was well known by employees, all fearing a bank "shut down" or bank closing.

Staying with this subject for a moment, staff learned at later time, one major reason the parent company (RG Financial) were experiencing major difficulty in raising the Regulators demand for the "Cash Reserves, was RG Financials stock had been de-listed from the NYSE. Guaranteeing its inability to generated sufficient cash to satisfy the above referred compliance issue. The former grand stature of a highly respected community bank – **Crown Bank** – would soon be history. Shameful, because in my heart of hearts, if original management had not been replaced by the parent Puerto Rican Company, none of the above would have occurred.

With the above circulating in my mind I begin interviewing again with different banks including Fifth Third, a large national bank and well managed. I received a standard loan officer position and pay grade but decline their offer. I sensed several similarities with their operating software to Wells Fargo and that underwriting was not local to each mortgage branch but centralized to one general location. Additionally, my selected branch was located in South Orlando, almost an hour's drive from Lake Mary. I could not envision driving 2 hours a day to attend work, this factor definitely added to my decision.

The obvious current position of the bank added severe concerns to funding the Seralago project. Should the bank be forced to close or be purchased by another competitive bank it might not result in a continuance with the previously approved lending brokers, putting the entire project, from my end, in serious jeopardy. The timing could not have been worse.

All of the above would soon serve to be inconsequential. While waiting for the bank to receive the Condo/Tel borrowers unit purchase documentation the mortgage industry sensing future difficulties, exacted an increase in loan rates. Particularly affected were interest rates for **Foreign Nationals.** The 30 would be buyers learned their quoted loan rates were immediately subject to a rate increase of 1.5% to 2.00% (9.00% was deemed a lot different than 7%) causing buyers to "place a buying hold" on the entire 80 units – including the 50 that planned to purchase through self financing. Adding further negativity to the project, the marketing teams now in England and Switzerland advised that potential buyers from that region chose to wait until the mortgage industry "settled down" and the marketing teams noted, group sale appointments were not "as well attended." I managed to keep the Regulator Compliance Issues quiet, not to difficult as Seralago Management and company partners had much to preoccupy their daily concerns as mortgage loan rates were universal and little anyone could do to alter the now changed buyers attitude.

Through out the summer and early autumn there were many turns, up and downs, hopes and plans the Seralago Developers tried to salvage but all were unsuccessful. For the Developer and his partners it was a massive financial loss with some forced to file personal bankruptcy. For me it was one of the many "almost magnificently successful projects" that didn't plan out. There is an old saying "timing is everything". Had the marketing of the project began when first scheduled we would have almost beat the economical clock and at least been partially successful. The flip side of that statement is who knows what the repercussions would have brought for the borrowers and related lending institutions. Hellish! Market values would have all plummeted, owners and lenders alike would all have suffered an equal result as the loan to property value ratio would have been deemed "under water" spurring massive foreclosures. I began to suspect as early as July that Seralago could be a failed project and turned more of my attention to regular business and a Banking Institution I could work with. Tied to that scenario was the announcement that **Fifth Third** had purchased RG Crown Bank with the official closing date set for October 1 2007.

With the above now a known fact I began more employment interviews. The bank's new ownership set into motion their business plan for former RG Crown Bank employees and schedule a host of training and orientation sessions for all employees, particularly affected were the mortgage personnel. The product and operating software that I now had the benefit of extensive orientation reconfirmed my original assessments back in April when I interviewed with 5/3rd. I disliked their operating software and possessed a negative attitude towards it. New Management advised the Underwriting Department most would be disassociated, meaning replaced. Their replacements would be incorporated with existing 5th/3rd Underwriters, however, there "might be" a few openings for former RG Crown Underwriters to fill new openings within their "General Underwriting Center". Added to that proclamation, throughout early stages of the "bank takeover" they began to subtly notify the remaining Loan Officers their compensation plan would be different than that of our former bank. When I interviewed with 5/3rd in April their Loan Officers compensation plan included a monthly sales objective of $650,000 and by successfully completing the monthly objective "bonus commissions' kicked in resulting in competitive sales commissions. But now, and unknown to any of the other former RG Crown Loan Officers who had not previously interviewed with 5th/3rd, learned their monthly objective was now mysteriously increased to $1 million! Clearly this was an intentional power play to discourage former RG Loan Officers and to cut to the chaste none (9 in total) chose to go with Fifth Third and not one of the Underwriters transferred citing a sub par compensation plan. For me there was no decision. I just was not going to be a Fifth Third employee.

I continued interviewing with several lenders finally finding a bank that interested me. I liked the Managing Director, understood their operating software, L/O's were permitted direct access to Underwriters, the Compensation Plan was competitive and my operating Branch Office was located in Lake Mary. The bank was a large national institution with its original roots centered in Wisconsin and had recently moved to Florida purchasing a "state bank" that found financial distress, much like RG Crown. The name of the bank was **M & I Bank**. I signed their employment "offer sheet" and agreed to a September employment date. When I signed the offer sheet I was required to list all loan applications in my current pipeline complete with supporting documentation– there were 8 in total and in various forms of loan processing. The norm in the mortgage industry sits with the Loan Officer to transfer any "pipe line" loan applications over to his new employer. This also best serves the interest of the L/O, as obviously he will collect the associated loan yield commissions. Exception to this usual arrangement are loan applicants that choose not to transfer to the new lender, remaining with the original lender or, the loan may have already closed and funded. In which instance the original bank is under no obligation to render the departing Loan Officer his commissions. Again, citing the norm within the industry, the new lender would then advance the calculated loan yield commissions that failed to move to the new employer/lender, thereby assuring the originating Loan Officer his rightful commissions. Most banks refer this commission structure as a "new signing bonus". One week prior to our agreed employment commencement date, M& I Management and I meet to sign all the required final employment forms, including commissions/volume bonus structures and the above referred "signing bonus".

I don't know the actual real reason, perhaps it was the nervousness that all lenders were beginning to experience fueling rumors of an approaching bad economic period, but now during the "pre-employment appointment" attended by my managing director and the area Vice President the signing bonus is void of mention or correctly stated, no longer listed. M & I Bank have changed their new hiring policies and inform me they will not pay the usual normal signing bonus for any and all loans that remain with RG Crown. The cited reason is the unpredictability of how many of my loans will remain with RG Crown. Ridiculous, as the bonus is never established until the very first day of the new employment. I don't even listen to the continuation of this dialogue but just declare that I will not be a party with an employer who reneges on the original pre-employment agreement and the basis of my decision to join M&I. My new Managing Director and VP refused to reconsider and I leave the meeting. No more **M & I Bank**. And I find myself doing a slow walk back to good old RG Crown soon to be Fifth Third Bank and one that I have already decided was not for me.

During my entire mortgage career I kept and filed a copy of my monthly sales reports. No longer with me since undertaking this writing, but by referencing these reports was how I was able to comment on my mortgage production. I closed all 8 of the loan applications I had related to M & I Bank by mid September and now everyone was aware of the October 1st takeover by **Fifth Third Bank.** With my decision made to resign which I did on October 1, I assume the position of doing little in originating any new loan applications, and just show up at the office taking long lunch breaks for the remaining two weeks. I did attempt closing a large Jumbo Loan (over 2.5 million) but failed as the interest rates were in acute acceleration and it was clear to most everyone in the mortgage industry things were going to be very different.

This decision process was in concert with the prior knowledge of booked Mediterranean Cruise celebrating our 10th Wedding Anniversary. So with that major date in mind I determine I would utilize the down time interviewing with other lenders. Plus a major event was in the works with the planned marriage of Julie and Harry at our home. Right behind my resignation, October 2nd, Julie's Grand Mother's birthday, they were married at our pool patio by a friend and former Seralago associate, Arden Clark, who also was a Justice Of the Peace. Very small in attendance, Gordon and Meade, who took videos and photographs and of course Fran & me. Following the ceremony we drank several bottles of Champagne and then journeyed to a local high-end restaurant, were a private dining room had been reserved. We dined and over engaged in several bottles of wines pleased as punch they chose to marry at our home and delighted welcoming Harry Cheek, a prince of a guy, into this crazy family.

One of the original RG Crown staff, a member of the former Wells Fargo episode, referred me to her Head Office, First Federal Savings & Loan, located only a few miles from my residence. They were a small bank but active in mortgage loans. I interviewed several times with senior management agreeing to join their mortgage team following the conclusion of our planned Anniversary Cruise, specifically December 10th.

We return from our cruise, exhausted and I continued experiencing severe knee pain, (more on that in a moment) well pleased that I had not agreed to commence immediately with my new employer. I checked in with Human Resources just as a formality. Nothing seemed irregular until my would be Operation Director called and advised they were having "scheduling" difficulties and would it be alright if we postponed our "start date" for a couple of weeks, until after the Christmas/New Year Holiday. Actually, it was welcomed news as I had a health issue to deal with. I was to check back with H/R after the Christmas Holidays to firm up a start date.

I had been a "jogger" for 35+ years. Not a serious one, only running 3 – 5 miles at a time about 3 times per week, but consistently doing so. Like everyone who is a jogger I suffered running injuries from time to time and after resting, the injuries would heal and I would resume the routine. A week before our cruse departure, I "tweaked" my knee experiencing only minor discomfort but curtailed any further jogging. While lifting weights one day during this running absence, I felt a sharp pain in the same right knee lasting only a few moments. Thinking nothing serious I played golf the following day and was unconcerned with the knee issue as the pain was barely noticeable.

I will return to the forming "dark clouds" clouding the future surrounding my new would be employer and my knee issue following the narrative of our Mediterranean Cruse.

But before doing so let me welcome a new member to the family. Genevieve Cheek was born on November 8th. She was not premature and not early. She was conceived early as Julie was measuring her biological clock in micro seconds and determined that birthing a baby was strategic to this clock and so while finishing her tour of Iraq she and Harry thought they "should hurry up". Never one to shy from "dare moves" Julie proceeded with their decision and hence one beautiful granddaughter was born healthy and remains that way and positions herself to remain very independent – sound familiar?

Our 10th Anniversary Cruise:

Following a short flight to Atlanta our overnight Air France flight (the most enjoyable flight to both our memories with superb food and wine) to Paris with a short connecting flight the next morning to Venice Italy. We have both previously visited the city built on seawater many times but enjoyed visiting the uniqueness of the old city once more. Fran had it in her mind she wanted to have a drink at the "world famous" (her words)

Cipriani **Harry's Bar**. After a couple of hours walking to find what I came to learn as just a neighborhood bar we found it and 58 USD later (for one special coffee and one scotch and water) with both eyes under an arched eyebrow we left this famous bar.

Our ship, a member of Celebrity Cruse Lines called **The Millennium** was huge, 13 levels, carrying 2300 guests and an equal number of staff. We departed the next morning for the old port city of Dubrovnik, Croatia. The city dates back to 1292 and while I found its harbor to be exquisitely beautiful it was my least favorite. Athens also sits next to my least favorite though not to be confused with the rich historical sites of 5th century Acropolis ruins. It is difficult for the human mind to absorb how these restored structures were originally built and how mankind had the wherewithal and resources to build such magnificent buildings. For all its gracious architecture I disliked Athens only for its people who seem to exude this attitude of unadulterated entitlement and rudeness. They were arrogant, bold and seemed only interested in themselves.

The Acropolis and other structures within the noted ruins are all built on large hills overlooking the city itself. It was during the 8hour walks climbing and descending these hills, necessary to view the ancient ruins that my knee blew up the size of a melon making it very painful to walk. There were little options. Either stay on board the ship and become non-mobile or, ignore the pain and treat it after returning shipside. My favorite recovery procedure was to sit on the upper rear deck with several glasses of Metaxa, a beautiful Greek Brandy, a rich Padron Cigar, with my knee wrapped in lots of ice. The pain would seemingly disappear much to the assistance of the brandy & cigar and swelling would reduce sufficiently for the next day of more walking. However, extended walking up and down hills only exacerbated the swelling and by mid cruise I consulted the ship Doctor were aid or medical advice was not to be found. By the time of our flight home I struggled with mobility and intense pain. Within days of our return I had an appointment with a knee Doctor and will write about my total recovery later.

From Greece our next stop turned out to be our favorite. Surprise for us too. Turkey! The port entry was Kusadasi where 100's of merchants ply their wares. We purchased, at highly reduced pricing (due mostly to our cruise being the last for the season) jewelry, spices, clothing, and a hand made carpet. All carried home with a bum knee! We had a 2day and 2night stay in Kusadasi affording us a splendid tour to the Biblical city of Ephesus, the showplace of **Aegean Archaeology** visiting the House of the Virgin Mary, where she was accompanied from an area of Israel by St. John and is buried there. Also buried a short distance from Mary's grave is a large memorial of the apostle, St. John. The Aegean ruins of this very old city are far more intact and easy to imagine life in that period than the ruins of **Pompeii.**

We celebrated our 10th anniversary at sea enjoying a magnificent six-course dinner with 6 wine pairings. Tremendous!

From Turkey it was up the Atlantic Coast of Italy with stops in Naples, (the most disorganized city I have ever visited) Civitavecchia, the port city for Rome. Having visited Rome twice previously, we chose to rent a car and tour the Tuscany area including the Etruscan ruins of **Tuscania.**

We continued to tour the Tuscany wine area outside of Florence and then cruised to the **French Riviera,** which included Monaco, Nice, and Villefranche. We visited the famous Monte Carlo Casino, where Fran actually walked away with some winnings and Prince Rainier and Grace Kelly's palace. The cruise terminated in Barcelona, a city we both wished we had more time to visit as it was limited to one day with a flight out early the next morning for Paris our departure city for home. Fran was overjoyed visiting the Picasso Museum and, if permitted, would have spent the night there in total glee.

It was truly a "lifetime vacation" and will be long remembered with the aid of short videos and tons of pictures.

I was able to schedule an appointment with a knee surgeon and within days I limped into his local office. X-rays and examination laid evidence and confirmation I had an **Arthritic Knee** along with a slight **Meniscus tear.** He proclaimed me to be a "project" but to garner a little time before the eventual knee replacement he injected my knee (the longest needle I could ever remember) with a form of lubricant jelly and I was instructed to return within a month where he would buy me another year or two with regular shots of Steroids. I wasn't happy with the prognosis but what can you do but accept the findings. The Doctors final words where "park the running shoes and we will see you in about a month". I do not exactly know what lubricant he injected me with, but magically, the knee pain disappeared (without knee replacement) and has to this very day, not limiting me to any mobility, other than jogging. I am more than lucky and the whys escape me.

One morning while reading the paper I came across the headline " First Federal Savings & Loan audited by Federal Regulators". The article went on to explain there were serious loan mortgage issues that unless ratified might restrict further future mortgage loans. I was able to speak to management and they strongly assured me the Federal Regulators would be completely satisfied with the internal actions already underway. Having lived through a previous situation I knew differently but because of the time of year, relented to doing anything akin to mortgages until after the Christmas/New Year holidays. Just to conclude this part of the narrative a month later, management and a host of new investors where unable to satisfy the Regulators. First Federal Savings & Loan was finally forced to discontinue their mortgage division. The entire banking division closed all its branches within 18 months.

I am not as familiar with the banking industry as I am with the mortgage business but I have my own version of the truthful real reasons the mortgage and real estate industry went into the dumper and so "over regulated" mortgage polices today. The explanation would prove to be too long, convoluted and intricate to verbalize within this writing.

As 2009 began I was unemployed with an interest to continue working recognizing that at an age approaching 70 there were few years remaining that my mind and body would permit the continuance of that notion. Prior to my resignation with RG Crown I participated in a "golf hole sponsorship" for a group of **homebuilders** the bank had previously agreed to sponsor. It was during this golf tournament that I met a number of builders, some that I had met previously and in particular a builder who I got to develop a relationship. Some time following my resignation he called me stating he had a customer that he contracted with to build a new home on a large lot in Clermont. Familiar with the construction scene from my days of working out of the Banks Branch there, I easily related to the lot area. He gave me his clients contact phone numbers, which I contacted, even though I no longer represented a lender. Having completed many Construction-Perm Loans I was well versed with the buzzwords and terms and after my personal meeting with the clients they chose me to represent them for financing their new home. At the time, I had been negotiating with First Federal and knew I would be employed with them beginning in January well before the commencement of construction. The client was a Sheriff Commander with Orange County and employed with that agency for over 20 years. His wife was a private school principal with a 4year contract under her arms and an income superior to her husband. I had reasons to presume this would be a very fundable loan.

Well of course as the New Year drew near, I fully realized I no longer had anything going with First Federal and it fell on me to negotiate something with a new lender so I would be able to capitalize on this jumbo loan, approaching $600,000. A probable fee for me approaching 8K

It was while attending an over the top New Years Eve party at one of our mutual friends, attended by 60 people, that I spoke with my old banking acquaintance and friend **Jack Koegel**. He was now president of a new bank in a brand new building located in Lake Mary. This current single branch was the first branch of an expansion into Florida by an Ohio Bank with its head office in Columbus Ohio. The name of the bank was **United**

Midwest Bank. Jack had long left the employ of RG Crown and was aware that I too had resigned from the same bank. I told him my disinterests with Fifth Third, and that I remained active in originating loans and had a loan application for a large "jumbo Loan". With that said I would appreciate a personal meeting to discuss some possible arrangement. He agreed and we met a few days later at his new office. The short story here is that I had simple conditions for joining his new branch. First, I did not want to be an "employee" but rather an "independent agent". As such I would not work at the branch but at my home or a private office and would be considered a "part time" agent. Second. I would adhere to all bank polices, take all their compliance tests on a regular basis and acknowledged I would be required to pass all compliance exams. Third. As an Independent agent I would not request a monthly draw, commissions only and would not request any medical insurance coverage including any 401K contributions. Finally, my compensations would be based on a 50/50 split of all loan yields and applied discounts. The only hitch was the legal authorization to access the banks operating software and pull client credit reports off bank site on my own computer. All of the above are issues pertaining to the Federal Privacy Act and of course the security issues pertaining to proprietary Bank Software, Loan Procedures and other facets of their mortgage modus operandi. Jack said he would need to converse with his board and get their ok to proceed. Eventually they all agreed to the exception and after completing an arrangement for an office and acquiring a computer I started immediately.

The first order of the day was to buy a computer and printer, which I did the same day Jack notified me of the boards decision. Attaining an office outside of my home was a personal preference, as I did not appreciate the natural interruptions. Over recent years I had remained friends with Chuck Turner, my former associate with the TEC/AIMCO Home Buying Plan. We often socialized together and of course, as a reminder, I was his best man at his marriage to Amy. Well now he had resigned from AIMCO and as a corporate settlement he was granted 7 rental properties, formerly managed by AIMCO as his corporate "parting gift", implemented to begin his own Property Management Company which he titled **Jeffery Charles Management** after his son's first name and of course his first name. Well, he grew the company from that original 7 to 17 properties located from Tampa to Jacksonville. He was doing exceptional well and had leased a 2000 sq. ft. office 1.8 miles from my home and exactly 1 mile to the new bank branch. It happened he had a spare office that was totally unoccupied. I asked if I could rent it on an "open end" monthly basis. He was the type of person that was delighted I would ask and said "absolutely" but under one condition. There would be no rental fees and he would consider it a favor if I would join his office and asked if he could consult with me on business and "personal" matters. I agreed but did not fully realize the depth of his personal and business problems. The office was fully furnished, complete with desk, credenza, office chairs, telephone and fax machine and so all I had to do was set up my computer/printer, load the banks various software versions and have the banks head office connect me to the 3 separate credit reporting agencies. I was all set for business within a week.

The first order of business for me, from my new office and lender was to assemble all the required documentation for the above referenced C/P loan for the Orange County Sheriff Commander, which will now be referred to as the **Steve Young Loan.** Documentation involved the Builders Financials, list of prior building construction completions, supplier referrals etc. Including the Architectural Drawings – all to scale, along with the building material lists and construction costs and the supporting material attesting to the borrowers credit worthiness and income history. Construction was to begin by mid June and I had all of the above approved in time for the initial foundation excavation.

Throughout the remainder of the year I managed to complete a couple of loans per month – nothing startling but I was ok with the production given that my effort was part time and the quickly changing rules within the mortgage industry. It was deteriorating at a pace few could believe. The glory days were long gone.

In April I sell my SUV for my asking price – it had close to 95,000 in miles – and I thought it time to sell before it blew over the 100,000mile threshold. I leased a new Lincoln MKZ that was perfect for me and I loved it.

For the May 28th long weekend Fran and I journeyed to Atlanta for a family gathering hosted by Colby and Nicky Leonard. Their spacious new home easily accompanied the 20 or so guests and we all enjoyed the excellent cuisine and the bevy of alcohol including two great rounds of golf.

After our return home, the Tuesday following Memorial Weekend, I was sitting at the kitchen table reading the paper with a cup of coffee when I spotted a headline concerning a local cop. It was at least a half page in size and as I read through it I could not believe what I was reading. Here is the "readers digest" version. The article detailed, with pictures, Commander Young in the company of a prostitute he picked up at 2:30 in the morning. How the photographer was able to take the picture remains a mystery, as surely an alert policeman would some how be cognizant of some one close to the scene with camera in his possession. Anyway upon further police questioning the prostitute later admitted that "yes" she was a Hooker and she and the Commander had several previous "rendezvous" similar to what the current newspaper article alleged, inclusive of a very damaging photograph. When you are working a large loan and several months away from loan closing, you always warn the borrowers not to apply for additional credit and avoid purchasing large items. I missed warning the Sheriff Commander to also avoid engagement in any illegal activities. This idiot and his approved builder, were both in possession of a **lenders loan commitment,** subject only to a final appraisal revue, the legal requirement of borrowers providing evidence of their last payroll stub and get this: three weeks away from loan closing, assuring them, as they often referred, "our dream home".

Three months of work down the drain and needless to explain "no more" Steve Young $620,000 Construction Perm Loan. The only follow up to the original newspaper report was his discharge of duties and I never heard a peep from him. I do know his wife continued with her lucrative management position with the private school for several additional years when her name appeared in another newspaper article accusing her of improper use of the Academy's funds to a level the school was forced to close due to insufficient operating funds. If you had met either of them, prior to all of this, your mind would simply not allow you to believe what you were reading. You just never know!!

There were other repercussions following this debacle, more serious than the loss of my fees. The builder, who had contracted with his suppliers, extending personal money to purchase certain equipment in readiness, assembled the necessary sub contractors and of course spent as much time as anyone pre-organizing the building of a 5000 sq. ft. home filed bankruptcy and left the state – divorced.

I close out the year humming along at a leisurely pace completing a couple of loans a month. Although it is easily noticeable one submits 4,5,6 loan applications to finalize 2 successful funded loans. Much wasted time and very frustrating.

We close out the year with Fran and I driving to Hot Springs AK visiting Harry, Julie and the now 3year old Genevieve, bugging them for 5 days before returning home via Memphis TN where Fran insists on visiting Elvis's "Graceland". She thoroughly enjoyed the visit. I thought it was somewhat boring, way over exaggerated and hugely expensive.

For the larger part of 2008 Gordon and Meade Owens were engaged in building a large home on the same property they had purchased several years prior. The new home construction, which included tearing down the old 50 year old home, was now completed and so in February 2009 Fran and I help them move into the new home on a fabulous large lot facing a small creek.

During this semi-retirement period Gordon helped me better understand the **Stock Market** which had been his "domain" since our initial introduction in 1995. Armed with the basics of basics understanding, I invest $25,000 so that his firm would some day turn that modest investment into something that would supplement my retirement income. Well like most everyone engaged in the stock market, 60% of the original investment just went "poof". John included, and later in the year I limped home with the remaining $11,000. You could not blame the investment brokerages, as all investors suffered the same fate. The stock market just plummeted like the rest of the economy.

The mortgage business became more dismal with little or no loans completed and so Mike Bernier and I consider teaming up with a law firm who assisted homeowners behind in their mortgage payments and/or underwater with their mortgage property. The objective of the law firm and our involvement with them was to restructure the existing mortgage loan providing "financial relief" to the borrowers. The banks all seemed in favor of working something out but in reality few did, resulting in little to no success for everyone. Having less than meager success with the entire exercise we decided we were wasting our time with banks talking a good game but in reality had no intention of assisting the battered borrowers.

In May, Jack Koegel was forced to resign his Presidency with United Midwest Bank. He and others were cited for appraisal fraud by investors who purchased land lots from previous owners. The new owners learned that the previous purchase transaction was very recent and now where purchasing the same lot for a much higher price. There is a real estate term for this and it is called **"flipping"**. The legalities of the case was based on **falsified appraisals** supporting the higher selling price and certain parties involved in the new mortgages had knowledge of the aforementioned "fraudulent appraisals". Jack was not on the front line but by association he was in the picture. When the news media got wind of this pending suit, Jack's name was included in the reporting media. The Columbus Ohio Head Office, in order to distance the bank from this suit, had no other alternative but to request his resignation. The branch remained open and managed by temporary Head Office Management but closed the mortgage operation.

While that was happening I had a sizeable loan application from a former client that wanted to purchase a large size "foreclosed" home currently owned by a bank and listed as a "short sale". The term meant that the bank owning the now foreclosed home was prepared to sell it on the open market for a reduced price – prepared to absorb a financial mortgage loss with the existing property. The problem, across the board with "short sales" was and remains, extremely difficult to finalize mortgage loans. Banks were famous for changing the former agreed selling price or choosing to reverse their decision to sell the property, instructing the realtor to remove and cancel the listing, all within weeks or days prior to new owners closing on the property. This resulted in huge struggles for the Realtor and the Lender. Many realtors and mortgage personnel quickly decided to remove their services from "short sales" and remained so until only recently.

When mortgage loans are in short demand and a loan officer finds one, he will do all he can to hang onto it. With this in mind I join a **Mortgage Brokers Office,** referred to me by Mike Bernier. The Brokerage, Maximum Lending Solutions, was a branch office of a well known long standing financing entity. This is hard to believe but over the next 3-4 months I submit 7 or 8 loan applications and none ever fund or close. With that unenviable record in mind I pretty much decided to discontinue mortgage acquisition efforts and as a matter of fact I do not close a single loan until mid 2010 where I co-venture a large jumbo loan that in fact did represent the conclusion of my mortgage career. But before commenting further on that last loan I want to turn my attention to an earlier comment about my friend Chuck Turner.

Chuck, and I had been friends for close to 15 years. You will recall he was instrumental in assisted me in forming the **AIMCO/TEC** program. It all began when he and his then girlfriend, moved into the home next to our Arrowmount residence.

In recent years Chuck was experiencing great stress with two major issues - his marriage and his company. He sought my business insight as a means of rectifying his current problems. The business correction was easy to resolve, as the sole cause of employee confusion, lack of operating funds and loss of client accounts was strictly through the actions of his wife, Amy.

To begin to understand the out of character poor decision making as it relates to his marriage and how it under minded his business one as to have some background information regarding Amy. Telling it like it is may cause the reader to consider my assessment of Amy as sexist, over judge mental and bias. But before you form that premature conclusion here are some facts to consider. First she was intellectually challenged due to a very early premature birth – like 6 months – where she suffered permanent "under brain development". The consequential results of this tragic birth were many, one of which were major issues with her parents that ultimately resulted in her decision to leave home and void herself of parental care during her early teenage years. I do not believe she completed high school due to the above conditions. She experienced great difficulty with memory recall, conversation with her was difficult as she found it difficult to "track", simple math equations and words to complete writing sentences escaped her, resulting in letter writing a near impossibility. Employment was based on menial jobs like stacking shelves, sales clerking and the like. So one would ask the question, "why in hell would Chuck, an executive, with a college degree choose to marry an Amy"? The single and simply answer: while Amy was not a good-looking girl she was 26, tiny (maybe weighed 100 lbs) had a nice butt, a small waist and always wanted a massive breast implant.

Before Amy there was the incident when Chuck, and his then live in girl friend had an argument and in her anger through the $10,000 diamond ring into the pond located right behind both of our homes. With that, Chuck through her out of the house and began his 2nd or 3rd career as a single person. Fran, in her infinite kindness would fix him up with countless blind dates. He was always disappointed with any number of stated reasons ranging from heavy makeup, overweight, to old, etc. We often enjoyed a "guys night out" where he acted like a wolf in heat. Nothing with a skirt was off limits. For the record those of you wondering did John aid and abet the situation? I never, never ever strayed from the vow of our marriage. But this guy was a propeller in motion when it came to the potential of sex.

Anyway, back to Amy. They were engaged 3 months after they met and married within 6months. Soon after he brought Amy into his business and not long after that promoted her **President** of the company. The staff could not stand her, tearing out their hair, as she was a detriment to production and constantly wanting to "talk" with the staff about Hollywood and Movie Stars. When I moved into sharing an office at his facilities I spent countless hours coaching Chuck on what he had to do to resolve the issues with his staff. Remove her from the office of Presidency, and seek an attorney instituting a separation or even divorce because I predicted "Chuck she will take you down". He would always agree. He responded to those advisements by bringing her to Tenant Board Meetings, after all she was the President of the Company. The stories the staff would relate to me (I was now occupying the spare office) would blow your mind on some of the comments she made to Board Members. To add wood to the fire she convinced Chuck to change the name of the company from Jeffrey Charles Management Company to **Amy Charles Management Company.** The logic behind that was his sons were rude to her. In honor of the company name change she stated she required a car significant with her name now on company letterhead. Soon she was driving a 328 BMW convertible. I asked him how he was able to justify this expense while the company was struggling having just lost a major apartment complex representing 700 units in Jacksonville. He stated he had no alternative and he began to weep. The office staff continued to despise her as they were well aware of the company's precarious financial position, remembering the incidents sited above, they also recalled he paid her American Express account for "over the limit" notices three times, each in the amount of $25,000. They, like me, knew the end to their employment was near.

I will abbreviate the next series of events that ultimately lead to the collapse of the company. From out of the blue Amy announced she wanted to enroll in a modeling school preparing her for her next career as she was finding no satisfaction with the company business and Chuck just does not turn her on any more. Matter of fact she would sit down in my office, uninvited, with little attention from me, complaining and actually "hitting" on me. Chuck enrolled her in a modeling school where she quit after 3 weeks – originally a 6month course. Realizing she was not going to graduate any modeling school, she proceeded to convince Chuck that her talent was more towards a model agency where she could book new graduate models into lucrative contracts. To my amazement and his staff, he proceeded to lease an office in neighboring Heathrow for a 6month period. She vacated the lease within a month. I now have given up on Chuck and tell him so. He admits he has not contacted the attorney contacts I had previously provided, as he is incapable of affording their fees. I repeat I am sorry but I too will leave his generosity provided me, as I cannot bear to watch the destruction that is sure to follow.

Before I leave his offices and set up an office at my home (I do move on Labor Day) I learn one Monday morning that Amy has now moved to Las Angeles where she intends to be a movie star. In the interest of deferring apartment rental cost she arranges to share an apartment with a limo driver who convinces Amy that if he had his own limo he would be able to afford the total apartment rent allowing her to live rent-free. Yep! You guessed it. Chuck buys a Lincoln Stretch Limo. Not long after Amy shows up in Lake Mary, broke without any money and her roommate and the Lincoln Limo can no longer be located. There are many other issues or misdeeds on her part that could be recited, but in the interest of not extending more to this sad narrative I will end with one final segment.

While living with Chuck once again (at least it was billed that way) she found herself a new boyfriend who operated a mall "fragrance kiosk" located in the "mall common area". He was married of course, but to impress this boyfriend, Amy decided on a strategy that natures her best interest. Overstating her true stature and someone she is not, she purchased $12,000 of his product using Chucks American Express card. When the bill arrived Chuck was perplexed with this charge knowing it wasn't his and questioned Amy. She disavowed any knowledge of this transaction. Upon review with A/E they provided copies of the $12,000 transaction and of course now Amy had no recourse but to admit it. She asked her boyfriend for permission to return the unpackaged merchandise, where he pleaded his case that he could not, as this action would serve cause to the cancellation of his licensed position and the high probability of loosing his franchise, resulting in no means of supporting his wife and children. Chuck could have refused payment but, guess what? He paid the bill in its entirety.

In the course of all this and just prior to moving my office, Chuck was successful in negotiating a final agreement he had worked on for some time. A competitor agreed to purchase Amy Charles for a highly discounted amount allowing the new owners to take over the management of the original 17 commercial communities, now reduced to 10 or 12. As to the agreed sales figure I am not comfortable in providing but the agreement also stated he would be employed as an advisor, under contract for 2 years at $50,000 per year. He was unsuccessful requesting the new owners retain part of his office staff. At the time a major disappointment for all involved but as the story unfolds not of much consequence as the entire agreement unraveled in less than a month.

While this nightmare seemed to continue forever, no one could imagine why and how Amy had such influence with Chuck when he surely knew her hair brain ideas were severely flawed and she possessed absolutely no sense of money. Zero! Amy, through no fault of her own, was not the brightest crayon in the box and all who knew her were aware of her intellectual challenges. Well, as will soon be revealed, Amy was in possession **of a vital and very unsuspecting secret** known only to Mr. & Mrs. Turner and in reflection to all who were acquainted with her, we clearly had underestimated her negotiating skills.

Here is the "bomb" that blew everyone's mind including the aforementioned unraveling of Chuck's salvation agreement. About a week after my office move Fran received a mid afternoon phone call from the former Amy Charles Resident Real Estate Broker. She informed Fran she was coming over with a case of beer. Fran replied that we did not drink too much beer whereupon she was told she would be drinking most of the beer once she learned of *why* and the *purpose of the visit*.

Holding my first beer in hand I learned that Chuck Turner was now **Nicole Turner.** Yes, that is correct he became a **Transgender.** Initially I refused to believe this report rationalizing that it was only a rumor to "deflect" the recent information of his failed business and his subsequent sale to a competitor. But his former real estate agent insisted that this was real, complete with the name change and that the procedure began three years prior, with final surgery completed only a week prior. My mind was in a jumble. How could anyone lie on a medical table and be a part of a decision to remove your "Johnson"? Before I finished my 3rd beer I received a 3page email from "Chuck" confirming the just received information followed by a phone call where he tried to explain his decision process. His explanation was he always felt like a woman and would often, in privacy only, dress in women's dresses/clothing. He wanted to remain friends stating he was the same person just now a different gender. The conversation went on for some time and I learned that Amy was totally aware of the procedure from the very beginning and agreed to never divulge her knowledge of Chuck's transgender decision. Now I was able to understand why she had such sway with him and how he had to be in concert with all her ridiculous ideas and spending – all guarding this dramatic secret. I closed the conversation noting I needed time to digest all of this.

In concluding this final segment concerning Chuck Turner, the new owners in learning of Chuck's new gender immediately cancelled his 2year advisory contract and Nicole now kissed "good bye" to $100,000.

I never was able to get my head around it and eventually told him so adding I felt deceived, reminding him of all the time spent, at his request, trying to help with his marriage and business. He could not control Amy's spending and subsequent business failure risking the probability that Amy would blow his cover and her initial agreement to "keep the family secret". I would continue to "boil" every time I remembered how his "man talk" over drinks and lunches relating story after story of coveted sex with many women. What rationalized bullshit of why he had no alternative but to proceed with this transgender procedure. It ended our friendship.

In closing 2009, with help from my neighbor, Carl Daniels, I began the study of FOREX (trading foreign currency) and Fran and I attended another Hockey Hall Of Fame Induction. Another super weekend and a reminder of how proud the family were of Kelly's super accomplishments.

Since the later part of 2009 I had been flirting with retirement but continued to "doodle" with past mortgage clients. The mortgage industry was so messed up that it was near impossible to consummate a loan. So I labeled myself as "semi retired" and continued learning foreign currency trading. It captivated my interest and motivation and I thought I understood the trading procedures. Eventually I invested 10K and began live trading. The thing you cannot learn attending seminars and re-reading the mounds of literature, is nothing teaches you how to control your emotions. It is called **trading psychology.** In lay mans terms there are two geckoes that sit on either side of your shoulders. They are not green in color but rather both are shit-yellow. One is called **greed** and the other **fear.** To be successful with live trading one has to learn how to control both and make decisions without their influence. The are very adept in masking their control of your mind. It requires many costly trading mistakes to learn how to ignore their influence and be successful in FOREX trading. It is estimated that 94% of FOREX traders fail. I promptly lost 50% of initial investment and a further $1000 in the following one and half years before I began to turn it in a positive direction. As of this date I currently am on the way to full recovery and believe I will soon be profitable. Once you understand and accept the trading psychology it becomes as easy to perform as I first falsely diagnosed it and those who stick with it can be **very profitable.**

Back to the closing chapter of the Mortgage Business:

I had pretty much entered the land of **retirees** but remained somewhat active fielding enquiries from past clients. So lets just say I was semi- semi - retired.

One of those enquiries was a call I received from my former RG Crown Bank Manager, from Puerto Rico, who barely spoke English at the time of his employ with RG Crown, contacted me with information that one of my past clients (whom he was acquainted with) wanted a "Cash Out Mortgage" to finance another Puerto Rican venture. I contacted the individual, introducing myself and the first thing out of his mouth was "Jesus Christ"! Sounded like a good beginning. He went on to explain that he had been to 9 banks – without success and the basis of his need for investment money – build another food super market on land he had an purchase option. His family owned a second home in an exclusive community in Bay Hill – the same Orlando suburb Tiger Woods resided before his famous 7iron golf club battle with his former wife's car. The property was clear of any loans or any encumbrances and valued in excess of 3.75 million $$. He needed $2.6 million in cash.

The reasons he was experiencing such difficulty in successfully finalizing a funded loan are easier to list in point form.

- *The loan was considered a "jumbo" loan - a red flag risk for lenders
- *The property was a second home - a lengthy history of foreclosures of any personal property types
- *Cash Out Mortgage – another red flag as deemed by lenders
- *The required amount of cash equaled a 70% loan to value of the collateral property. Considered a high LTV loan for any cash out mortgage.

In summary it was a very difficult loan to complete. But excited me and propelled me to compete. Because of my inactivity within the mortgage business, my state mortgage license had lapsed and given all circumstances I decided it would be wasteful to re-engage schooling and more tests to re-apply. So I brought Mike Bernier into the equation where I would "piggyback" onto his license. This of course would enable him to participate in the commission structure – of which I was willing to concede in exchange for his knowledge of lenders and his legal mortgage license. I knew there would be healthy commissions due to the anticipated loan difficulty and loan amount.

The agreed arrangement was I would be the contact person with the borrower and Mike would deal with the direct lender. Lender after lender declined to even consider the loan. We ended concluding a deal with a Hedge Fund Management Firm who agreed to complete the loan. In the end (glorious borrowers who do not act within certain time frames) he had not provided the required documents in time before the Hedge Fund Management Company invested it's entire portfolio in other investments and was now deplete of any funds. Back to the beginning and through a contact that Mike had we found another lender that had the funds and was in agreement to close and fund the loan. But that contact of course wanted a piece of the pie and so we ended each agreeing to 1% of the available 4 discount points. Not as much as we first anticipated but still a handsome payoff for what would represent my final loan closing and my final curtain in the mortgage industry.

I thoroughly enjoyed the business and I often commented I had wished I had entered into it long before 1999. I had a reputation as good loan officer and possessed an ability to communicate well with would be clients. Plus I loved the challenge of difficult loans.

Now I was fully retired. Retirement is another stage of adjustment and one requiring a new attitude. Finding things to do after almost 55 years of work is not easy and I cannot recall not ever being employed. Boredom comes easy and lends itself to a deterioration of the mind. But if you are resourceful you bounce around and eventually, if you don't give up, you become reactive in a host of activities and some how the days become full, not like they were, but acceptable.

CHAPTER THIRTEEN

FINAL THOUGHTS AND SUMMARY CONCLUSIONS:

Resources:

Readers may wonder how I was able to assemble this writing accurately or possibly even question it's validity. Almost exclusively, my resources were my daily journals, day timers, subject files and yearly diaries, that I retained from the near beginning of my working career. My memory may appear acute but only after reading notations and records, as stated above, triggering a "memory recall". Admittedly, early in my career, I had fleeting moments when I thought I might write a "leaner version" of it and thus the motive for retaining boxes and boxes of the aforementioned resources. To be sure, without this resource, this narrative in its current form would have been impossible.

Regrets:

There are some, though not many. High up the totem pole would have been to be a better father and husband, particularly in the early stages of my young family. Secondly, I am guilty of not accomplishing much more in life. Within me sits a knowing, I had the ability to do more. The why is a "life mystery" some of us are incapable to fully explain. Perhaps it was destiny or just human weakness to partake in wine, women and song. Mother encouraged me to enter the priesthood and the other maternal wish, – Politics. Though I cannot imagine any of these maternal wishes, either, would have dictated the necessity of a higher education. I regret my parents not "pushing" me towards a higher level. Many of my early teachers made it known to me I had the ability to go beyond high school. Giving ground to my parents, never achieving grades sufficient only to "getting by" was most likely a major factor in their thought process. The education decision was purely mine and the teenage mentality, including a saxophone, clearly was more predominate than a better or improved cause.

The opposite to my listed regrets were demonstrated many times through my inbred ability and internal will to get up off the "defeat mat" and gather myself for another try, learning from mistakes and failures. A reminder to all young readers, as in my grand children: Never give up, no matter the damages. There is no greater failure than to stop trying. I sometimes marvel at the entitlement attitude of today's youth and how this impacts our nation. I do not recall not ever working for any extended period and I also know I never drew a single unemployment benefit check.

Belief: A key ingredient to a successful objective, no matter how trivial or challenging, begins with your <u>faith</u> and <u>commitment,</u> *imagining* your success, to the selected goal. I am often reminded of a poem (by Blake I believe) recited by Dr. Wayne Dyer, former resident of Detroit, while I attended one of his meetings during my residence in Michigan. Try to memorize it to me it helps encourage the above.

To see the world in a grain of sand, or the heavens in a wildflower

To hold infinity in your hand and eternity in an hour

We are lead to believe a lie, when we are told to see with the eye - not through the eye.

We were born in the night to perish in a night

When the souls slept in beams of light.

Family:

I marvel at the strength and willpower of my children. If there were any cause for failure amongst them surely they would qualify. The product of single parents, while loving, we were not always there for them. I did hold a field of influence but was often absent from the call of family duties and responsibilities and on site direction. They are resilient beyond comparison and no one will never know the immense pride and love I hold for all of them.

My siblings. How could anyone write any comment expressing the bond that was somehow instilled within us? Without exception, any of my sisters and brother would fight to death in honor and preservation for the other. Not lost in my memory are the extraordinary efforts my sisters took upon themselves to foster loving care and family examples towards John and Jane's children in the early years of separation. I know without a doubt, their influence rests with them to this day. I love you all so.

Myra Frances.

What an extraordinary woman I was blessed to marry! Was it an accident? Not an iota of chance. I have been lucky to been chosen to be a part of this Destiny. I firmly recall New Years Day in 1995. While driving to Florida for the expressed purpose of starting a new company, the Florida State Conservatory of Music, I could not shake an overpowering sensation that there was another real reason for this new venture. Eight days after my arrival Fran and I met on what was really a "set up date" and as we now know the rest is history. I will not ever forget the magnitude of that overflowing, unshakeable strange spirit that washed my soul and mind during that 2day drive. Fran possesses an unshakeable, immeasurable capacity to love, is the ultimate partner, always supporting me with a prevailing attitude the glass is always half full never half empty. We share a saying I have believed in for longer than I recall. "At the eleventh hour nothing is more important than family" which runs in concert with her family and mine. I am fortunate beyond deserving.

This writing exercise, while intended for the young people in our family is for you Fran. No one could love and respect you as I. A large "thank you" for your encouragement and help with this book.

I learned to enjoy this writing as it provided me another look at my life from the early days to present with the flow of life both up and down and the marvelous experiences it provided me. It is my hope readers enjoy this book and are able to gain any amount of thought provoking history and possibly something of an acquired learning quality.

Respectfully,

John Masse

2013

Made in United States
Orlando, FL
29 April 2024